Law and Economics

Market, Non-market and Network Transactions

Edited by

Panta Murali Prasad
Indian Institute of Technology Kanpur, India

Ranita Nagar
Gujarat National Law University, Gandhinagar , India

Series in Economics

VERNON PRESS

www.vernonpress.com

In the Americas:
Vernon Press
1000 N West Street,
Suite 1200, Wilmington,
Delaware 19801
United States

In the rest of the world:
Vernon Press
C/Sancti Espiritu 17,
Malaga, 29006
Spain

Series in Economics

Library of Congress Control Number: 2018963327

ISBN: 978-1-62273-452-8

Cover's image used with permission by Prof. Praveen Kulshreshtha. Edited by Mr. T Das

Cover design by Vernon Press

Table of Contents

Preface

Market and non-market institutions under capitalism will mobilise and allocate resources efficiently for economic growth and development. However, asymmetric information, pervasive subsidies, misuse of dominant position, negative externalities, and bounded rationality limits the efficacy of the institutions on mitigation of techno-economic and legal challenges. Moreover, competition among the nations' national security in terms of environment, economy, and sovereignty further results in protectionist market and non-market transactions. As a consequence, sovereign debt, jobless growth, double trust dilemma, weapons of mass destruction, commercialisation of merit goods, and unfair trade practices prevail. Thus, there is a need for efficient property, contract, tort, and business legal rules to provide incentives to change the behaviour of individuals to achieve sustainable development. Law and Economics applies economics as a method to formulate efficient legal rules that provide incentives to parties to meet reasonable and rational standards in order to minimise costs and maximise benefits, jointly on their activities. In essence, legalisation of economic freedom will mitigate risks and uncertainties and promote overall social wellbeing.

Innovation plays a major role in achieving sustainable development in the knowledge economy. However, the innovator and investor – who have opposing goals, interests and fears, and suffer from "Double Trust Dilemma" – share one thing in common: they both want the new venture to succeed and make very high profits! Consequently, to circumvent the "Double Trust Dilemma", both innovator and investor must rely on a mutually agreeable and dependable legal framework, to lower risks and maximise individual returns.

Industries in capitalism will have a little concern for environmentalism and safety standards. This will impose social costs on households that will hinder the attainment of sustainable development. Similarly, producer sovereignty prevails over consumer sovereignty in a goods and services market in an underdeveloped market system. The supply of substandard quality of goods and services under the standard form of contracts will impose financial and health risks on ignorant consumers. In addition, liability and regulatory systems, on product defects and services deficiency, have little effect in providing incentives to the wrongdoer to reduce the risk of harm on consumers.

This book is published from the proceedings of the 2nd International Law and Economics Conference on Market, Non-market and Network Transactions. It was held at the Indian Institute of Technology Kanpur (IIT Kanpur) on 3rd and 4th September 2016, under the consortium of the Indian Institute of Technology Kanpur, Gujarat National Law University (GNLU) and Indian Institute of Management Ahmedabad (IIMA). The consortium stressed that there is a need for efficient legal rules to change the behaviour of individuals, of societies, and basic social structures and trends, to achieve societal well-being. It has also emphasised the institutional conditions that might promote efficient legal norms. Accordingly, the consortium has concentrated its efforts on:

- Research-based teaching and teaching-based research on Law and Economics by initiation of National and International collaborative academic activities;
- Creation of an association (Indian Association of Law and Economics) for generation and dissemination of knowledge to academicians, technocrats, professionals and policy makers; and,
- Participation in the formulation and implementation of efficient legal rules to minimise transaction costs of the parties and to achieve sustainable development.

It has received 444 abstracts against the announced seven conference themes. They were:

1) Law and Economics of Private and Public Laws;
2) Environmental Challenges;
3) Consumer Contracts;
4) Crime against Women;
5) Intellectual Property Rights;
6) Law and Finance; and
7) Constitutional functionaries and the Public Trust, from the academic fraternity, professionals and decision makers.

The double review process of the abstracts helped us to select 42 oral and 26 poster presentations. We had 27 oral presentations in nine sessions and 11 poster presentations. Based on the recommendations of the oral sessions' chair and combined with a few keynote talks, we had developed 12 chapters for publication.

The contributors have developed their chapters by keeping in view globalisation, that not only enhances the Gross Domestic Product of the member nations of United Nations, World Trade Organization, World Bank and the International Monetary Fund but brings market (Competition) and non-market (Gender discrimination) conflicts that requires ex-ante (Administrative Laws) and ex-post (Private Laws) effective remedial measures. The chapters emphasise in a nutshell:

- Law and Economics have continued to improve and expand, introducing behavioural insights from psychology and, most recently, empirical methods to the study of law. The chapter urges law and economics scholars around the world to engage with local, regional, and national decision makers to create a process for the routine collection of empirical evidence about a wide range of legal matters. (Chapter 1);
- The role of innovative leadership (R&D) and its challenges in value creation for the stakeholders and ecology in one of the Fortune 500 Companies. (Chapter 2);
- The docket - explosion results in docket-radiation (Accumulation of court cases) and in turn will contribute to high transaction costs where there are no disputes in credit transactions that ultimately hinders overall economic growth and development. (Chapter 3);
- Mergers & Acquisitions, In-house R&D and Selling techniques increase the market share of firms in the Indian cement sector. Thus, there is a need for an ex-post scrutiny of M&A by antitrust authorities in combination with other business strategies to curb the anti-competitive behaviour of the firms. (Chapter 4);
- The chapter focuses on the relationship between gender identity, perceived gender discrimination and stress among working professionals. The empirical work reveals that gender identity significantly predicts perceived gender discrimination and that gender identity and perceived gender discrimination together predict stress. (Chapter 5);
- An Analytic Hierarchy Process (AHP) model and its usefulness to policy makers on the structured implementation of financial inclusion in India. The model states that among the various drivers of financial inclusion, the role of rural intermediaries assumes the highest importance for the adoption of a financial inclusion policy in the country. (Chapter 6);

- The chapter examines the factors that determine the level of financial inclusion in India. According to the study, banks' accessibility and enhancement of information communication technology will help to achieve financial inclusion and in turn achieve social wellbeing. (Chapter 7);
- The chapter analyses the institutional arbitration and its efficacy in providing redressal to aggrieved contractual parties in the construction sector in India. The study highlights that a speedy and cost-effective method of dispute resolution between parties will enhance their economic performance. (Chapter 8);
- The chapter examines TRIPS and TRIPS plus the pharmaceutical industry and healthcare in India. According to it, the pharmaceutical product patent provisions shall trade off between the growth of pharmaceutical industry and the improvement of public healthcare in India under the TRIPS regime. (Chapter 9);
- This chapter analyses the extent to which the European REACH Regulation contributes to adequate risk control of nanomaterials. It introduces an analytical framework which may support the Indian legislator in identifying the "most harmonious fit" to solve the regulatory choice problem of ensuring safe and sustainable management of nanomaterials in chemical legislation. (Chapter 10);
- People's demand for more anti-corruption constitutional provision will result in more corruption. According to the study, the Constitution should control and limit the power and authority of the state; thus, it will reduce corruption in that manner. (Chapter 11); and,
- The chapter explores, within the context of law and economics, some key ideas in the movement of towards 'social economics'. May we instead of law and economics consider law as economics and economics as law? Are there ways to integrate considerations of 'efficiency' with 'justice'? How is one to view 'efficiency' both as a 'static' and 'dynamic' social process? How do the judicial process and law shape the free market and stand shaped by it? Does the 'nudge' theory implicitly extend to Indian social action litigation? (Chapter 12).

The interdisciplinary subject Law and Economics is gaining momentum among academicians, practitioners and policy makers in India. The higher educational institutions viz., National Law Institutions, Indian Institute of Technologies, Management Institutions carry out teaching, research and outreach activities on Law and Economics. The Apex Court Justices Sapre A. M., Sikri A. K. and Chandrachud D. Y., apply law and economics principles to the cases of Shivshakti Sugar Mills v. Shree Renuka Sagar and Justice K.S. Puttuswamy (Retd.) v. Union of India in the year 2017. The Government of India in its legislations viz., the Real Estate (Regulation and Development) Act and the Insolvency and Bankruptcy Code use the principles. The Indian Association of Law and Economics (IALE) was formed in the year 2016.

Panta Murali Prasad
Ranita Nagar

Acknowledgements

The book is the outcome of the 2nd International Conference on Law and Economics at Indian Institute of Technology Kanpur, 2016. The conference was organised by Indian Institute of Technology Kanpur, Gujarat National Law University-Gandhinagar and Indian Institute of Management Ahmedabad.

Grateful thanks are due to the Directors of Indian Institute of Technology Kanpur, Gujarat National Law University-Gandhinagar and Indian Institute of Management Ahmedabad. Grateful thanks are also due to Prof. H. B. Schäfer, at Bucerius Law University, Germany, for his helpful advice as on teaching, research and outreach activities of Law and Economics in India.

Thank are due to the contributors of book chapters: Thomas S. Ulen, Uday S. Racherla, Ramanand Mundkur, Neha Jaiswal, Pulak Mishra, *Indrajit Dube*, Navya Jain, Meena Osmany, Syed Hameedur Rahman Zaini, Asif Akhtar, RavindraTripathi, Priyanka Tandon, Nikhil Yadav, Mohana Raje, Kavita Kalyandurgmath, Jagdish Raje, Hardik H. Parikh, Julian Schenten, Supruet Thavornyutikarn, Upendra Baxi.

Emanuela Carbonara, University of Bologna, Manoj Dalvi, Long Island University, Errol D'Souza, Indian Institute of Management Ahmedabad, T. C. A. Anant, University of Delhi,Y. V. Reddy, Former Governor, Resrve Bank of India, Satish Jain, Jawaharlal Nahru University, D Narasimha Reddy, University of Hyderabad, Ariel Porat, Tel Aviv University, Vikramadita Khanna, University of Michigan Law School, Bandi Kamaiah, University of Hyderabad, Jaivir Singh, Jawaharlal Nahru University, Avinash S. Ganu, Visiting Faculty, GIPE, Sayali Ganu Dabake, Visiting Faculty, GIPE, Hitesh Kumar Thakkar, Gujarat National Law University, Marisport A., Gujarat National Law University, Tarun Gupta, Indian Institute of Technology Kanpur, Praveen Kulshreshtha, Indian Institute of Technology Kanpur, RavindraTripathi, MNIT Allahabad, Navin Bali, IBBI, New Delhi, Rahul Arora, CUTS, Jaipur, Kamonluck Daensophon, Thammasat University, Shantanu Braj Choubey, Lawyer, Patna High Court, Jasmine Kaur ,Lawyer, Punjab and Haryana High Court, Bedanta Chakraborty, Gujarat National Law University, Cheta Sheth, Gujarat National Law University, Jagrati Gupta, Gujarat National Law University, VidhiKatiyar, Punjab university,

Nitin N. Zade, TISS, Amitava Roy, St. Xaviers' Kolkata, Ashu Arora, Allahabad University, Nishant Vats, Centre of Advanced Financial Research and Learning, Nabarun Ray, Gujarat National Law University, Lalit Panda, Alumni, Gujarat National Law University, Ram Singh, Delhi School of Economics, VivekRanjan Pandey, Advocate, Anish Sugathan, Indian Institute of Management Ahmedabad, YugankGoyal, Jindal School of Liberal Arts and Humanities, Nalin Bharti, Indian Institute of Technology Patna, Anand S. Dayal, Koura & Co., Advocates, Vikas Kumar, AzimPremji University, Sarbjit Singh, CUTS, Jaipur, Mamta Kumari, Indian Institute of Technology Patna, Dereje Asfaw, Indian Institute of Technology Kanpur, Smeshekar, NLIU, Kartin Meyer-Renschhausen, University of Applied Sciences Darmstad, Sital Kalantry, Cornel Law School, Viswanath Pingali, IIMA, Ravindra Kumar Singh, GNLU, contributors of oral and poster presentations and participants of the ICLE, 2016, and many others. Many thanks to all of them.

Grateful thanks are due to Indian Council of Social Science Research (ICSSR), and India Infrastructure Finance Company (IIFCL) which provided us the financial assistance to organize the Conference.

We are responsible for any error of fact or interpretation which may remain, and which will be corrected as the fascinating issue at the book's heart, Law and Economics: Market, Non-market and Network Transactions, continues to unfold.

Chapter 1

Introduction

Thomas S. Ulen [1, 2]

Abstract

Law and economics has demonstrated an allure to scholars and practitioners around the world. That allure arises from the numerous important insights and avenues for understanding the law that law and economics has provided. Additionally, the field has continued to improve and expand, introducing behavioral insights from psychology and, most recently, empirical methods to the study of the law. Focusing on that latter development, this chapter explores the lack of reception to early empirical work, such as Farber and Matheson's important article eliminating the distinction between bargain and gift promises, and contrasts that cool reception to the explosion of and warm reception for recent empirical legal studies. The chapter concludes by urging law and economics scholars around the world to engage with local, regional, and national decisionmakers to create a process for the routine collection of empirical evidence about a wide range of legal matters.

Keywords: Behavioral Law and Economics, Empirical Legal Studies, Law and Economics, Private Law.

---

[1] Swanlund Chair Emeritus, University of Illinois at Urbana-Champaign, and Professor of Law Emeritus, University of Illinois College of Law; Faculty Fellow of the Hagler Institute for Advanced Studies, Texas A&M University, and Visiting Professor, Texas A&M University School of Law, 2016-2018; Distinguished Lecturer, Hagler Institute for Advanced Studies, Texas A&M University, 2018-2019.

[2] This is a revised version of a talk that I gave by Skype to the ICLE at IIT Kanpur on Sunday, September 4, 2016. I would like to thank Professor and Dean Ranita Nagar for her very kind invitation to speak to the conference and to apologize to her and the conferees for not being able to be there with you. I had the delightful duty and pleasure of spending the week of the conference taking care of our two granddaughters.

My subjects today are the allure of law and economics and of evidence-based law. I shall seek to offer some thoughts on why this field has grabbed the attention of legal scholars all over the world and has been such a fertile source of insights into the law and of practical wisdom for the legal profession. I also want to make a preliminary case for using empirical methods to provide an evidentiary basis for law.

I have been doing law and economics for nearly 40 years, and I find it just as interesting and exciting today as I did when I first discovered the field in the late 1970s. And I think that many people, including all of you, have noticed that allure yourselves or are in the early stages of succumbing to that allure. During the time that I have had the honor and pleasure to be affiliated with great law schools and universities in the U.S. and abroad, I have also found that the people who have been attracted to law and economics are among the most intelligent, enthusiastic, and hard-working scholars that I have had the good fortune to meet and interact with.

These facts lead me to ask: Why has this field been so alluring to so many faculty, students, and practitioners for so long and in so many countries? Relatedly, why has the rate of scholarly progress toward a greater understanding of the law been so deeply associated with law and economics over the past 30-plus years? And finally, what can we do to bring the power of empirical legal studies to bear on legal debate, government officials, and practitioners?

Here are a couple of reasons for the continuing allure of law and economics. One is the inherent interest of the topic. I mean not just that law and how it operates and serves modern society are fascinating topics, although they certainly are. I mean, rather, that the most fascinating aspect of law and economics is that it brings two great and distantly related disciplines into close connection to throw remarkably bright light on each of those scholarly disciplines. We are, of course, most familiar with the insights that economics has brought to bear on law.[3]

---

[3] The amount of new knowledge that has been generated by law-and-economics scholars around the world over the past 40 years is breathtakingly large. See, for example, any of the superb texts by Richard Posner, Steven Shavell, A. Mitchell Polinsky, Thomas Miceli, and Jim Leitzel; the text by Robert Cooter and me; the two-volume *Handbooks of Law and Economics*, edited by A. Mitchell Polinsky and Steve Shavell; and the various volumes of the second edition of the *Encyclopedia of Law and Economics*, series editor Gerrit de Geest.

Just as remarkable are the less-noticed insights that the law has been able to throw on topics in economics. For example, I did not fully appreciate the power of the work being done in cognitive and social psychology (and now known as behavioral economics) by scholars like Daniel Kahneman, Amos Tversky, Richard Thaler, Paul Slovic, George Lowenstein, and others for understanding *economics* until I saw it applied by legal scholars. As yet another example that I do not believe has been adequately recognized, consider the powerful insights into bargaining and other transactions that contract law could confer on the economics of contracts.[4] The economic analysis of contracts by economists could profit greatly from a close study of contract law (especially the economic analysis of contracts).[5]

A second – and, I think, more important reason – for the continuing allure of law and economics is that the field keeps changing for the better. It is not the same field today that it was 40 years ago. Nor is it the same field that it was 20 or 10 years ago. And I am confident that the field will have made further advances in the next 20 years.

To give just three examples of these continuing improvements, consider these: First, during the late 1970s and the 1980s law-and-economics scholars wrote principally about (and elaborated) the theoretical aspects of bringing economic analysis to the study of the law. For instance, they showed how an economic understanding of tort liability might have important answers to open questions in the analysis of tort law (such as the significant differences between negligence liability and strict liability). They also showed that an economic understanding of contract law helped to explain how best to enforce bargain promises and the circumstances under which gift or donative promises might be enforceable.

The principal tool that scholars used in this first phase of law and economics was standard microeconomic theory. Legal decision makers, like economic decision makers, were thought to be rationally self-interested. As a result, they took actions that were well-suited to maximizing their well-being. So, for example, if the law imposed liability on a tortfeasor who failed to take as much precaution as required by the

---

[4] For a compelling example, see DOUGLAS G. BAIRD, RECONSTRUCTING CONTRACTS (2013).

[5] See an explanation of the Nobel Prize in Economics awarded to Oliver Hart in 2016 for his scholarship in the economics of contracts at https://content.ubs.com/microsites/together/en/nobel-perspectives/laureates/oliver-hart.html.
The possibilities for cross-fertilization between that work and contract law are many.

legal duty of care, rational potential injurers would comply with their legal duty and, therefore, the social costs of accidents would be minimized.

Second, in the late 1980s and early 1990s, law and economics discovered behavioral economics and began to apply that field to the study of law.[6]And those applications have been transformative.[7] Because behavioral economics focuses on the *actual* observable regularities of human behavior rather than on the normative ideal of the rational decisionmaker, behavioral economics was inherently of much greater interest to lawyers and law scholars (who, despite their interest in theory, are practical and pragmatic at heart).

Third, beginning in the early 1990s and continuing through to today, law and economics has taken a very empirical turn. In part, this is because the economic theories of the various areas of the law had, by that time, been so thoroughly elaborated that there was very little more to do in the way of theorizing.

I want to use the remainder of my talk to focus on this ongoing work in empirical legal studies as an explanatory factor in the continuing allure of law and economics.

I shall seek to make four central points about empirical legal studies. First, traditional doctrinal analysis, for reasons about which I shall speculate shortly, was neither capable of doing empirical studies nor, more surprisingly, interested in what those studies might reveal. Second, a widespread interest in empirical work about legal issues blossomed with the spread of law and economics, largely because economics, as a social science, had been deeply interested in confirming or rejecting its theories through empirical work since at least the 1950s. However, and third, even when the desire to do empirical legal studies appeared after the spread of law and economics, it proved difficult for that work to begin because the legal system did not routinely provide data that were well-suited to assessing empirical propositions about the law. That situation induced empirically minded legal scholars to modify their empirical techniques

---

[6] Incidentally, this application of behavioral economics to law occurred before it occurred in economics and much more thoroughly than in economics. One indication of this assertion is that I do not know a single law-and-economics scholar who was surprised by the awarding of the 2002 Nobel Memorial Prize in Economic Sciences to the psychologist Daniel Kahneman, but I do know economists who were surprised by that selection.

[7] See Russell B Korobkin & Thomas S Ulen, *Law and Behavioral Science: Removing the Rationality Assumption from Law and Economics*, 88 CAL. L. REV. 1051 (2000).

from those that they would have otherwise adopted from economics. Fourth and finally, I will make a modest proposal for something that you and I can do to make empirical legal studies better and more interesting and persuasive to legal and policy decisionmakers.

Now to some background information.

By "empirical data" I mean systematically collected information about a particular phenomenon or phenomena. Further, when I refer to "empirical data," I mean that someone has arranged those data so that they reveal as much as possible about the phenomenon. These data are typically referred to as "descriptive data" or "descriptive statistics." For example, they show us the observations that are the most common – the mean, median, and mode. They also show us the range of the data – from the lowest number to the highest number or, more technically, the variance or the standard deviation of our data. Finally, we may use these data to perform analysis of the data – for example, to search for correlations among the various elements of the data or to find causal relations through regressions.

Let me give a very brief example. Suppose that the legal phenomenon in which we are interested is crime. So, we collect as much data as we can from a variety of jurisdictions (say, cities) about a set of property and personal, nonviolent and violent crimes over a given time period. We also collect information about a variety of other matters – the number of police in each of the cities; the number of crimes that are solved by an arrest; the number of criminal defendants who are found guilty; and the punishments they are sentenced to. We then compute our descriptive statistics for all these data. We know the numbers for each city in our sample for each of, say, the last 10 years. We know the average number of crimes per city per year, and we compute the variance and standard deviation for those crimes within each city over the last 10 years.

Those *descriptive* data can tell us a lot. For example, they can tell us whether crime has been constant over the last 10 years, going up, or going down. They might tell us that crime seems to be becoming more serious or less violent. They can help us to understand variations in crime. Does crime (All crime? Only some crimes?) move countercyclically, going up when the economy goes down and going down when the economy goes up? How effective are criminal justice system variables, such as the number of police, the presence of public cameras, and the length and certainty of sanctions, in deterring crime?[8]

---

[8] For a marvelous recent summary of these and other matters, see Magnus Lofstrom

Yet another important revelation from these descriptive data can be comparisons across regional and national boundaries. Still confining ourselves to crime, our first instinct might be to believe that crime rates in Country *A* are likely to be determined by factors in Country *A*. But suppose that we discover that the pattern of crime and crime rates in Country *A* follows the pattern of crime and crime rates in Countries *B*, *C*, *D*, and so on. We know that the culture, demographics, economies, and criminal justice systems of those countries are very different. And yet our descriptive statistics reveal that the pattern of crime and crime rates is very similar in all those countries. That strongly suggests that there are some common factors across the countries that account for this similarity of patterns.

This is not merely a theoretical possibility. It is, in fact, precisely what is going on among the high-income Western countries with respect to crime rates. The patterns are eerily similar across those counties. Specifically, crime rates in all high-income Western countries peaked in the early 1990s and have been declining ever since. This is an intriguing puzzle. Why should the patterns be similar, given the many and big differences among the countries?[9]

We might wish to go beyond description to offer explanation. That typically means a causal explanation relating the variations in crime within a city, region, or country to distinct causal factors. This calls for care and sophistication regarding technique. But these matters are not so sophisticated that they should frighten away any aspiring legal scholar. I have already mentioned some of the causal factors that might be of interest. For example, we might be eager to see if stronger and longer punishment causes less crime or whether more police means less crime and vice versa.

As one of my favorite examples of the allure of law and economics (and the surprises that careful empirical work can reveal), consider the remarkable work of John Donohue and Steve Levitt. In 2001 they published a famous article demonstrating that half of the decline in both

---

& Steven Raphael, *Crime, the Criminal Justice System, and Socioeconomic Inequality*, 30 J. ECON. PERSP. 103 (2016).

[9] See Michael Tonry, *Why Crime Rates Are Falling Throughout the Western World*, 43 CRIME AND JUSTICE 1 (2014); Lofstrom & Raphael, supra n. 8; Franklin E. Zimring, *The Necessity and Value of Transnational Comparative Study: Some Preaching from a Recent Convert*, 5 CRIM. PUB. POL'Y. 615 (2006); and FRANKLIN E ZIMRING, THE GREAT AMERICAN CRIME DECLINE (2006).

violent and nonviolent crime since 1991 in the United States can be attributed to the legalization of abortion in the famous U.S. Supreme Court case of *Roe v. Wade*, decided in January 1973.[10]

There is one last background concept that I want to discuss. This will be important in what comes later. I think that empirical work is an absolutely vital second step in any serious scholarly inquiry. But what is the first step? The absolutely vital first step is to do good theoretical work.[11] By this I mean that it is important to give a general causal account of or meaningful hypothesis about the legal phenomenon that you are discussing. To give an example, consider this hypothesis: Exposure to tort liability for negligently harming another person will lead most people, such as product manufacturers, to take more care than if they were not exposed to tort liability.

There are at least two implications of this hypothesis. First, if something causes a reduction in the likelihood of an injurer's being held financially liable for harms his or her negligence causes, then potential injurers will, in the future, take less care. Second, if something causes an *increase* in the likelihood of an injurer's being held financially liable for harms that his negligence has caused, then potential injurers will, in the future, take *more care.*

Those hypotheses seem to be straightforward, and I think that most of us who have studied law and economics find those hypotheses to be both plausible and more likely than not to be true. But, importantly, that belief in the efficacy of liability on precautionary decisions is contingent on being confronted with data. The hypothesis that there is a causal connection between liability and precaution makes sense. It is plausible. But it may not be true.

This is a central point of what I want to say to you. A logically consistent hypothesis could be wrong! And indeed, the history of science – including of economics and of law and economics – provides many examples of plausible hypotheses that are simply wrong. Consider the hypothesis that the Earth is at the center of our solar system and that the other planets and the Sun orbit around the Earth. In law and economics, an example from

---

[10] See John J. Donohue III & Steven D Levitt, *The Impact of Legalized Abortion on Crime*, 116 Q. J. ECON. 379 (2001). But see also Christopher L. Foote & Christopher F. Goetz, *The Impact of Legalized Abortion on Crime: A Comment*, 123 Q. J. ECON. 407 (2008).

[11] As I've already indicated, this is precisely the pattern that law and economics has followed: Theoretical work first; empirical work second.

which we should all derive instruction is that in which scholars over the past nearly 50 years have sought to find an inverse causal relationship between the execution of the death penalty and homicide. It is perfectly reasonable to hypothesize that the possibility of being put to death may deter people from committing death-eligible crimes. But the evidence brought to bear on this hypothesis has not yet persuaded many scholars, including me, that the hypothesis is correct.[12]

The principal corrective to make sure that we do not put too much of our faith in logically consistent and attractive hypotheses is to do empirical work. That consists of collecting data relevant to establishing the truth or falsity of our hypothesis and then confronting the hypothesis with those data to see whether the world agrees with or rejects our hypothesis.

This is particularly important in a field like the law where so much of what we think about ultimately results in real actions – that is, in policies, pronouncements, and law about what is right and wrong, what is acceptable, and what is unacceptable. And these policies are frequently extremely important, such as whether some important societal values are well-served by taking a life through the death penalty.

That is to say this: We in the legal academy are not merely a debating society. We are a group of academics and practitioners whose work has the most important consequences for our societies. We teach those who will guide society in the future. As a result, we have a duty to go beyond theory to provide our students and our societies with *evidence* that our theories are much more likely to be correct than incorrect.

I will argue that we have not – until very recently – fulfilled this duty to back up our legal theories with empirical evidence.

Let me return to my four central points.

My first point is that prior to approximately 1990, very few practitioners and law professors ever mentioned that there ought to be more empirical work in law. Rather, the complaint was that if there needed to be more of anything from legal scholars, it was more and broader theorizing.

One of the most curious aspects of the pre-1980 period in legal scholarship was that there *was* some empirical legal research being done, but no one seemed to find it interesting.

---

[12] I very highly recommend John J. Donohue III & Justin Wolfers, *Uses and Abuses of Emprical Evidence in the Death Penalty Debate*, 58 STAN. L. REV. 791 (2005), and John J. Donohue III & Justin Wolfers, *Estimating the Impact of the Death Penalty on Murder*, 8 AM. L. ECON. REV. 249 (2009).

Let me give you an example. In 1985, Dan Farber and John Matheson, then of the University of Minnesota Law School, published "Beyond Promissory Estoppel: Contract Law and the 'Invisible Handshake,'" 52 *U. Chi. L. Rev.* 903 (1985). The article concerned a principle of contract law called "promissory estoppel." That principle provided a justification for enforcing a contract in which someone promised to give a gift or other benefit – what is called a "donative promise" – to another party without receiving anything explicit back from the other party.[13]

Under central principles of contract law in the common law countries, only a "bargain promise" is said to be enforceable. A "bargain promise" is one in which one party promises to do something for another party in exchange for that party's doing something in return. Because gift or donative promises do not have this reciprocal nature, they were thought not to be routinely enforceable.

Despite traditional doctrine against the enforceability of a donative promise, most courts in the common law countries found a means of making a promise to give a gift enforceable – through an equitable doctrine called "promissory estoppel." That doctrine held that if the party (called the "promisee") to whom the promise to give a gift believed the promisor to have been serious about giving a gift, that if believing that promisor to be serious was reasonable, and if the promisee incurred detrimental reliance expenditures,[14] the promise became enforceable.

Farber and Matheson undertook to see if, in actual practice, this is the manner in which courts in the U.S. determined the enforceability of gift promises. They looked at every case they could find in the United States in the 10 years before their paper was published in which someone had asked for enforcement of a contract on the basis of promissory estoppel.

---

[13] I would like to sidestep the issue of whether to consider a nonpecuniary benefit (such as a feeling of pride or happiness) conferred on the donor by the donee might count as "receiving [something] explicit back from the [donor]."

[14] Suppose that Smith promises to give the University of Illinois a gift of $150 million in order to build a new law school. The University believes Smith to be serious, and Smith intends for the University to believe her to be serious. So, in reliance on the promise's being fulfilled, the University purchases land for the new law school, hires architects to draw up plans for the new building, publicizes the good news of the gift and the new building, and more. These and other expenditures (including, perhaps, opportunity costs incurred) taken by the promisee (the University), if they are reasonable and if it was reasonable to believe the promisor, constitute "detrimental reliance expenditures" and almost certainly make Smith's promise enforceable.

They expected this doctrine to have been raised in cases in which there was no bargain – that is, in disputes involving gift or donative promises. They also anticipated that because most U.S. courts had incorporated the equitable doctrine of promissory estoppel, most gift or donative promises in which there was reasonable detrimental reliance, would be enforced.

What they discovered was somewhat different. First, promissory estoppel was not being applied just to donative promises. It was being applied to a broader class of promises, including bargain promises, including commercial contracts. Second, the courts did not inquire into the matter of what reliance expenditures were made and whether those were reasonable. Third, the courts' principal concern, Farber and Matheson found, was whether the promise was a serious one upon which a reasonable person would have relied.

Farber and Matheson said that they believed that this empirical evidence showed that judges did not distinguish between bargain and gift promises; rather, courts behaved as if any serious promise triggered enforceability. Courts are apparently prepared to enforce any promise made in furtherance of a legitimate economic goal.

This is not what contract law professors teach their students (or taught those judges when they were law students). Even if those professors distinguish between bargain and gift promises and have different doctrines that they say trigger enforceability of those different forms of promising, that is apparently not what courts are doing. In short, Farber and Matheson's empirical work seemed to have found that what was actually going on in contract disputes was subtly but importantly different from what contract law professors were (and are still) teaching their students.

What was the effect of this remarkable empirical finding? You might have expected that the community of contract law scholars would have taken note, at least to the extent of mentioning this finding to students in lectures, casebooks, or treatises. So far as I can tell, they did not do so. The legal academy did not change anything at all. I find this astonishing. It is as if a medical study found that a particular medical procedure was completely ineffective, but the medical profession continued to teach and use the procedure.

So, to summarize: Prior to 1990 or so, not only was there very little empirical legal work but even when dramatic empirical legal scholarship appeared, as in the Farber and Matheson study, very few paid attention.[15]

My second central point is that all this changed around 1990. By that date, law and economics had become a central part of modern legal scholarship. And because law and economics began by bringing the precepts of economics into the study of law and because economics has for the last 80 years made a commitment to do empirical work regarding its theories, the rise of law and economics invariably meant the (eventual) rise of empirical legal studies. That is, the rise of empirical scholarship in the law – not just the work (that was done before) but having the legal profession pay attention to this work – is due to the rise of law and economics.

My third point is that there have been substantial impediments over the past 25 years to doing empirical legal research. The first and most obvious is that law professors and practitioners were not taught or skilled in doing empirical work. This fact began to change with the rise of law and economics and the hiring of joint J.D./Ph.D. degree-holding professors with empirical skills from other disciplines.

A second impediment was that few, if any, legal systems around the world routinely collect data about legal matters that is well-suited to allowing researchers to describe and explain the extent to which laws are working well or ill. Even if a jurisdiction collects data about litigated disputes (as, for example, is being done by the PACER system in the U.S.[16]), that is not very helpful. Litigated disputes account for less than 5 percent of all disputes and are, therefore, only a fraction of legal disputes. Many of the other things that might interest us about the law, such as records of the number of contracts successfully concluded, the number of parcels in a jurisdiction that change hands in arms-length exchange, and the number and kind of parcels taken by governmental or delegated private entities in a given time period, are currently unrecorded.

---

[15] Another example, also from contract law, of a remarkable empirical finding that has had, to my knowledge, very little impact is Douglas Laycock, *The Death of the Irreparable Injury Rule*, 103 HARV. L. REV. 688 (1990), and DOUGLAS LAYCOCK, THE DEATH OF THE IRREPARABLE INJURY RULE (1991).

[16] PACER stands for "Public Access to Court Electronic Records." See www.pacer.gov. PACER is a system for the electronic storage of U.S. federal court documents. The system began in 1988, and by 2013 was said to contain 500 million documents.

Early empirical researchers were ingenious in finding relevant data in archives or creating data through randomized controlled trials, surveys, and experiments. But there is only so far that this creativity can take us.[17] Now that a significant portion of the legal academy – if not practitioners, public policy decisionmakers, and the public – is eager to do and report on empirical studies of legal issues, we need to take steps to provide them with data.

The fourth and final point that I would like to make about evidence-based law is this: Because data about the law are not being collected regularly, we in the legal field can all do something to help. In fact, we can do two things. First, we should make, as forcefully as we can, repeated demonstrations to our own profession and to public decisionmakers of the importance and value of empirical legal studies. People often seem to be beguiled by wonderful-sounding legal and policy reform proposals that suggest the many ways that those proposals might make society happier, wealthier, fairer, and more efficient. But those proposals can be, at best, coherent and plausible. They may still be wrong or oversold. Much stronger is the proposal that is coherent, plausible, and supported by powerful evidence.

Second, once we have made a case for doing (even *requiring*) empirical evidence, we can, and should, urge the legal system – the legislature, agencies, the courts, private lawyers, and others – to begin to collect systematic data. Perhaps we can help to form a committee with public and private officials that can examine what data could be cheaply but routinely collected and stored in a publicly accessible form. The time to begin that project is yesterday, not today or tomorrow.[18] The sooner we all begin, the greater will be the thanks of future legal researchers, policy students, and everyday citizens.

---

[17] A common, but not necessarily good criticism of behavioral findings, has been that these findings were generated by laboratory experiments, not by real choices made in the field. To the extent that real decisions are different from laboratory decisions, this is a criticism that would lose some sting if there were better data about real legal decisions.

[18] There is precedence for this development in the history of economics. When economics developed an interest in macroeconomics, including economic growth, in the 1940s and early 1950s, Simon Kuznets devoted considerable energy to getting the U.S. government to develop national income accounts. Those accounts are now so extensive that they serve as benchmarks of how society is doing with regard to many economic variables, such as growth and unemployment.

Bibliography

Baird, Douglas G., (2013) *Reconstructing Contracts*. Cambridge, MA: Harvard University Press.

Cooter, Robert D., &Thomas S. Ulen, (2016) *Law and Economics* (6th ed). Available without charge at http://scholarship.berkeley.edu/book2.

De Geest, Gerrit, (2012 – 2018) *Encyclopedia of Law and Economics* (2nd ed). Cheltenham, UK: Edward Elgar.

Donohue III, John J., & Steven D. Levitt. (2001) *The Impact of Legalized Abortion on Crime*, 116 Q. J. Econ.379.

Donohue III, John, J., &Justin Wolfers. (2009) *Estimating the Impact of the Death Penalty on Murder*, 8 Am. L. Econ. Rev.249.

Donohue III, John J., & Justin Wolfers. (2005) *Uses and Abuses of Empirical Evidence in the Death* Penalty *Debate*, 58 Stan. L. Rev. 791.

Foote, Christopher L., and Christopher F. Goetz. (2008) *The Impact of Legalized Abortion on Crime: A Comment*, 123 Q. J. Econ. 407.

Korobkin, Russell B.&Thomas S. Ulen, (2000)*Law and Behavioral Science: Removing the Rationality Assumption from Law and Economics*, 88 Cal. L. Rev. 1051.

Laycock, Douglas, (1990),*The Death of the Irreparable Injury Rule*, 103 Harv. L. Rev.688.

Laycock, Douglas, (1991) *The Death of the Irreparable Injury Rule*. Oxford: Oxford University Press.

Leitzel, Jim, (2015) *Concepts in Law and Economics: A Guide for the Curious*. Oxford, UK: Oxford University Press.

Lofstrom, Magnus, &Steven Raphael, (2016)*Crime, the Criminal Justice System, and Socioeconomic Inequality*, 30 J. Econ. Persp.103.

Miceli, Thomas J. (2017) *The Economic Approach to Law* (3rd ed). Stanford, CA: Stanford University Press.

Polinsky, A. Mitchell, & Shavell, Steven, eds. (2007) *Handbook of Law and Economics*. (ed) Vols. 1 & 2. Amsterdam: North Holland.

Polinsky, A. M. (2011) *An Introduction to Law and Economics* (4th ed). New York: Wolters Kluwer.

Posner, Richard A., (2014) *The Economic Analysis of Law* (9th ed). Boston: Little, Brown and Company.

Shavell, Steven, (2004) *Foundations of Economic Analysis of Law*. Cambridge, MA: Harvard University Press.

Tonry, Michael, (2014) *Why Crime Rates Are Falling Throughout the Western World*, 43 Crime and Justice 1.

Zimring, Franklin E., (2006) *The Great American Crime Decline*. Oxford, UK: Oxford University Press.

Zimring, Franklin E., (2006) *The Necessity and Value of Transnational Comparative Study: Some Preaching from a Recent Convert*, 5 Crim. Pub. Pol'y.615.

Chapter 2

What is Innovative Leadership? An industry perspective

Uday Racherla [1, 2]

"A leader is one who knows the way, goes the way and shows the way."
-John Maxwell

Abstract

Based on the analysis of autoethnographic experiences from the Fortune 500 companies, my research shows that "innovative leadership" is, "*leadership that solves the needs/wants/challenges faced by the company, by creatively leveraging ideas and resources to overcome constraints, risks and uncertainties – to create "value" for all stakeholders.*" This is not an academic study, but a study that analyzes and narrates "*real-world personal learnings*" of crisis leadership in a Fortune 500 company. Thus, in this talk, I take a page out of my R&D executive leadership in Fortune 500 Companies, and show how *innovative leadership* can be *very complex* and involve *doing many right things* under challenging circumstances–such as, setting the right vision and strategy in an unchartered territory; reframing constraints, risks and uncertainties; inspiring others in adversity; pioneering solutions when experts predict failure; persuading others through evidence when their interests are different; overcoming crises with courage and conviction; resolving conflicts; and doing what is ethically right rather than politically right – to achieve results. Finally, in this talk, I demonstrate how *innovative leadership* is worth its struggle as it creates "value" for all the stakeholders,

---

[1] Uday Racherla, Ph.D., M.B.A., Professor of Innovation and Intellectual Property Management, Industrial & Management Engineering, Indian Institute of Technology Kanpur, Kanpur 208016 (2012-2017); udays@iitk.ac.in

[2] This work is based on the key note address delivered at the 2nd International Conference on Law and Economics at IIT-Kanpur (2016).

namely– "win" for consumers, "win" for the company, "win" for shareholders, and "win" for the environment.

Keywords: Innovation, Value Creation, Innovative Leadership.

Peter Drucker said,[3] "*Management is doing things right,*" while "*Leadership is doing the right things.*" Indeed, we agree with this philosophical position.

According to Dave Ulrich of the University of Michigan,[4] there are four principles that are critical for *leadership.* They are (quoted as such):

1. Effective leaders *should start with results.* Leadership is equally about *what we deliver* as it is about *who we are, what we do, and what we know.* Some leadership results are *outside the organization* (customer share, investor confidence, community reputation) and some results are *inside the organization* (employee productivity and organization capability).
2. Effective leaders have *nailed the fundamentals.* There are some basic rules that all leaders need to master. Absent mastery of these *five basics,* leaders will be burdened by their weakness. Leaders *need to (a) shape the future, (b) get things done, (c) manage others, (d) invest in others, and (e) demonstrate personal proficiency.*
3. Effective leaders *build leadership* more than leaders *by creating a leadership brand.* Individual leaders matter, but *leadership matters more.* Leadership comes from *building the infrastructure* that develops the next generation of leaders. When leadership *starts with and focuses on customers, it is more likely to endure.*
4. Effective leaders ensure *leadership sustainability.* Leadership is an *enduring pattern not an isolated event.* When leaders change their pattern of behavior to make the requirements of their position, they are sustainable."

---

3 https://www.ukessays.com/essays/business/management-is-doing-things-right-leadership-is-doing-the-right-things-business-essay.php

4 https://michiganross.umich.edu/sites/default/files/uploads/RTIA/pdfs/dulrich_wp_what_is_leadership.pdf

Thus, Ulrich's research emphasizes that *leadership must achieve results*, that it *requires doing the right things* (basics), that it *needs to focus on customers*, and that it *requires resilience and flexibility* to be sustainable. Thus, this perspective is fully in step with the realistic personal experiences I will narrate in this talk.

Today, we find companies facing challenging times: *technologies* are advancing at lightning speeds; *customer* wants and *market* needs are constantly evolving; competition is becoming global; *social pressures* are mounting; *environmental concerns* of public are growing; *governmental regulations* are demanding higher operational standards from the businesses; *business models* need to be flexible to meet evolving global needs.

In my own experience, in today's dynamic and challenging world, businesses need *innovative leadership- in order to succeed and deliver sustainable results to all the stakeholders involved.* Then, the question is, *"What is innovative leadership?"*

To answer this question and explain what *innovative leadership "actually looks like in the real world,"* I will show you a personal example from my own 20+ year R&D global leadership experience in the Fortune 500 companies.

Innovative leadership – a case study

The ABC Company is an FMCG Company[5] in the USA. It is an approximately $10 billion company with five divisions, and multiple global brands that are either #1 or #2 in America. I was the Head of R&D for one of its divisions.

My division had been facing incredible *competitive pressure* from an FMCG Giant in the world, due to its strategic acquisition of another major competitor of ours; Customers were *demanding newer innovations* in our products, as their needs were evolving; The California Air Resources Board (CARB) passed a *tough new environmental regulation* that required one of our major brands to reduce the Volatile Organic Chemicals (VOCs)[6] from 7% to 4% within 3 years or remove the products from the market entirely! I was hired by the ABC Company as the Worldwide Director of R&D for this division as soon as the CARB regulation was announced, to bring newer

---

[5] The identity of this company is purposely masked.

[6] The Piston-Can packaging had 3% VOCs and the Gels themselves carried 4% VOCs (Total = 7% VOCs).

innovations into our products as well as get the entire product line compliant with the regulation. Everything looked normal from outside the company before I actually took charge of the R&D.

At the outset itself, I realized that bringing completely new innovations to create adjacent brands for this division was a different kind of challenge, as compared to achieving regulatory compliance that required Draconian reduction of VOCs in a major product line that consisted of 24 SKUs.

Stances of the Board of C-Level Officers. To get the ball rolling, I requested for a meeting with the board of C-level officers consisting of the CEO and his top advisors, namely Chief Marketing Officer (CMO), Chief Operations Officer (COO), and Chief Financial Officer (CFO), among other principals to strategize potential future directions for my R&D workforce. Therefore, as part of this discussion, I suggested three *strategic options* for CARB VOC compliance:

- Change the Packaging, Don't Change the Gels (Option-A)
- Don't Change the Packaging, Change the Gels (Option-B)
- Change the Packaging and Change the Gels (Option-C)

First, I tried to propose Option A. Immediately, the COO remarked, "You can do that over my dead body! *No packaging change allowed*!" Obviously, I found his position rather inflexible. Therefore, I asked him to explain. He then stated that *packaging change would cost the company* at least, $30 million in capital investment, not easily recoverable through product sales (risk). He wouldn't let that happen on his watch. The rest of the board agreed with the COO's position.

Next, I tried to explore Option-B with the board of directors. Immediately, the CMO jumped into the conversation and remarked, "Are you kidding? *Do you think anyone will allow any changes to gels? No way!*" Naturally, I found his answer unsettling, considering the meagre options available for solving this particular challenge. So, I asked him to explain. The CMO stated, "Our gels are #1 in the market place! Any changes to gels will be easily detected by the customers (constraint)." The rest of the board members also echoed this opinion.

Once Options-A &B were rejected outright, it was amply clear that Option-C became an orphan. So, I didn't see any point raising it. The net result was that no one liked the Options that I suggested, and no one offered any alternatives either. Indeed, this was a stalemate.

Expert Opinions. As this was *unchartered territory* for me, and I was not an expert in this field, I wanted to talk to experts in the field. Accordingly, I asked my research engineers who each had 15-25 years of experience in making and selling aerosols, for their advice. When I explored Options-A&B with them, they all told me in a singular voice that these gels and packaging were optimized over 10 years of R&D. Thus, the expert opinion summed up to the following: *there was no scope for any modifications of either packaging or gels.*

Uncertainty. As CARB regulatory compliance within a 3-year window was unchangeable, what everyone agreed was *not doing anything was not an option,* though everyone appeared to dislike the Options suggested and no one had any clue about what to do next. Without a solution in hand, future looked uncertain.

Reframing Constraints, Risks and Uncertainties* (CRUs) *and setting Vision. At this stage, I *reframed the CRUs* in my own mind and carved out a "*unique vision.*" In line with my vision, I designed *mental solutions* for solving the problem, *to persuade the experts and the board of directors.* The goal was to make them see my vision under reframed CRUs, so they would allow me to explore Options-A &B.

Creating Opportunity When there was no Clear Way Forward. I called for another meeting with the Board of C-Level Officers. I reframed the CRUs. I asked COO whether he would still oppose Option-A if the capital investment was about $5 million and not $50 million, and the manufacturing lines would see minimum modifications, but not radical changes. The COO, who wanted to look reasonable, agreed with me in front of the entire board of officers and said that *he would be perfectly fine with that.* Next, I asked the CMO whether he would still oppose Option-B, if I could make changes to gels which the consumers might not be able to detect. He too, like the COO, said that *he would be perfectly fine with that.* This was the opportunity I was waiting for!

Implementing Vision, Persuading the Same Experts. Now I had to win over my own experts (senior engineers) to take a second look at the problem. For this, I *questioned the status quo* in a way that was rational to them and opened their minds to look at what must be done in a new light. Then, I suggested a "*whole new approach*" to address the "knowledge gaps," which they could not refuse to work on. So, they conducted "new research" according to my technology strategy, and under my supervision. This resulted in "*inventions*" *that were very encouraging*:

> **Option-A.** The same engineers who originally said that packaging had been optimized over 10 years of R&D and had no possibility for any change found an *improved packaging solution that would allow us to reduce VOCs from* 3% to 1%, *ensuring that it still worked*

efficiently. This solution might allow us *to retain the gels without any change* (4% VOCs), provided our competitors agreed to join us to lobby the CARB to accept VOC reduction from 7% to 5% (1% from packaging, 4% from gels).

Option-B. Similarly, extensive research by my group using an array of "new" experiments revealed that *the VOC content in gels also could be reduced from* 4% to 2%, *without being detected by users, at least on laboratory scale.* This confirmation was done by the same experts who said that the gels could not be improved. This added more credibility.

Option-C. Now that we can change packaging as well the gels, I asked my team to quickly "put together" a *modified gel* with 2% VOCs and *improved packaging* with 2% VOCs (this is indeed Option-C, about which I didn't even discuss with the board members). This worked beautifully, far better than what anyone could imagine. Everyone who tested our "new solution" felt that it was better than our market product. We have a CARB compliant gel and packaging in our hand!!!

At this point, I realized that we needed to communicate our *invention successes* and get the company's commitment to moving ahead.

Blind Testing the New Products with Board Members. Thus, the stage was set for upwards communication. Therefore, once again, I requested a meeting with the board of C-level officers so that they could blind test the *new products* against our *actually marketed products* and experience the outcome of our *product innovation.* There was a miraculous outcome. Every single board member, without exception, loved and picked our *new products* over *actually marketed products.* They also said that they could easily recognize the actually marketed products, even in sleep (words they had to later swallow!).

When they were told about what they had picked, *they all stood up and gave a standing ovation in amazement.* So, everyone blessed Option-C. The stage was next set for large-scale consumer testing of all the products as per Option-C.

Testing Option-C in three large U.S. Cities. The gels of the entire product line of 27 SKUs were changed, and packaging modified and tested in 3 large U.S. cities. The results came out as amazingly positive! *Consumers preferred the new products over the products actually sold in the market.*

Launching our new innovation in the market. Compliance with CARB. Finally, we successfully launched the new products in changed packaging in the market place. Thus, we fully complied with the CARB deadline and saved the entire aerosol business.

Overall Leadership Outcome. Thus, the lesson here is that *innovative leadership* creates real results *value for the company* (complied with CARB and saved 50 million capital investment)[7], *value for the customer* (they got their preferred products to meet their needs), *value for the shareholders*(the company was later divested for a huge profit), and *value for the environment* (less VOCs in the environment).

Thus, based on the analysis of autoethnographic experiences, I propose that *innovative leadership* is, "*leadership that solves the needs / wants / challenges faced by the company, by creatively leveraging ideas and resources to overcome constraints, risks and uncertainties – to create "value" for all stakeholders.*" In doing so, leaders *shape the future, get things done, manage others, invest in others, and demonstrate personal proficiency.*

Bibliography

Drucker P. F., (2013). Management and Leadership Principles, Essays, UK. Online. Available at https://www.ukessays.com/essays/business/management-is-doing-things-right-leadership-is-doing-the-right-things-business-essay.php?vref=1 (Accessed October 16, 2018).

Ulrich, D., and Small wood, N., What is Leadership? The RBL Group. Online. Available athttps://michiganross.umich.edu/sites/default/files/uploads/RTIA/pdfs/dulrich_wp_what_is_leadership.pdf (Accessed October 16, 2018).

[7] We invented alternative packaging that used no VOCs but costed $50 million in capital investment, which we did not mention in this paper.

Chapter 3

From explosion to radiation: Why court delays affect loan EMIs and the wider economy

Ramanand Mundkur [1]

Abstract

The docket-explosion has led to docket-radiation, where as a result of court delays, transaction costs have increased even in transactions where there are no disputes. The additional costs inflict a huge burden on economic growth in India. Eliminating court delays should, conversely, have a knock-on effect in reducing these transaction costs–thereby accelerating economic growth. Some have also postulated that eliminating court delays should increase access to credit, thereby also stimulating economic growth. The chapter examines these issues and assesses approaches that might be used to address the problem. To begin, the first part of this chapter briefly examines the current state of affairs by reviewing the scale of the docket-explosion and concerns regarding docket-exclusion in India. Thereafter, it turns to assess how the docket-explosion has led to docket-radiation, by increasing transaction costs in credit transactions. The final part of the chapter examines the various reasons for the current state of affairs and identifies possible approaches to address the problem.

Keywords: Law's delay, credit transactions, transaction costs

---

[1] LLM (Harvard), BA, LL B (Hons) (NLSIU). The author would like to thank his associates, Midhika Joseph and Apurba Kundu, for their invaluable assistance in preparing this paper.

3.1. Docket explosion and docket exclusion

In June 2016, a total of 597,887 new cases were filed in the Indian courts, and 582,205 pending cases were disposed of in the same month. In July 2016, a total of 687,551 new cases were filed, while 659,900 cases were disposed of. A similar pattern is seen in most months, and the number of new cases filed each month normally exceeds the number of pending cases disposed of by the courts. In the circumstances, and given prior delays, there are now about 22 million cases pending in the courts. As the following table shows, in July 2016, over 12 million cases were pending for at least two years, out of which more than 2 million were pending for more than 10 years.[2]

Table 3.1.: Pending Cases

Status in July 2016	Civil		Criminal		Total	
	Cases	%	Cases	%	Cases	%
Over 10 years	670,936	8.97%	1,608,808	10.82%	2,279,744	10.20%
Between 5 and 10 years	1,177,969	15.75%	2,573,168	17.30%	3,751,137	16.78%
Between 2 and 5 years	2,229,164	29.80%	4,303,283	28.94%	6,532,447	29.23%
Less than 2 years	3,401,403	45.48%	6,384,999	42.94%	9,786,402	43.79%
Total pending cases	**7,479,472**	**100.00%**	**14,870,258**	**100.00%**	**22,349,730**	**100.00%**

Source: National Judicial Data Grid

Civil litigation can take several years to reach resolution in India. Some conjecture that a commercial dispute could take 15 years to reach final resolution depending on the nature of the case and the remedies sought.[3] The problem becomes even more worrisome when one considers that more than two-thirds of the 22 million pending cases are criminal cases (and involve situations where individuals have been incarcerated pending trial—without any determination of guilt).

Alternative dispute resolution methods and special tribunals appear, for the most part, to be bogged down in a similar morass. Although comprehensive data on alternative dispute resolution methods,

[2] National Judicial Data Grid (2016).

[3] KPMG-CII (2014).

particularly arbitration, is lacking, anecdotal evidence and court records suggest that a substantial number of arbitration proceedings also get dragged to court in any event; and delays in enforcement of arbitration awards in India have become chronic.

In the 2011 *White Industries* case, the International Chamber of Commerce's arbitral tribunal was asked whether a 10-year delay suffered by White Industries in enforcing an arbitration award in India breached India's investment treaty obligations. The Tribunal had "no difficulty in concluding the Indian judicial system's inability to deal with White's jurisdictional claim in over nine years, and the [Indian] Supreme Court's inability to hear White's jurisdictional appeal for over five years amounts to undue delay and constitutes a breach of India's voluntarily assumed obligation of providing White with "effective means" of asserting claims and enforcing rights."[4]

Commentators such as the former director of the National Judicial Academy, Dr G Mohan Gopal, have noted that a larger problem presented for India's judiciary is not the *docket explosion* described above, but a problem he refers to as *docket exclusion.* This is, in essence, a description of the current situation where the poorer and more marginalized sections of Indian society have been frozen out from accessing the judiciary.

Dr Mohan Gopal illustrates this concern by using the example of the US, where some 330 new cases are filed for every thousand people, while Bihar has an annual filing of about four new cases per thousand. The annual filing for India as a whole is 17 cases per thousand. Within India, Kerala has about 40 new cases per thousand population and Delhi has about 52 new cases per thousand.

This significant difference is not attributed to fewer violations or breaches in Bihar or Kerala compared to the US. Rather, the problem is attributed to a mix of an overloaded judiciary coupled with approaches that prevent the judiciary from working efficiently.[5]

A corollary of Dr Mohan Gopal's observations concerns trial costs. Since trial costs are linked to trial length, in order to keep costs down and ensure

---

[4] White Industries Australia Limited v Republic of India final award dated November 30, 2011, at p 119, available at http://www.italaw.com/sites/default/files/case-documents/ita0906.pdf (accessed July 24, 2016).

[5] Mohan Gopal (2016).

wider access to justice, it is important to ensure that trial lengths are also kept short and reasonable.

3.2. Docket radiation

The scale of the problem is not limited to the extremely worrisome docket explosion and docket exclusion described above. Judicial delays aren't just affecting the millions of cases languishing in courts, or the hundreds of millions of instances where disputes are not settled and rights are not enforced through the courts.

The problem appears to be affecting the billions of transactions carried out each year—where there are no disputes at all. In effect, the docket explosion has led to a toxic radiation that's affecting the entire economy.

This radiation is evident in India's private sector lending where virtually all loans (other than credit card debt) are secured. Lenders insist on collateral because of the cost, delay and uncertainty associated with enforcing creditor rights. Borrowers have no choice but to provide the collateral, as alternative sources of funding are unavailable. Making secured lending easier and more reliable for creditors (as has been done through the SARFAESI Act)[6] addresses the symptom and—for the reasons explained below—exacerbates the problem. This is because, in the Indian context, secured lending comes with high, hidden, economic costs.

At least five such hidden costs appear self-evident–particularly in the Indian context. First, more often than not, with secured lending, the loan decision is no longer primarily driven by the potential economic benefit or likely success of the financed activity. Rather, the lending decision is more closely linked to the value of the collateral provided to secure the loan. Second, loan defaults and non-performance don't just impact the financed activity (for which the loan was taken)–they also impact the (possibly healthy) assets provided as collateral. Third, encumbering capital assets creates artificial scarcity in those assets and prevents the use of those assets for additional (potential revenue-generating) economic transactions. Fourth, secured lending makes the encumbered capital assets vulnerable to value erosion from unrelated transactions (as the pledged or secured assets cannot be dealt with until the security is released by the lender). Fifth, because of the artificial scarcity in capital

---

[6] The Securitisation and Reconstruction of Financial Assets and Enforcement of Security Interests Act, 2002.

assets created, and because of the inability to deal with those assets during the tenure of the loan, secured lending masks clear market signals on the price and value of encumbered capital assets, which in turn affects capital allocation by markets.[7]

Take the example of a publicly listed borrower, B, that borrows Rs 1,000 million, and pledges the publicly traded shares it holds in another publicly listed company, C, as collateral to secure this loan. The pledged shares cannot be traded until the loan is repaid. Therefore, until the loan is repaid, the supply of company C's shares is artificially lowered. Economic transactions involving the pledged shares are also frozen for this period. As a result, the pledged shares are also more vulnerable to value erosion during this time. If company C were to make a poor business decision, then while the pledge is valid, B would not be able to sell those shares in response to C's poor business decision. In such case, B would have no option other than to sit by and watch asset value erode. This also shows that B has no way of managing or limiting the adverse effects of a poor economic decision by C, while the shares are pledged. And, for the same reason, the markets would not be able to effectively signal responses to bad business decisions by C.

While the above principles apply most acutely when the collateral is in the nature of assets like shares, the principles would also hold to a varying degree if other capital assets, such as real property, were pledged as collateral.

Other aspects of the economy are being affected as well. Court delays are seen as an opportunity to game the system. Unscrupulous high-value borrowers identified as 'wilful defaulters' have been using court delays to buy time and delay or defray the impact of their defaults. The resulting costs are being picked up by the banking system. This, in turn, affects capital adequacy and overall systemic risk within the banking system.

The following table compares the average time taken by courts to decide a case in each of the G20 countries, with the percentage of non-performing assets (NPAs) in each such country, as reported in early 2016.

---

[7] Mundkur (2016).

Table 3.2.: Percentage NPAs and Time to Enforce Contracts

Country	NPAs as Percentage of Total Loans	Time to Decide Case (in Days)
Argentina	1.7	590
Australia	1.00	395
Brazil	3.30	731
Canada	0.50	570
China	1.50	453
France	4.00	395
Germany	--	429
India	5.90	1420
Indonesia	2.40	471
Italy	18.10	1120
Japan	1.60	360
Mexico	2.50	389
Russia	8.30	307
Saudi Arabia	1.20	575
South Africa	3.10	600
South Korea	0.60	230
Turkey	3.00	580
UK	1.40	437
USA	1.50	420

Sources: IMF, World Bank

Admittedly, the above data contain inherent limitations (such as on the manner in which the period of time taken for a court to decide a case has been computed and differences on the manner in which non-performing assets are recognised and reported in different countries). However, as the following scatter diagram of the same data shows, there appears to be a slight positive correlation between judicial delays and overall non-performing assets. Moreover, in outlier countries, such as India and Italy, where the time taken by courts far exceeds the average time in other G20 countries, it is not surprising that the percentage of NPAs is also very high.

Figure 3.1.: Relationship Between NPAs and Time Taken by Courts

The link between a country's robustness in enforcing the rule of law and a country's economy cannot be overstated. A 2013 paper by the OECD reviewed trial processes in OECD countries and recognised the key economic role of judicial systems. By guaranteeing property rights, judicial systems strengthen incentives to save and invest. By guaranteeing enforcement of contracts, judicial systems stimulate agents to enter into economic relationships by dissuading opportunistic behaviour and reducing transaction costs. This has a positive impact on growth through various channels.[8]

Economists have also found that improving judicial systems increases credit growth generally. In a 2002 paper, Prof Jappelli and his colleagues, postulated a model that illustrated how improvements in judicial efficiency reduce credit rationing and increase the volume of lending.[9] A later paper examining evidence from India's debt recovery tribunals similarly found that legal enforcement of lender rights increases credit access for all borrowers, by expanding the set of incentive-compatible loan contracts.[10]

Given these economic benefits, it is disappointing that judicial delays continue to plague the Indian economy a quarter of a century after India

---

[8] OECD (2013).

[9] Jappelli et al (2002).

[10] von Lilienfeld-Toal et al (2012).

undertook structural reforms to liberalise its economy in 1991.The next section turns to examine why these problems persist in India and how they might be addressed.

3.3. Causes and responses

In any country, factors affecting delays in courts can arise both on the supply side and on the demand side.[11] In India, though, supply-side issues appear to play a larger role.

On the supply side, one of the most significant factors affecting court delays is the grossly inadequate number of judges in the country.[12] The Supreme Court of India reported that at the end of last year the sanctioned strength of judges in the country was 21,669 judges. Not only is this number of judges itself inadequate, but there are also numerous vacancies in the sanctioned strength of judges. With nearly 5,000 posts vacant, in effect, the country's 1.25 billion people are served by barely 16,000 judges. This has resulted in judges being overburdened with a high volume of cases and insufficient time to dedicate to that large workload of cases.

In addition, systems and processes followed by Indian courts (both in terms of workload administration and legal procedures followed) add to the delays. For instance, judicial rosters are frequently rotated in courts throughout the country. When such rotations occur, judges who have been previously hearing a case get allotted to other cases and new judges have to start hearing the same cases from the very beginning. This process results in a significant duplication of work and wastes time previously spent. In addition, there are few incentives to prevent lawyers from adopting delaying tactics as litigation strategy—i.e., often with the intention of pushing up litigation costs for the other side. Lawyers file frivolous motions or interlocutory appeals and seek multiple adjournments (often for trivial reasons), such measures are frequently frowned upon, but they will be rarely sanctioned. For instance, if and when costs are awarded to a successful party, the costs are nominal and completely unrelated to actual legal costs incurred. Even in the infrequent instances where 'punitive' costs are awarded, the award falls short of actual costs incurred. This overall lack of rigor in sanctioning improper delaying tactics allows these malpractices to continue unchecked, thereby adding to the problem of court delays.

---

[11] OECD (2013).

[12] Law Commission of India (2014); Mohan Gopal (2016).

The technological infrastructure of India's court systems also cries for attention. While computerization is used in workload management in the Supreme Court and the High Courts, even in these higher courts, filings and service processes still rely on physical delivery of documents. In the lower courts, computerization of workload management and court records is extremely deficient.

In sum, the quantity (and quality) of financial and human resources devoted to justice, inefficiencies in the production process due to the lack of techniques for efficient management of cases and the diffusion of information and communication technologies and the improper structuring of the incentives for judges and lawyers are just a few of the factors fomenting court delays on the supply side.

The costs of litigation, including lawyer fees, availability of and faith in the judicial system, inconsistencies affecting the certainty of judicial outcomes, and the diffusion of alternative dispute resolution methods are all factors influencing court delays on the demand side.

In addition, it has been recognized by the courts that the government, government companies and government agencies comprise the single largest group of litigants (often in disputes involving only government departments and entities).[13] The government's careless and callous over-use of the judiciary has also resulted in overburdening the courts, increasing court delays and limiting overall access to courts for ordinary citizens.

The above list of causes is by no means exhaustive and is, in fact, barely illustrative. However, as with many issues, what is most telling in such situations, is a review of the nature and amount of financial resources being dedicated to the judiciary at present.

The total scheme-wise budgetary allocation for law and justice for 2016-17 is Rs 5,100 crores (i.e., the equivalent of just US$ 763 million at July 2018 exchange rates). Of this, Rs 5,011.99 crores (or approximately US$ 750 million) is on account of plan and non-plan *revenue* expenditure, and the remaining Rs 88.01 crores (or approximately US$ 13 million) is on account of non-plan capital expenditure. Even within the revenue expenditure allocations, Rs 3,649.29 crores (or approximately US 546 million) has been

---

[13] Chief Conservator of Forests v Collector, (2003) 3 SCC 472.

allocated for non-plan revenue expenditure on *elections.*[14] The actual expenditure by the Ministry of Law and Justice in the previous year shows little variation from these overall themes.

In effect, the bulk of the government's expenditure in relation to law and justice is either for elections or by way of revenue expenditure (essentially salaries, professional fees, and maintenance). Less than 2% of the government's, already meagre, budgetary allocation to law and justice is towards capital expenditure. In other words, no investment is being made in creating or building the essential 'judicial' infrastructure that is so desperately needed in India.

Given the long history of court delays, there have been numerous suggestions on reforms that can address the problem of court delays.[15] Many of these suggestions have focussed on the essential area of strengthening judicial manpower—both by filling existing vacancies and by increasing the sanctioned strength of judges. Other suggestions have sought to also examine productivity and efficiency issues towards addressing court delays, such as through the effective use of technology, changes to case administration procedures, and changes to litigation procedures.[16]

To be fair, efforts are ongoing towards better management of litigation. For instance, a draft National Policy of Litigation is being formulated with the aim of reducing the government's over use of courts. Efforts are also being made to develop a web-portal that would allow the government to monitor all the court cases in which it is involved. An 'e-Courts' project (which has been underway since 2007) continues to be implemented, with the goal of universal computerisation of district and subordinate courts. Measures have also been undertaken to repeal obsolete laws and enact new laws associated with the administration of justice.[17]

3.4. Conclusion

While efforts are being made to address the problem, the Government's budgetary publications demonstrate that not enough is being done. All the

[14] Ministry of Law and Justice (2016a). Although the Election Commission is an autonomous body, election related expenses appear to be booked through the Ministry of Law and Justice.

[15] Law Commission of India (2014); George (2014).

[16] OECD (2013).

[17] Ministry of Law and Justice (2016b).

efforts being made are conducted on a shoe-string budget—and the monetary allocations have no relationship to the sheer scale of the problem. Hence, there is a need for a change in mindset. To begin with, it would be useful to recognize the role of the judiciary and the administration of justice within the overall economic infrastructure of the country. In fact, the rule of law is effectively the key ingredient without which the factors of production in any economy cannot work. Labour, capital and land simply cannot be effectively utilised without the rule of law. There has been and continues to be significant investment and structural reform in other areas of infrastructure–roads, rails, ports, airports, power, irrigation, networking and telecommunications. There is a need for investment of a similar scale and wider structural reforms of similar calibre in this area of infrastructure too–i.e., infrastructure that supports and enables the rule of law. Sadly, until this happens, we are doomed to continue using teaspoons to tunnel through the landslide of court cases that blocks the country and its economy from inclusive and meaningful progress and growth.

Bibliography

George S. R., (2014) *Releasing India's Supreme Court from the Shadow of Delay: A Proposal for Policy Reform,* March 16, available at https://www.hks.harvard.edu/index.php/content/download/66823/1240102/version/1/file/SYPA_SimiGeorge_2014.pdf (accessed August 4, 2016).

Jappelli T., Pagano M., and Bianco M., (2002) *Courts and Banks: Effects of Judicial Enforcement on Credit Markets,* available at https://ideas.repec.org/p/sef/csefwp/58.html (accessed July 24, 2016).

KPMG-CII, (2014) *Ease of Doing Business in India, 2014,* KPMG-CII Survey, *available at* https://www.kpmg.com/IN/en/IssuesAndInsights/ArticlesPublications/Documents/KP

MG-CII-Ease-of-doing-business-in-India.pdf (accessed July 24, 2016).

Law Commission of India, (2014) 245th Report, *Arrears and Backlog: Creating Additional Judicial (wo)manpower,* July, available at http://lawcommissionofindia.nic.in/reports (accessed April 20, 2016).

Mathur S. and Bolia N., (2016) *In India's District Courts a Crisis is Revealed,* April 5, 2016, *available at* http://www.indiaspend.com/cover-story/in-indias-district-courts-a-crisis-is-revealed-79079 (accessed April 20, 2016).

Ministry of Law and Justice, (2016a) *Outcome Budget 2016-17,* Government of India—Ministry of Law and Justice, *available at* http://lawmin.nic.in/ld/Outcome-2016-17.pdf (accessed August 4, 2016).

Ministry of Law and Justice, (2016b) *Initiatives Taken by the Ministry of Law and Justice During the Two Years of the Present Government,* available at http://lawmin.nic.in/la/2year-achi.pdf (accessed August 4, 2016).

Mohan Gopal G., (2016) *Justice and the Two Ideas of India*, in Frontline, May 27, 2016 available at http://www.frontline.in/cover-story/justice-and-the-two-ideas-of-india/article8581178.ece#test (accessed July 24, 2016).

Mundkur R., (2016) *Investing in the Right Infrastructure*, in LiveMint, January 6, available at http://www.livemint.com/Opinion/tkCfqdl34UPNHdOsAOc9rM/Investing-in-the-right-infrastructure.html (accessed July 24, 2016).

OECD, (2013) *What Makes Civil Justice Effective?* OECD Economics Department Policy Notes, No 18, June.

von Lilienfeld-Toal U., Mookherjee D., and Visaria S., (2012) *The Distributive Impact of Reforms in Credit Enforcement: Evidence from Indian Debt Recovery Tribunals*, Econometrica, Vol 80, No 2.

Chapter 4

Mergers, acquisitions, competitiveness and competition: A study of the Indian cement sector

Neha Jaiswal[1], Pulak Mishra[2], and Indrajit Dube[3]

Abstract

The emergence of mergers and acquisitions (M&A) as strategies for restructuring and growth of firms during the post-reform period is well recognized in existing studies. However, it is also observed that the distribution of such deals is highly skewed towards a few industries like cement, thus raising concerns about market concentration therein. In the cement industry, in particular, emerging oligopolistic market structure following M&A and cartelization by the firms has become a matter of serious concern for the antitrust authority of the country. In this perspective, the present paper makes an attempt to examine how M&A along with other business strategies have affected the structure of the market in the Indian cement industry. The paper uses panel data estimation techniques for a set of 12 firms over the period from 2000-01 to 2013-14. It is found that the strategies of M&A have resulted in greater market shares of the merging and acquiring firms. In addition, the strategy

[1] Doctoral Research Scholar, Rajiv Gandhi School of Intellectual Property Law, Indian Institute of Technology Kharagpur, Kharagpur 721 302, Email: sainehajaiswal@gmail.com

[2] Professor, Department of Humanities and Social Sciences, Indian Institute of Technology Kharagpur, Kharagpur 721 302, Contact: +91-3222-283692(O), Email: pmishra@hss.iitkgp.ernet.in

[3] Professor, Rajiv Gandhi School of Intellectual Property Law, Indian Institute of Technology Kharagpur, Kharagpur 721 302, Contact: +91-3222-81732(O), Email: id@iitkgp.ac.in

of in-house R&D and selling related efforts have also caused an increase in the market share of these firms, whereas vertical integration and inventory management are found to have a negative impact on the same. Interestingly, profitability, capital intensity and technology purchase do not have any statistically significant impact on firms' market share. Hence, an ex-post scrutiny of M&A by the antitrust authorities in combination with other business strategies is necessary to restrict anti-competitive behavior of the firms.

JEL Classification: *D43, G34, L1, L2, L4*

Keywords: Mergers and Acquisitions; Market Concentration; Competitiveness; Antitrust; Cement Sector; India.

4.1. Introduction

With the opening up of Indian economy through deregulation and policy reform measures since the 1990s the strategy of mergers and acquisitions (M&A) has emerged as a predominant strategy by which firms either restructure their business or/and grow (Basant, 2000). The incidence of this strategy is not felt equally by all the firms and in all the sectors of the economy (Basant and Mishra, 2012). The sectoral variation in M&A can be linked to the difference in market structure for each of the sector. Considering this fact, the present study looks into the Indian cement sector which is characterized to be purely oligopolistic in nature and has shown cartelized behavior as well as a consolidation drive in recent years.

It is interesting to note that the sector stands to be the second largest producer of cement in the world with an expected increase in its production for about more than 50 percent by 2020. With an oligopolistic market structure, the sector is dominated by a few dominant private players capturing most of the market. Regardless of the increase in capacity and production by the firms, the sector contributes negligibly to the trade volumes of the country. This is contrary to China's position where it contributes around 50 percent of the global output. Since a large part of the demand catered by the sector is domestic in nature, this makes the firm to underutilize its capacity. The Indian cement sector had previously witnessed a fragmented structure less concentrated, but recently the share of top players rose to 65% from its low base of 30%. This consolidation drive saw active participation by the foreign players (Anand, 2009).

About this consolidation drive, it is said that the infrastructure initiatives and the boom within the infrastructure during the late 1990s made firms raise their capacity to expect a rise in demand. The capacities exceeded the demand which in turn led to a decrease in the prices. This caused the weaker firms to sell their assets to efficient firms (Anand, 2009). Consequently, the sector has marked an unprecedented increase in the number of mergers and acquisitions. In a sector which is characterized with oligopolistic market structure, having a high level of market concentration and highly capital intensive a consolidation is a matter of concern for the market regulator (in India market is regulated by Competition Commission of India). Therefore, the present paper attempts to find out how the strategy of M&A along with various measures of competitiveness adopted by M&A incidental firms have affected the level of market concentration within the sector. In order to obtain the need and the importance of M&A within the sector, one needs to understand the decadal change or shifts in the strategies and performance of the sector since the reform era until today. The interlinkages between the structure of the market and the strategy are the crucial aspects which will be addressed in this paper.

4.2. Literature review

The theory of competition has evolved from its limited static view based on the assumption stationary state to dynamic view. Works done by Schumpeter (1950) introduced the concept of dynamic competition emphasizing the technology-driven rivalry in the market rather than price and output-based competition within the market. According to him, concentrated industries are more favorable for innovation as firms in such industries operate in a way that more closely approximates imperfectly competitive markets. This raises the market power and thereby innovative effort and R&D effort in particular. This is further supported through the findings of a number of studies that find a positive relationship between market concentration and R&D and that support the Schumpeterian proposition (Williamson 1965; Scherer 1967; Levin 1981; Weiss 2005; Jefferson et al. 2006). On the other hand, studies done by Cohen et al. (1987), Geroski (1990), and Blundell et al. (1995) have shown that industry concentration has either no effect or a negative impact on innovation. A rise in the innovative effort necessarily is linked to the amount of competitive pressure particularly by new entrants (Aghion et al., 2002).

Apart from innovation, there are a number of strategies which are being adopted by the firms in order to earn greater profitability and raise their market share. Several theories[4] have been developed postulating M&A as a

---

[4] Trautwein (1990) has discussed various theories related to motives of mergers. There are five different theories explaining the motives behind mergers. These

measure to raise market power. For example, the monopoly theory suggests that mergers are intended planned as well executed to gain market power (Steiner, 1975; Chatterjee, 1986 and Trautwein, 1990).

It is important to note that Mitchell and Mulherin (1996) in their study stated that M&As are industry-specific activities. Thus, the impact of M&A on market concentration may depend on the number and size distribution of firms in the industry, entry of new firms, import competition, expansion of the market, other business strategies, etc. In addition, the motive of the particular synergy is also important (Banerjee and Eckward, 1998)[5]. Hence, the impact of M&A on market concentration should be explored with adequate control for other related factors.

While the efficiency theory views mergers as being planned and executed to achieve synergies. This synergy may be financial, and/or operational in nature (Trautwein, 1990; Porter, 1985; Jensen and Murphy, 1988). Further, the theory suggests that M&A are planned and executed to reduce costs through the scale of economies (Porter, 1985 and Shelton, 1988). The synergies gained through M&A may enhance productive efficiency, innovative efforts, dynamic efficiency, and competitiveness of the weaker firms. Besides, entry of MNCs through acquisition may cause spillovers of technology and managerial competencies enhancing the competitiveness of domestic firms. This may prevent market concentration in the long run. In the case of India, firms are more inclined towards horizontal M&A (Khanna, 1997; Beena, 2000, Kumar, 2000; Agarwal, 2002; Basant and Mishra, 2012) and the share of vertical and conglomerate types has been less (Agrawal, 2002). According to Venkiteswaran (1997), a large number of mergers during the post-reform period are aimed at consolidation of business to achieve critical mass and size in operations, reduce costs and minimize inter-group competition.

Apart from innovating and M&As, there are another set of strategies as well which raise the firms market concentration and power. Like in oligopolistic markets, strategies for non-price competition can be crucial to firms for differentiating their products and enhancing extract market power (Kim and Vale, 2001). According to Meurer and Stahl (1994), where price competition is weak, advertising helps the consumer to understand

---

theories of M&A include the monopoly theory (Steiner, 1975; Chatterjee, 1986) the efficiency theory (Porter, 1985; Shelton, 1988), the valuation theory (Holderness and Seehan, 1985), the empire-building theory (Mueller, 1969; and Black, 1989), and the process theory (Jemison and Sitkin, 1986).

[5] There are studies (e.g., Weiss, 1965 and Mueller, 1985) that have shown either no significant change or decline in market concentration following M&As.

distinct characteristics of different brands. This makes the demand for the product less elastic resulting in increased control over price and hence higher profitability. Advertising may also act as an important strategic entry barrier and thereby limit market competition (Basant and Mishra, 2012)[6]. Besides, it helps in product differentiation and image advantage, establishing a brand, creating barriers for the new firms and thus raising incumbents' market share (Comanor and Wilson, 1967; Martin, 1979 and Shepherd, 1982). As observed by Pagoulatos and Sorensen (1981), advertising significantly influences both concentration and profits leading to entry barrier in the US food processing industry. Similarly, Mishra (2011) finds a significant influence of advertising on consumer' welfare in the Indian manufacturing sector.

In addition to advertising, marketing and distribution are important selling efforts made by the firms. While marketing helps firms in product promotion and reach consumers, a well-defined distribution network results in the timely access of products to consumers. Thus, both strategies tend to raise the level of market concentration. According to Basant (2000) and Mishra (2007), firms spent less on product differentiation vis-à-vis developing marketing and distribution related complementary assets during the post-reform period.

The regulatory and policy dimension dealt under the theory of competition gives it further dynamism. In the case of India, studies either looked into the regulatory or economic aspect of competition and moreover the law itself is in a very nascent stage. A series of work done by Bhattcharjea (2003, 2006, 2010 and 2012) made a distinction between the MRTP Act and Competition Act, 2002[7]. Agarwal and Bhattacharjea, (2006) studied the relationship between mergers in India and the regulatory changes (for the period 1973-74 to 2002-03). The study found the abolition of premerger scrutiny under MRTP Act during 1991 left a positive and significant impact over the merger behavior. The study lacks in tracing out the impact of competition law on merger activity in terms of the above-mentioned issues.

As pointed out by Tirole, (2014) the role of regulation and competition policy is to scientifically guide the beneficial public interventions which are required to be made in less competitive industries. This guiding should be made on the functioning of these imperfectly competitive markets, i.e.,

---

[6] However, it is also argued that advertising can help new firms to enter into the market through making the product known quickly to the consumers.

[7] For greater clarity see section 4.3.3, given below.

the firm's behaviour when they have market power, its consecutive effect on suppliers, customers, and competitors. Therefore, the present study is an attempt in this direction, where we try to look into the behavior of firms within the cement sector, its successive effect on the level of concentration and competition. The section below, i.e., section 4.3 gives a detailed understanding about the structure of the cement sector in India in terms of the level of M&A activities within the sector, competitiveness within the sector and competition issues seen in the past within the sector. Under section 4.4 the model specification and probable impact of the independent variable, data and methodology adopted, along with the results and discussion have been discussed. Lastly, section 4.5 discusses the conclusion of the study.

4.3. Structure of Cement Sector in India

4.3.1. Mergers and Acquisitions within the Indian Cement sector

Since the adoption of liberalization, globalization and privatization policy by the Indian economy a series of consecutive strategic changes were seen of which M&A is the predominant one. The Indian cement sector like other sectors of the economy have also reacted to the consecutive wave of M&A and adopted it as one of its vital strategies. The reasons behind the adoption of M&A within the sector could be many folds. Firstly, the creation of fresh Greenfield capacity requires a huge amount of investment. Secondly, the sector is located in only a few geographical pockets because of restricted raw material availability along with its demand and supply constraints. Additionally, there lies limitation in terms of area for setting up of new business along with a gestation period of 3-4 years. Therefore, acquiring or merging with other firm provides a feasible solution for the players within this sector. On studying the nature of deals within the sector, it was found that most of the deals were concentrated along with a rise from 2004 to 2007 (Table 4.1). This is due to the entry of leading foreign players within the domestic market. In terms of the nature of deal[8] the sector witnessed the majority of the deals to be horizontal in

[8] In the present study the categorization of M&A deals into horizontal, vertical and conglomerate is based upon analyzing the details of the deal and sub-industry grouping of target firm, acquiring firm and selling firm. A horizontal deal is one in which both the firms sell homogenous or similar goods. On the other hand, in a vertical deal a firm acquires or merges with either a consumer or supplying firm. While in a conglomerate deal apparently there is no relationship between the two entities.

nature (Table 4.1). A rise in an horizontal deal could imply that the firms concentrated more on raising the market share and raising profitability through efficiency gains which might be in the form of production reshuffling through utilizing the unused capacities, the scale of economies and using the technological and innovative capacities of each other[9]. Therefore, the present section analyzes shift in the market structure of the Indian cement sector along with its strategic decision making and their performance during the period of 1993 to 2015.

Table 4.1.: Mergers and Acquisitions deal within the Indian Cement Sector

		Nature of deal		
Year	Deal Frequency	Horizontal	Vertical	Conglomerate
1997-98	1	1	-	-
1998-99	6	1	1	4
1999-00	1	1	-	-
2000-01	3	1	1	1
2001-02	8	5	1	2
2002-03	2	1	-	1
2003-04	2	2	-	-
2004-05	8	5	1	-
2005-06	8	4	-	4
2006-07	12	8	2	2
2007-08	9	3	3	3
2008-09	5	4	1	-
2009-10	6	3	2	1
2010-11	6	5	-	1
2011-12	5	1	2	2
2012-13	5	2	1	2
2013-14	5	2	1	2
2014-15	7	3	3	1

Source: Bloomberg database

[9] Here, it is to be noted that one needs to check for the tradeoff between the welfare-reducing price effect and welfare-increasing gains in productive efficiency known as Williamson tradeoff (Belleflamme and Peitz, 2010). This tradeoff is often checked by the domestic antitrust agencies. Further, in case of India prior to Competition Act, 2002 the Monopolies and Restrictive Trade Practices Act existed but post 1991 chapter III which dealt with the restriction on M&A had became inoperative. The merger regulation within the Competition Act had also come into force since July 2011. Thus, one needs to be skeptical while assessing the effects of these deals because of its lack of scrutiny from the competition perspective.

Entry of new firms into the sector has been observed over the years. Still, the overall contribution of these firms in terms of their average market share has been negligible (i.e., less than 1%). This indicates that although the new economic reforms and the consequent boom in the infrastructure sector created enough incentive for the new firms to enter into the market and grow. The new entrants face problems in terms of the high capital cost and long gestation period along with the lack of accessibility to the raw materials (Parliament Standing Committee Report, 2011). The distribution of firms has been the same along with their market share remains the same from 1993 to 2008 except for the period 2009-2015. The global economic slowdown could be a reason for the decline in firm's participation and their respective average market share. Given the number of firms and its average market share distribution, it becomes important to understand the level of market concentration within the sector.

Table 4.2: Trends in market share distribution of the firms since (1992-93 to 2014-15)

Range	1993-2000		2001-2008		2009-2015		1993-2015	
	No. of firms (%)	Avg Mkt Share (%)	No. of firms (%)	Avg Mkt Share (%)	No. of firms (%)	Avg Mkt Share (%)	No. of firms (%)	Avg Mkt Share (%)
0 < Mkt Share < 1	38 (61.30)	0.21	46 (66.67)	0.26	53 (71.62)	0.21	45 (66.18)	0.23
1 < Mkt Share < 5	18 (29.03)	2.07	18 (26.09)	2.24	15 (20.27)	2.39	17 (25.00)	2.22
5 < Mkt Share < 10	4 (6.45)	6.87	2 (2.90)	7.43	4 (5.41)	6.63	3 (4.41)	6.99
10 < Mkt Share < 15	1 (1.61)	13.89	2 (2.90)	12.06	1 (1.35)	10.49	2 (2.94)	12.22
15 < Mkt Share < 20	1 (1.61)	16.54	1 (1.45)	16.47	1 (1.35)	14.09	1 (1.47)	15.83
Mkt Share> 20	0		0		0	20.63	0	20.63
Total (%)	62 (100)		69 (100)		74 (100)		68 (100)	

Source: Prowess, CMIE

In order to assess the level of market concentration of the firms within the cement sector the present study undertakes HHI, Entropy, GRS and CR4. The average HHI has remained the same over the years indicating towards a stagnant level of concentration for the industry as a whole. Overall since 1993 to 2015 the level of concentration has declined with the majority being contributed in the first phase followed by the second but after 2009, the concentration has increased.

Table 4.3: Trends in various indices of Concentration, its Skewness and Standard Deviation since (1992-93 to 2014-15)

	HHI			Entropy			GRS			CR4		
Year	AV	GR	S.D.	AV	GR	S.D.	AV	GR	S.D.	AV	GR	S.D.
1993-2000	0.07	-2.93	0.01	8.57	1.04	0.23	0.17	-3.34	0.02	0.46	-1.12	0.02
2001-2008	0.07	-0.33	0.00	9.41	1.88	0.45	0.15	-0.64	0.02	0.44	0.11	0.02
2009-2015	0.07	4.72	0.01	10.64	1.35	0.32	0.17	8.62	0.04	0.43	2.19	0.03
1993-2015	0.07	-0.29	0.01	9.49	1.40	0.91	0.16	0.24	0.02	0.44	-0.33	0.02

Source: Prowess, CMIE

Mishra et al. (2011) in his study has noted the problems with the widely accepted measures of market share and its limitation. Therefore, the table above gives a fair glimpse about the structure of Indian cement sector. In the year 2011, the sector which came under the scanner of Competition Commission of India for cartelization activity by the top 11 firms and a penalty of 50% of the average profit for 2009-10 and 2010-11 imposed respectively[10]. Interlinking the structure of the market and how the strategy of M&A affects the structure of the market. It is important to understand the implications of the decrease in concentration and the subsequent rise in the number of small firms into the market since 2009 along with a rise in M&A activities since 2004. Can M&A be credited to the decline in the concentration and the rise in the number of entrants within the market as its post effect? Another important aspect is to check whether M&A has been an alternative to escape from the penalties of cartelization and if not than what are its actual motives. For this one needs to see the subsequent efficiency gains from such strategy other than just raise in market concentration. Therefore, the next section looks into the competitiveness scenario of the sector over the years.

4.3.2. Competitiveness within the Indian Cement sector

This section aims to give an overview of the existing level of competitiveness shown by the firms within the sector. In terms of competitiveness, the firms are assessed in three ways- first on the bases of non-price and technology strategy, second in terms of their cost efficiency and lastly in terms of performance. Among the various non-price strategies advertising is one of the most important strategies. Here one needs to remember that this strategy stands vital only for firms selling

[10] See, CCI Case No. 29 of 2010

differentiated products. But in an oligopolistic market structure where firms are selling only homogenous commodities adoption of such a strategy hardly helps them. Thus, total expenditure made on this strategy is less than one percent of the total sales from 1993 to 2015 (Table 4.4). But it is interesting to note that although the advertising intensity has continued to be less than 1 percent, it has still relatively increased.

Strong marketing and distribution network help the firms in two ways. On the one hand, a well-knitted marketing and distribution network of a firm can help in raising accessibility and enhances efficiency which in turn raises the demand for the product. On the other hand, such assets increase the bargaining power of the firm in equity-based foreign collaborations as they help the firms to have greater access to distribution channels which may be useful for the MNCs (Basant and Mishra, 2012). The cement sector firms have given greater importance to distribution strategy by raising the amount spent on it (Table 4.4). As the sector is divided in terms of geographic location in India based on the accessibility of raw materials and demand. Therefore, in order to both access raw material and the supply of goods, both requires an efficient distribution network. While over the years marketing intensity has been more or less consistent over the years. Selling strategy which gives an overall view of the firms spending on advertising, marketing and distribution has shown an increasing trend for the sector. Studies in context are indicative of the fact that selling expenses have significantly affected market concentration (Mishra and Behera, 2007) and patterns of M&A activity across industries (Mishra, 2011).

Table 4.4.: Trends in non-price and technology strategies in Indian Cement Sector since (1992-93 to 2014-15)

Year	Advertising /Sales (%)	Marketing /Sales (%)	Distribution /Sales (%)	Selling /Sales (%)	R&D /Sales (%)	Domestic Tech. Pur (%)	Foreign Tech. Pur (%)	Total Tech. Pur (%)
1993-2000	0.44	2.29	11.00	13.73	0.15	0.73	1.26	1.99
2001-2008	0.59	2.01	13.12	15.71	0.09	1.18	1.28	2.46
2009-2015	0.70	2.34	15.23	18.27	0.06	1.23	1.87	3.10
1993-2015	0.58	2.21	13.11	15.90	0.10	1.05	1.47	2.52

Source: Prowess, CMIE

Technological expenditure[11] is also an important factor which helps us to understand the structure of the market in a better manner. Market-driven with a high amount of competition makes technological expenditure one of their vital strategies. As this helps them in two ways- firstly, it raises the efficiency in terms of increased output, better utilization of resources and having an edge over the competitors in terms of the better quality of the product. Secondly, increased technological advancement also helps to create a kind of barrier for new entry within the market. Although in a purely oligopolistic structure of market the cement sector has shown an increasing trend towards total technological expenditure. This implies the firms are driven with some amount of competition within the sector which would compel them to adopt cost reducing or higher value added product technique reflected in increasing technology expenditure. This increasing trend could also be due to raised M&A activities within the sector where the firms come together in order to raise their selling efficiency along with technological advancement.

Table 4.5.: Trends in cost-efficiency in Indian Cement Sector since (1992-93 to 2014-15)

Year	Raw material/Sales (%)	Power and Fuel/Sales (%)	Salaries and wages/Sales (%)	Total Production cost/Sales (%)
1993-2000	12.88	24.75	1.69	39.32
2001-2008	10.63	24.77	5.24	40.65
2009-2015	12.39	21.36	5.18	38.93
1993-2015	11.97	23.63	4.04	39.64

Source: Prowess, CMIE

One of the widely discussed objectives behind any M&A is the efficiency gains that are obtained by economies of scale through access to cheaper raw materials due to the increased size of purchases, better management, etc. In a sector like cement the production cost in terms of raw material, power and fuels and salaries constitute the majority of the cost. The sector has been more or less consistent in terms of these types of costs. Adding to

[11] Here total technological expenditure intensity comprises of domestic technology purchase and foreign technology purchase by the firms. This basically signifies the technological motivation of the firms.

this is a long term overview which shows an increase in the raw material expenditure within the sector. This can mainly be due to lack of domestic availability of raw material which has raised its import raising its overall cost. There is an overall decline in the power and fuels[12], salaries and wages and total production cost as a whole. Thus, one needs to check whether this consistency and decline could actually be attributed to an increase in M&A activity by the firms over the years or are due to any other factor.

Table 4.6: Trends in Corporate Performance of Indian Cement Sector since (1992-93 to 2014-15)

Table 6: Trends in Corporate Performance of Indian Cement Sector since (1992-93 to 2014-15)						
Year	ROCE (%)	ROA (%)	PBITA/Sales (%)	PAT/Sales (%)	Export/Sales (%)	Import/Sales (%)
1993-2000	13.57	14.63	14.88	0.48	3.17	1.14
2001-2008	20.95	19.08	22.27	5.71	3.96	1.21
2009-2015	19.74	22.67	26.33	11.03	1.54	1.73
1993-2015	18.09	18.79	21.16	5.74	2.89	1.36

Source: Prowess, CMIE

Profitability rises with a decrease in cost. As observed in the table above over the year's firms have increased total technological expenditure have tried to reduce their production cost causing a rise in its profitability. Firms have also been efficient in terms of raising their return on capital employed and net fixed assets. While the cement sector which has been known over the years for its high capital intensiveness has declined its capital intensity. Technological advancement also facilitates exporting intensity of the firms as it makes them internationally competitive. The tables above are indicative of the fact that the Indian cement sector

[12] There has been a steep decline in the supply of coal due to diversion of coal to power sector. This has made firms to opt for more economized option fuel for their plants (See, report on Valuation Analysis of Indian Cement sector).

although has improved its technological base but still lacks in technological advancement to compete internationally. Moreover, cement is a bulky commodity, and thus transportation cost comprises of a huge part of its cost. Thus, the plants within the sector are domestic in nature distributed in various geographical locations and catering the demand of that region. This can be one of the vital reasons for the sector's incompetency to contribute to trade balance[13]. This is contrary to China's position where it contributes to around 50 percent of the global output. The short fall of raw material causes the firms within the sector to import. As still the sector highly depends on domestic raw material availability this causes the firms to have fluctuating but increased importing intensity over the years.

4.3.3. Competition issues within the Indian Cement sector

As the sections above look into the market structure and behavior of the firms within the cement sector. Now in the present section the level of competition and the role of market regulator have been analyzed. On assessing the level of competition on the bases of market structure and competitiveness shown by the firms one needs to check the behavior of the firms shown in the past. The industries characterized by high overhead costs like cement, mining, chemicals, steel and aluminum are particularly subjected to pricing disciplines breakdowns. It is when a cyclical or secular decline in demand forces member firms to operate well below designed plant capacity (Scherer, 1980). Studies on the sector rightly pointed out that without a change in costs, price increases indicate changes in market power and hence changes in profitability, which is the main reason for any collusive agreement (Anand, 2009 and Singh, 2013). In this regard, the Indian cement sector is no different and has shown the act of cartelization[14].

---

[13] According to Cement Manufacturers Association the country's cement production was 330 million tonnes in 2013 which is expected to double to reach almost 550 million tonnes by 2020.

[14] Collusive (or price fixing) behavior by the firms arises in the form of cartel where the firms stop competing with each other has always been under the scanner of antitrust agencies. On the one hand it is said to affect the market in the form of increase in price, lower product variety and quality reduced innovation in the effected market all these affects the long-run economic growth and productivity (Ghosal, 2011). On the other hand, a possible argument is that collusion increases the price cost margin of the firms further raising their profits. This raised profit may incentivize new firms to enter into the market. Consequently, this entry may

In order to understand the market structure, strategic behavior and the consequent performance of the firms, it is important to study the behavior of the firms followed by the reaction of regulatory authority in the past. The Competition Commission of India (CCI) has detected cartelized behavior among the firms within the Indian cement sector. The Builders' Association of India had alleged Cement Manufacturing Association and other top performing eleven cement manufacturing companies[15] in the year 2010 to indulge in anticompetitive activities. The Commission judged the case in respect of violation of section 3 (1) (a) and (b) of the Competition Act, 2002[16]. Therefore, with the help of analyzing the factors[17] mentioned in section 19 (d) to (f) to establish the contravention of section 3(3) (a) and (b) stood established. The commission thus exercised its powers and penalized the parties imposing a penalty of Rs 6,300 crore (i.e., 10% of their turnover for all 11 firms respectively) and Cement Manufacturer Association of India was fined 10% of its total receipt since 2009 to 2011.

---

socially desirable to ameliorate the previous social under provision of the number of products. Along with this the sharing of information within a cartel addition helps in efficient allocation of resources leading to decline in overall production cost in turn raising the welfare (Belleflamme and Peitz, 2010). However, the antitrust agencies have always taken cartels "per se" to be anticompetitive. In the present case we discuss the Indian cement cartel case of 2012.

[15] These eleven companies were ACC, Gujarat Ambuja Cements Limited (now Ambuja Cements Limited), Ultratech Cements, Grasim Cements (now merged with Ultratech Cements), JK Cements, India Cements, Madras Cements, Century Textiles & Industries Limited, Binani Cements, Lafarge India and Jaiprakash Associates Limited.

[16] For details about the section see competition act, 2002.

[17] Broadly the judgment was based on firstly studying the market structure were 12 companies comprised of 75% of the total capacity rightly pointing towards oligopolistic structure of the market. Secondly the commission found that the CMA is engaged in collecting competition sensitive data which it circulated among its members which facilitated coordination among the companies. Next there was immediate increase in price just after the high powered committee meeting took place. On investigating with the participating members there were some inconsistencies in terms of their reply. Again, there were traces of price, product and dispatch parallelism and artificially limiting and controlling the capacity utilization (i.e., under the investigation it was found that year on year bases there was decline in capacity utilization by the firms). Due to inelastic nature of good along with the above said actions caused firms to artificially raise its price, formation of price leaders and enjoying high profit margins.

Again, with the amendment of merger regulation[18] within the Competition Act reviews the M&A related deals. Even though there were a number of deals within the cement sector (see Table 4.1) since the coming up of this regulation still only these seven deals crossed the threshold limit[19] and did the filing. It is important to note that out of the eleven firms penalized for cartelized behavior three of them were engaged in M&A deals that required filing with CCI. These deals fell under section 5 dealing with the combination (i.e., according to the act M&A both fall under this section) and were judged under section 20 (4) whether the said deal would appreciably affect the relevant market (Table 4.7). Section 20 (4) of the act catalog a number of issue like actual or potential level of competition through imports into the market; extent of barriers to entry; level of combination in the market; degree of countervailing power in the market; whether the combination could lead to a rise in price and profit margin; extent of effective competition likely to sustain in the market; availability of substitutes; market share of both the entities; combination causing removal of vigorous or effective competitors; nature and extent of vertical integration and innovation and benefits obtained through the proposed combination.

Despite the fact that these three firms showed cartelized behavior in the past according to judgment, their strategy of combination was not to make any appreciable adverse effect on competition. Again, most of the deals passed were horizontal in nature.

---

[18] Under section 5 of the act discusses about the mergers and acquisition under the broad heading of combination. The various competitive strategies adopted by the players such as merger, acquisition of shares, assets, acquiring control of an enterprise has been addressed by the composite expression "combination" under section 5 of the act. Here combinations have been defined in terms of assets and turnover a) exclusively in India and b) in India and outside India. Thus, the section is guided by the following basic principles where a combination would result, subject to the other prescriptions of the section, such as the monetary thresholds of assets or turnover of the enterprises specified therein.

[19] For detailed thresholds limits see, Central Government notification S.O. 479(E) dated 4th March, 2011.

Table 4.7: M&A deals approved by CCI since 2011 to 2015

Year	Acquirer/Investor	Target	Nature of Combination	Penalty under cartel detection
2013	Paris Cement Investment Holdings Limited	Lafarge India Private Limited.	Conglomerate	Yes (Target)
2013	JSW Steel Limited	Heidelberg Cement India Limited	Vertical	-
2013	Ultratech Cement Limited	Jaypee Cement Corporation Limited	Horizontal	Yes (Acquirer)
2014	Shree Cements Limited	Jaiprakash Associates Limited	Horizontal	Yes (Target)
2015	Holcim Limited	Lafarge S.A.	Horizontal	-
2015	UltraTech Cement Limited	Jaiprakash Associates Limited	Horizontal	Yes (Acquirer & Target)
2015	Financiére Lafarge S.A. S	Paris Cement Investment Holdings Limited	Horizontal	-

Source: Various approved combination orders under Form I/II by Competition Commission of India

As observed from the sections above there is an improvement in the various competitive strategies and performance of the firms within the market. Therefore, it is interesting to find that although the sector has such a high level of concentration and a history of cartelized behaviour, the firms are still acquainted with the strategy of merger and acquisition. Another noteworthy thing is the period of the study i.e., during a large part of our study there was an absence of antitrust agency[20]. Thus, an absence

[20] The regulatory mechanism during the period could be dealt under, the Monopolies and Restrictive Trade Practices Act (MRTPA) of 1969 abolished in the year 2009. MRTPA dealt with concentration of economic power, permission for substantial expansion of business, establishment of new undertaking and mergers. The MRTPA concentrate on curbing the monopoly and dominance behavior by the firms whereas Competition Act, 2002 looks into the anticompetitive and abusing the dominant position by the firms. It is to be noted that until 2009 the MRTPA existed but the cases which came under it were not more on anticompetitive perspective rather on consumer protection. Therefore, from the given condition it is clear that the period of the study marks a transition phase when the reform measures were actually fetching its dividends through increased foreign direct investment, exports and overall growth of the economy. Moreover, the merger regulation under MRTPA was abolished long back in the year 1991.

of a market regulatory mechanism for the period 2000 to mid of 2009 can also be linked to one of the causes for such cartel to sustain. This is substantiated through the detection of cartel and constitution of the CCI in 2009. Similarly, it is expected that the firms will react to the amendments in the merger regulation. A shift from MRTP to Competition Act, 2002 is ought to affect the behavior of the firms within the market. Given the said regulatory framework which keeps a keen eye on the behavior of the firms in the market, one need to systematically study the driving forces behind such M&A and successive changes on market structure.

4.4. Model specification

The traditional model in order to determine the cause and effect relationship between the structure-conduct-performance as proposed by Mason (1939) and Bain (1956) has been challenged. Later the work by Tirole (1988) abandoned this unidirectional framework and the notion of the dual causalities was established within the SCP frameworks. Moving a step further the influence of public policy was included by Scherer and Ross (1990) into the present framework. In the case of India, studies conducted by Mishra (2011) and Basant and Mishra (2014) were able to discuss the SCP framework by adding the much-required policy and regulatory changes into it.

$$MKT_{it} = f(M\&A\ IN_{it}, SELL_{it}, CI_{it}, PBT_{it}, R\&D_{it}, TTP_{it}, VERT_{it}, INVT_{it})$$

In the following model market share (MKT) is said to be a function of intensity of mergers and acquisitions made by the firms (M&A IN), level of selling intensity of the firms (SELL), capital intensity of the firms (CI), profitability of the firms (PBT), R&D intensity of the firms (R&D), total technology expenditure made by the firms (TTP), degree of vertical integration (VERT) and management of inventory by the firms (INVT).

4. 4.1. Probable Impact of the Independent Variables

4.4.1.1. Mergers and Acquisitions (M&A IN): M&A can affect the firm within the market in two ways. According to the monopoly theory, mergers are intended to raise market power (Steiner, 1975; Chatterjee, 1986 and Trautwein, 1990). But on the contrary, the efficiency theory view suggests that the synergies caused by M&A help the firm to reduce costs through the scale of economies (Porter, 1985 and Shelton, 1988). Therefore, as M&As are more of sector-specific activity the objective of the firm and the reaction of the other firms within the market will decide, how M&As effect market concentration of the firm i.e., whether it raises or decreases the level of concentration within the market.

4.4.1.2. Selling Intensity (SELL): Selling intensity can be seen as a firm's non-price strategy in the form of advertising, marketing and distribution. It represents the efforts firms make in order to have the edge over its competitors. Now as it consists of three vital components, this widely varies from one form of market to another. Now in a monopolistic competition, it is seen that advertising plays a much important role than the distribution. On the other hand, in the case of pure oligopoly like that of cement, a well-knitted distribution network is highly important. Greater distribution expenditure implies capturing a greater part of the market ensuring it has an edge over its competitors. Therefore, increase selling intensity in a purely oligopolistic sector may lead to greater concentration.

4.4.1.3. Capital Intensity (CI): High capital intensity may act as a barrier for other firms to enter into the market. Firms with greater capital intensity may raise their level of market concentration. But a set of other diverse factors such as M&A or another competitive strategy may act as a source of new entry into the market and raising efficiency gains and making the firm more competitive. Therefore, capital intensity on the face of it looks like a barrier for new entrants but one needs to look into a mix of other strategies in order to assess its true impact on the level of concentration.

4.4.1.4. Profitability (PBT): Higher Profitability, on the one hand, could be seen as a measure of greater market power. This could lead to a greater amount of concentration within the market. On the other hand, profitability cannot be seen in isolation of the other strategic decisions by the firm in order to detect the cause of this raised profitability. If the profitability is caused due to greater innovative efforts made by the firm this may also attract new entrants to enter into the market. If this raised profitability is due to structural and higher capital base, this may act as an entry barrier. Therefore, the impact of profitability may depend on the market structure and a set of other factors adopted by the firm.

4.4.1.5. In-house R&D intensity (R&D): Firms with greater R&D effort may act in both ways for the firms. It may cause the firm to earn greater profitability through greater efficiency raising its market share and concentration. This raised profitability may incentivize new firms to adopt this strategy reducing the incumbents' market share and level of concentration. While it may act as a constraint i.e., the rise in R&D efforts allows the incumbent to have an edge over its competitors which raises its market share and level of concentration. Therefore, R&D intensity's impact may largely depend on the level of R&D base, kind of sector and players within the market.

4.4.1.6. Total Technology Purchase (TTP): Total technology purchase is a mix of a firms R&D efforts, domestic technology purchase and foreign technology purchase. This is the firm's total expenditure in order to improve its technological base. Here the type of market plays an important role i.e., the firms in a more concentrated market structure are less inclined towards efficient means of production through greater technological effort. While firms in a concentrated market try to be efficient through raising technological efforts, it may lead to an increased profit and a rise in their market share. Therefore, it largely depends on the type of market whether it would increase or decrease.

4.4.1.7. Vertical Integration (VERT): Vertical integration means the extent to which the multiple stages of production are combined under common ownership. Firms adopt such a strategy in order to decrease the dependence in terms of outsourcing which in turn decreases their risk. A greater vertically integrated firm is cost-effective and has a better utilization of resources which makes them more competitive. This may act as a barrier for new entrants as they lack such access to well established and timely access to resources which may ultimately lead to a rise in the level of concentration. On the other hand, vertical integration may also cause profits to rise attracting new firms to enter into the market. Therefore, it is difficult to predict the actual effect of this strategy due to the other strategy adopted by the firm.

4.4.1.8. Inventory Management (INVT): Inventory management ought to be a crucial factor for manufacturing firm. Firms with effective inventory management schemes means are ought to be more efficient, are utilizing their resources in a better manner and are faced with a greater demand. This rise in efficiency may fetch them greater profit in the market raising their level of concentration. On the other hand, firms with greater profits may cause new entry leading to a decrease in concentration level. Thus, vertical integration might cause an increase or decrease in market concentration.

4.4.2. Data and methodology

The above function is estimated by using panel data estimation technique for a set of 12 firms within the cement sector which have adopted the strategy of M&A over the period 2000 to 2013.

Applying Panel data estimation not only helps in raising the size of the sample, consecutively raising its degrees of freedom and efficiency of estimates. This technique also helps to capture the process of adjustment made by different firms over the period of time. Here the data set is an unbalanced panel[21] one. In addition to this, it helps in understanding the impact of M&A on the market structure of the firms within the sector in a better manner. M&A related data has been extracted from Bloomberg database which has been successively matched with the financial data from Prowess, CMIE.

Three models have been estimated i.e., the pooled regression model, the fixed effects model (FEM), and the random effects model (REM). The pooled regression model assumes that the intercept, as well as the slope coefficients, are the same for all the 12 firms within the sector. On the other hand, in the FEM the intercept is allowed to vary across the firms to incorporate special characteristics of the cross-sectional units. In the REM, it is assumed that the intercept of a particular firm is a random drawing from a large population with a constant mean value.

In other words, in the REM the intercept of a firm is expressed as a deviation from the constant population mean (Gujarati and Sangeeta, 2007). Therefore, the choice amongst the pooled regression model, the FEM, and the REM are very important as it largely influences conclusions on the individual coefficients. Further a restricted F-test is carried out in order to make a choice between the pooled regression model and the FEM. This test validates the FEM over the pooled regression model on the basis of the null hypothesis that there is a common intercept for all the firms[22]. The FEM is chosen over a pooled regression model only if the

---

[21] If each individual in the data set is observed the same number of times, usually denoted T, the data set is a balanced panel. An unbalanced panel data set is one in which individuals may be observed different numbers of times. We will denote this Ti (Greene, 2007).

[22] Here the following test statistics is used: $F = \frac{\left(R^2_{UR} - R^2_{R}\right)/_{d-1}}{1-R^2_{UR}/_{n-(d+k)}} \sim F_{[(d-1),(n-d-k)]}$;

where R^2_{UR} stands for goodness-of-fit of the model (i.e., FEM), R^2_R for goodness-of-fit of the restricted model (the pooled regression model), d for the number of groups, n calculated F-value is greater than the critical F-value. Now in order to choose between the pooled regression model and the REM Breusch and Pagan Lagrange Multiplier test is applied (Breusch and Pagan, 1980).

This test is based on the null hypothesis of no random effect and uses a test statistic that follows χ^2 distribution. If the null hypothesis gets rejected, then the REM is chosen over the pooled regression model. Lastly to choose between REM and FEM the Hausman test[23] is applied.

The said test is based upon the null hypothesis that the estimators of the FEM and the REM do not differ significantly and uses a test statistic that has an asymptotic χ^2 distribution.

4.4.3. Results and discussion

This section consists of three tables- Table 4.8 representing the summary statistics of the variables used in the regression analysis in order to get a brief overview about them. Within Table 4.9 it is seen that the F-statistic of the pooled regression model, FEM and Wald χ^2 of the REM all are statistically significant. The explanatory power for the REM model is reasonably high than that of pooled and the FEM. According to Gujarati and Sangeetha (2007), low values don't mean one should reject the model. Additionally, neither does a high R^2 values favor's a model, nor its low value makes it worth rejecting.

Table 4.8.: Summary statistics of variables used in regression model

Variable	Obs	Mean	Std. Dev.	Min	Max
MKT	168	4.67	5.57	0.00	22.75
M&A IN	168	0.15	0.36	0.00	1.00
SELL	157	13.00	6.01	0.28	23.25
CI	159	82.55	73.35	17.52	911.58
PBT	159	8.12	10.82	-18.19	31.81
R&D	91	0.06	0.08	0.00	0.40
TTP	128	1.22	1.16	0.01	4.30
VERT	159	0.52	0.11	0.07	0.68
INVT	159	7.17	2.18	3.84	20.74

---

for the total number of observations, and k for the number of explanatory variables (for details see Gujarati and Sangeeta, 2007).

23 For details see Hausman (1978).

Further in order to check the problem of multicollinearity variance inflating factor (VIF) these explanatory variables respectively show no multicollinearity. The t-statistics and z-statistics for the individual coefficients are computed by using White's (1980) robust standard errors to control for heteroscedasticity and autocorrelation.

Table 4.9.: Regression results with Market share as a measure

Ordinary Least Squares Model				Fixed Effects Model			Random Effects Model		
Variable	Coeff	t-Stat	VIF	Variable	Coeff	t-Stat	Variable	Coeff	Z-Stat
Intercept	-3.55	-1.23		Intercept	9.80	2.06**	Intercept	-1.80	-0.57
M&A IN	1.14	1.07	1.12	M&A IN	1.43	2.74***	M&A IN	1.26	1.59*
SELL	0.65	4.37***	2.24	SELL	0.49	2.77***	SELL	0.87	7.1**
CI	0.05	2.44**	1.82	CI	0.01	0.93	CI	0.02	1.58*
PBT	0.26	6.03***	3.07	PBT	0.14	1.48	PBT	0.43	5.87**
R&D	28.91	6.69***	1.18	R&D	10.05	2.45**	R&D	28.38	6.4**
TTP	-0.12	-0.32	1.3	TTP	-0.37	-1.34	TTP	-0.43	-1.22
VERT	-4.26	-0.77	3.09	VERT	-17.36	-1.68*	VERT	-18.64	-2.38**
INVT	-0.48	-2.55***	1.55	INVT	-0.53	-1.91**	INVT	-0.71	-3.32**
F-Stat	48.06**			F-Stat	3.54**		Wald-c^2	273.45**	
R^2	0.76			R^2-Within	0.31		R^2-Within	0.16	
Adj- R^2	0.74			R^2-Between	0.65		R^2-Between	0.92	
				R^2-Overall	0.61		R^2-Overall	0.79	
Number of Observations	80			Number of Observations	80		Number of Observa-tions	80	

*** Statistically significant at 1 percent;
** Statistically significant at 5 percent;
* Statistically significant at 10 percent

The tests for the appropriate selection of the appropriate model between the three. Now in order to choose between pooled and the fixed effect model with the help of restricted F test. As depicted by the value F Statistic which is statistically significant which implies FEM to be a better model than the pooled model. Again, in order to choose between pooled and the REM the Breusch and Pagan Lagrange multiplier test[24] is performed. The

[24] See Breusch and Pagan (1980)

χ^2 value doesn't stand to be statistically significant which implies that the REM is not suitable. Lastly, Hausman test is applied in order to choose between FEM and REM. The Hausman test stands to be statistically significant implying the systematic difference between the coefficients and the FEM is a better fit than the REM. Therefore, the regression results of the FEM are chosen in order to explain the implications of individual coefficients.

Table 4.10: Test for selection of appropriate model

Purpose	Null Hypothesis	Test	Test Statistic
Selection between Pooled Regression Model and Fixed Effects Model	All $u_i = 0$	Restricted F Test	$F(7{,}64) = 15.82^{***}$
Selection between Pooled Regression Model and Random Effects Model	$\sigma_u^2 = 0$	BreuschPagan Lagrange Multiplier Test	$\chi^2(1) = 0$
Selection between Fixed Effects Model and Random Effects Model	Difference in coefficients is not systematic	Hausman Test	$\chi^2(8) = 47.03^{***}$

*** Statistically significant at 1 percent

As shown in Table 4.9 the t-statistic of fixed effect model M&A_IN, SELL, R&D, VERT and INVT are statistically significant. This implies that the market share is higher for firms with greater M&A intensity, selling intensity and R&D intensity. On the other hand, firms with greater inventory stocks and vertical integration lead to the lowering of the market share of firms. While the variables like profitability, capital intensity and total technology purchase don't influence or significantly impact the market share of the firms within the Indian cement sector.

The regression results have an important implication for the Indian cement sector. Firstly, the extent of M&A has essentially proven to raise their market share. In the case of India, studies in the past the results are indicative that the firms are more inclined towards horizontal M&A (Beena, 2000; Agarwal, 2002 and Basant and Mishra, 2012). In the present study for all 12 firms the majority of the M&A deals are also horizontal in nature. This made the firms rise their market concentration. Further, this gain in the market share through the greater inclination towards M&A has also added to their selling intensity. As noted above, selling intensity is a combination of advertising, marketing and distribution intensity. In the case of cement sector, a well-knitted distribution network is vital in order to cater for a larger market in a cost-efficient manner. Consequently, studies are indicative of the fact that selling expenses have significantly affected market concentration (Mishra and Behera, 2007) and patterns of M&A activity across industries (Mishra, 2011). Therefore, in the case of the cement sector a similar kind of result has also been found. The firms increasing their R&D intensity ought to have increased their market share in the sector. The results are high in the line of findings made by Levin (1981), Weiss (2005), and Jefferson et al. (2006), which support the Schumpeterian (1942) that concentrated industries are more favorable for innovation. Additionally, it is also to be noted that this rise in innovative efforts could be due to the adoption of a strategy of M&A by the firms within the sector.

It is interesting to note that firms having a greater market share negatively influences the extent of vertical integration within the sector. This means that the firms within the sector that have greater reliance on sub-contractual production agreements in order to reduce the risks and cost of production. Linking it to the findings above firms within the Indian cement sector is more induced to have horizontal integration within the market. This means that the firms find it more beneficial to merge or acquire firms producing similar or homogenous products in the market. On the one hand this, in turn, makes the acquiring firm to access their selling efforts and R&D development. On the other hand, it makes the firms outsource the goods or services required rather than to develop it oneself. M&As which Basant and Mishra (2012) found that the extent of vertical integration has declined over the years for sectors within the Indian manufacturing sector. The firms having greater market share had declining inventory stock. This could be due to many reasons first cement is a perishable product maintaining huge inventory may add to the cost and raise the risk for the firm. Moreover, the cement market is located in a restricted geographic location, maintaining the cost firms can only supply within this location. Thus, the firms face less fluctuation in the demand which makes them produce according to the demand and minimize inventory.

Lastly, the factors like profitability, capital intensity and total technology purchase have no effect on the market share of the firms. As stated the study intends to identify the factors influencing the market share of M&A adopted firms. This more or less is indicative of the motive of the firm behind an M&A and the efficiency gains obtained through it. The probable implication of profitability and capital intensity of the firms within the sector already have a stable capital and profit base and intend to raise their market share through other factors. For total technology purchase which is a combination of both domestic technology purchase and foreign technology purchase, it can be said that the sector is not a technology-intensive sector which makes a purchase of technology domestically and internationally completely futile. Rather the results show that the merged firms which intended to raise market share had opted for in-house R&D base either of oneself or their merging partners in order to raise their level of concentration within the market.

4.5. Conclusion

The study throws the much desired light on a sector which although had been under the scanner of regulatory agencies still lacked a detailed analysis of the said situation. The study has intended to see the factors influencing the market share for the firm's incidental to the strategy of M&A. Some of the major findings of the study are that the greater the extent of M&As the greater the market share of the firm. The strategy of M&A has helped the firms to grow within the sector. Further, in terms of competitiveness parameters like In-house R&D intensity and selling intensity significantly influences the market share of these firms positively. While the presence of vertical integration and inventory stock negatively influences the market share of the firms. The much-hyped theoretical motives of M&As profitability, capital intensity and total technology purchase have hypothetically not stood up, thus creating no impact upon on a firm's concentration.

Given the following results, it is important to link it with the existing regulatory mechanism within the country in order to derive proper implication for future policy. In order to do this, the present study is not limited to capturing the competitiveness behavior of the M&A led firms but also to makes an attempt to study the existing market regulatory mechanism i.e., the Competition Act, 2002 and link them. On studying the regulation related to M&A and the combination related orders passed by CCI in the past a greater amount of emphasis is given upon the concentration, profit and capital base measures while making the judgment. The results of the present study are important in order to understand the behavior and motives of the firms along with present regulatory framework. Along being argued in the theoretical literature that the firms earning greater profits, possessing greater capital and greater technology expenditure are ought to capture and enjoy a greater portion of the market. But the Indian cement sector has shown conversely a different understanding i.e., that these factors might not influence the market concentration. Again, this is to be kept in mind that these firms are incidental to M&A strategy. Rather the efficiency motive of the competitive factors like the rise in Research & Development and improved selling intensity makes the firms to access the greater portion of the market. But at the same time, it is also seen that the M&As are capable of raising market concentration. This means there is a relationship between M&A and the competitive efficiency of the firm. This indicates that the approval of the deals by the market regulator requires an emphasis on the competitiveness of the cement firms. However, our study does not pinpoint the role of market regulator as the Competition Act, 2002 and the merger regulation (2011) is covered only in the later period of our study. As the market regulatory mechanism is new, it creates scope for a future study to completely trace the role in terms M&A strategy and Competitiveness of the firm.

But as the study has covered some portion since the coming of Indian competition act which suggests for drawing certain implication from the result. The regulatory authority as given in Table 4.7 has approved the entire cement sector deals from 2011 to 2015 among which a few were made by or among the cartelizing firms have higher market concentration. This means that although on the face of it the deal might not seem to be adversely affecting the competition in the later years it might turn out to be anti-competitive. Saraswathy (2015) studied the efficiency gains from M&A is also affirmative of this. The study criticized the existing procedural norms for no provision in the Indian Competition Act to examine, whether the approved deal is actually bringing efficiencies, technical know-how and ultimately the consumer satisfaction since the merger control provisions are *ex-ante* in nature. Therefore, in order to curb the anticompetitive behavior made by these firms, the role of antitrust authorities should not be limited to *ex-ante* analysis but should observe the behavior of the firms once the deal is effective into the market.

Appendix: Measurement of the Variables

In the present paper, annual values are used over the period of time. Such a measure can also account for the process of adjustment along with reducing the potential simultaneity bias in the envisaged relationship. Accordingly, all the variables are measured as the simple moving average of the previous three years with the year under reference being the starting year.

Market Share (MKT): The market share of the firm is measured as the ratio of the sale of the firm (S) to its total sales (S), for all the firms during the given year i.e.,

$$MKT_{it} = \frac{\left[\frac{S_{i,t-1}}{\sum_{i=1}^{n} S_{i,t-1}} + \frac{S_{i,t-2}}{\sum_{i=1}^{n} S_{i,t-2}} + \frac{S_{i,t-3}}{\sum_{i=1}^{n} S_{i,t-3}}\right]}{3}$$

Here, MKT_{it} stands for the market share of firm i in year t.

Mergers and Acquisitions (M&A IN): Mergers and Acquisitions deal taken place within the Indian cement sector from 2000 to 2013 have been compiled from Bloomberg database. The present model only those firms have been considered who have adopted the strategy of M&A. This gives certainty towards incidence of the strategy of M&A by all 12 firms. Next was to calculate the extent of M&As adopted by these firms. For this, a cumulation of the deals was taken together for all 12 firms (from 2000 to 2013).

Selling Intensity (SELL): SELL as the sum of the ratio of distribution (D) to sales, marketing expenses (M) to sales, and the ratio of advertising expenditure (A) to sales, i.e., the sum of distribution intensity (DI), marketing intensity (MI), and advertising intensity (AI).

$$SELL_{it} = \left[\frac{\left[\frac{\sum_{i=1}^{n} D_{i,t-1}}{\sum_{i=1}^{n} S_{i,t-1}} + \frac{\sum_{i=1}^{n} D_{i,t-2}}{\sum_{i=1}^{n} S_{i,t-2}} + \frac{\sum_{i=1}^{n} D_{i,t-3}}{\sum_{i=1}^{n} S_{i,t-3}}\right]}{3} + \frac{\left[\frac{\sum_{i=1}^{n} M_{i,t-1}}{\sum_{i=1}^{n} S_{i,t-1}} + \frac{\sum_{i=1}^{n} M_{i,t-2}}{\sum_{i=1}^{n} S_{i,t-2}} + \frac{\sum_{i=1}^{n} M_{i,t-3}}{\sum_{i=1}^{n} S_{i,t-3}}\right]}{3} + \frac{\left[\frac{\sum_{i=1}^{n} A_{i,t-1}}{\sum_{i=1}^{n} S_{i,t-1}} + \frac{\sum_{i=1}^{n} A_{i,t-2}}{\sum_{i=1}^{n} S_{i,t-2}} + \frac{\sum_{i=1}^{n} A_{i,t-3}}{\sum_{i=1}^{n} S_{i,t-3}}\right]}{3}\right]$$

Here, $SELL_{it}$ stands for the selling intensity of firm i in year t.

Capital Intensity (CI): The capital intensity of an industry is measured as the ratio of capital employed (CE) to sales (S), i.e.,

$$CI_{it} = \frac{\left[\frac{\sum_{i=1}^{n} \mathrm{CE}_{i,t-1}}{\sum_{i=1}^{n} S_{i,t-1}} + \frac{\sum_{i=1}^{n} \mathrm{CE}_{i,t-2}}{\sum_{i=1}^{n} S_{i,t-2}} + \frac{\sum_{i=1}^{n} \mathrm{CE}_{i,t-3}}{\sum_{i=1}^{n} S_{i,t-3}}\right]}{3}$$

Here, CI_{it} stands for capital intensity of firm i in year t.

Profitability (PBT): The profitability of a firm is measured as the ratio of profit earned by a firm before tax (P) to sales (S), i.e.,

$$CI_{it} = \frac{\left[\frac{\sum_{i=1}^{n} \mathrm{P}_{i,t-1}}{\sum_{i=1}^{n} S_{i,t-1}} + \frac{\sum_{i=1}^{n} \mathrm{P}_{i,t-2}}{\sum_{i=1}^{n} S_{i,t-2}} + \frac{\sum_{i=1}^{n} \mathrm{P}_{i,t-3}}{\sum_{i=1}^{n} S_{i,t-3}}\right]}{3}$$

Here, PBT_{it} stands for profitability of firm i in year t.

In-house R&D intensity (R&D): The in-house R&D intensity of a firm is measured as the ratio of R&D (RD) in the industry to sales (S), i.e.,

$$\mathrm{R\&}D_{it} = \frac{\left[\frac{\sum_{i=1}^{n} RD_{i,t-1}}{\sum_{i=1}^{n} S_{i,t-1}} + \frac{\sum_{i=1}^{n} RD_{i,t-2}}{\sum_{i=1}^{n} S_{i,t-2}} + \frac{\sum_{i=1}^{n} RD_{i,t-3}}{\sum_{i=1}^{n} S_{i,t-3}}\right]}{3}$$

Here, R&D $_{it}$ stands for in-house R&D intensity of firm i in year t.

Total Technology Purchase (TTP): The ratio of expenditure on domestic technology purchase (DTP) to sales, foreign technology purchase (FTP) to sales and in-house R&D (R&D) to sales, i.e., sum of domestic technology purchase (DTP), foreign technology purchase intensity (FTPI) and R&D intensity (RDI) is used as a measure of technology strategies.

$$TTP_{it} = \left[\frac{\left[\frac{\sum_{i=1}^{n} DTP_{i,t-1}}{\sum_{i=1}^{n} S_{i,t-1}} + \frac{\sum_{i=1}^{n} DTP_{i,t-2}}{\sum_{i=1}^{n} S_{i,t-2}} + \frac{\sum_{i=1}^{n} DTP_{i,t-3}}{\sum_{i=1}^{n} S_{i,t-3}}\right]}{3} + \frac{\left[\frac{\sum_{i=1}^{n} \mathrm{FTP}_{i,t-1}}{\sum_{i=1}^{n} S_{i,t-1}} + \frac{\sum_{i=1}^{n} \mathrm{FTP}_{i,t-2}}{\sum_{i=1}^{n} S_{i,t-2}} + \frac{\sum_{i=1}^{n} \mathrm{FTP}_{i,t-3}}{\sum_{i=1}^{n} S_{i,t-3}}\right]}{3} + \frac{\left[\frac{\sum_{i=1}^{n} \mathrm{R\&}D_{i,t-1}}{\sum_{i=1}^{n} S_{i,t-1}} + \frac{\sum_{i=1}^{n} \mathrm{R\&}D_{i,t-2}}{\sum_{i=1}^{n} S_{i,t-2}} + \frac{\sum_{i=1}^{n} \mathrm{R\&}D_{i,t-3}}{\sum_{i=1}^{n} S_{i,t-3}}\right]}{3}\right]$$

Here, TTP $_{it}$ stands for the total technology purchase of firm i in year t.

Vertical Integration (VERT): The vertical integration made by a firm is measured as the ratio of value added (VA) to value of output (VO), i.e.,

$$VERT_{it} = \frac{\left[\frac{\sum_{i=1}^{n} \mathrm{VA}_{i,t-1}}{\sum_{i=1}^{n} \mathrm{VO}_{i,t-1}} + \frac{\sum_{i=1}^{n} \mathrm{VA}_{i,t-2}}{\sum_{i=1}^{n} \mathrm{VO}_{i,t-2}} + \frac{\sum_{i=1}^{n} \mathrm{VA}_{i,t-3}}{\sum_{i=1}^{n} \mathrm{VO}_{i,t-3}}\right]}{3}$$

Here, VERT$_{it}$ stands for vertical integration of firm i in year t.

Inventory Management (INVT): The inventory management of a firm is measured as the ratio of inventory (IN) to sales (S), i.e.,

$$INVT_{it} = \frac{\left[\frac{\sum_{i=1}^{n} IN_{i,t-1}}{\sum_{i=1}^{n} S_{i,t-1}} + \frac{\sum_{i=1}^{n} IN_{i,t-2}}{\sum_{i=1}^{n} S_{i,t-2}} + \frac{\sum_{i=1}^{n} IN_{i,t-3}}{\sum_{i=1}^{n} S_{i,t-3}}\right]}{3}$$

Here, INVT$_{it}$ stands for inventory management of firm i in year t.

Bibliography

Agarwal M., (2002) *Analyses of Mergers in India.* (Unpublished M. Phil thesis). Delhi: University of Delhi.

Agarwal M., and Bhattacharjea A., (2006) *Mergers in India: A Response to Regulatory Shock,* Emerging Markets Finance and Trade, 42(3), 46-65.

Aghion P., Carlin W., and Schaffer M., (2002) *Competition, Innovation and Growth in Transition: Exploring the Interactions Between Policies,* (Working Paper No.501). MI: The William Davidson Institute, University of Michigan Business School.

Anand S. (2009) *Identifying cartels using economic evidence, a case study of Indian cement Industry,* Competition Commission of India, New Delhi.

Banerjee A., and Eckard E. W. (1998) *Are Mega-Mergers Anticompetitive? Evidence from the First Great Merger Wave,* RAND Journal of Economics, 29(4), 803-827.

Basant R., (2000) *Corporate response to economic reforms,* Economic and Political Weekly, 35(10), 813-822.

Basant R., and Mishra P., (2012) *How has the Indian Corporate Sector Responded to Two Decades of Economic Reforms in India? An Exploration of Patterns and Trends,* (Working Paper No. 2012-02-02) Ahmedabad: Indian Institute of Management.

Basant R., and Mishra P., (2014) *Determinants of inter-industry variations in research and development efforts in Indian manufacturing sector: a dynamic panel data analysis,* Innovation and Development, 4(1), 91-109.

Beena P. L., (2000) *An Analysis of Mergers in the Private Corporate Sector,* (Working Paper No. 301). Trivandrum: Centre for Development Studies.

Belleflamme P., and Peitz M., (2010) Industrial *organization: markets and strategies.* Cambridge: Cambridge University Press.

Blundell R., Griffith R., and Reenen J. V., (1995) *Dynamic Count Data Models of Technological Innovation,* The Economic Journal, 105(429), 333-344.

Breusch T. S., and Pagan A. R., (1980) *The Lagrange multiplier test and its applications to model specification in econometrics,* The Review of Economic Studies, 239-253.

Chatterjee S., (1986) *Types of synergy and economic value: The impact of acquisitions on merging and rival firms,* Strategic management journal, 7(2), 119-139.

Cohen W., Levin R., and Mowery D., (1987) *Firm Size and R&D Intensity: A Re-Examination,* Journal of Industrial Economics, 35(4), 543-565.

Comanor W. S., and Wilson T. A., (1967) *Advertising, market structure and performance,* Review of Economics and Statistics, 47 (4), 423–440.

Gerick P. A., (1990) Innovation, *Technological Opportunity and Market Structure,* Oxford Economic Papers, 42(3), 586–602.

Ghosal V., (2011) The law and economics of enhancing cartel enforcement: Using information from non-cartel investigations to prosecute cartels. *Review of Law & Economics,* 7(2), 501-538.

Greene, W. H. (2007) *Econometric analysis.* Upper Saddle River: Prentice-Hall.

Gujarati D. N., and Sangeetha, (2007) *Basic Econometrics.* New Delhi: Tata McGraw Hill Publishing Company Limited.

Hausman J. A., (1978). *Specification Tests in Econometrics. Econometrica,* Journal of the Econometric Society, 46(6), 1251-1271.

Holderness C. G., and Seehan D. P., (1985) *Raiders or Saviors? The Evidence on Six Controversial Investors,* Journal of Financial Economics, 14(4), 555-579.

Jefferson G. H., Bai H., Guan X., and Yu X., (2006) *R and D performance in Chinese Industry,* Economics of Innovation and New Technology. 15 (4-5), 345-366.

Jemison D. B., and Sitkin S. B., (1986) *Corporate Acquisitions: A Process Perspective,* Academy Management Review, 11(1), 145-163.

Jensen M. C., and Murphy K., (1998) *Performance pay and top management incentives,* (Working Paper). Harvard: Harvard Business School.

Khanna S., (1997) *Industrial Deregulation and Corporate Restructuring: Understanding India's First Merger Wave (Mimeo).* Calcutta: Indian Institute of Management.

Kim M., and Vale B., (2001) *Non-price strategic behavior: the case of bank branches,* International Journal of Industrial Organization, 19(10), 1583-1602.

Kumar N. (2000) *Multinational Enterprises and M&As in India: Patterns and Implications,* Economic and Political Weekly, 35(32), 2851-2858.

Levin R. C. (1981) *Toward an Empirical Model of Schumpeterian Competition,* (Working Paper Series A, No. 43). New Haven (U.S.A): Yale School of Organization and Management.

Martin S., (1979) *Advertising, concentration, and profitability: the simultaneity problem,* The Bell Journal of Economics, 10(2), 639-647.

Meurer M., and Stahl D., (1994) *Informative Advertising and Product Match.* International Journal of Industrial Organization, 12(1), 1-9.

Mishra P., (2007) *Determinants of R&D Efforts: A Study of Indian Manufacturing Sector,* Vidyasagar University Journal of Economics, 12, 68-81.

Mishra P. and Behera B., (2007) *Instabilities in Market Concentration: An Empirical Investigation in Indian Manufacturing Sector.* Journal of Indian School of Political Economy, 19(3), 419-449.

Mishra P. (2011) *Determinants of Inter-Industry Variations in Mergers and Acquisitions: Empirical Evidence from Indian Manufacturing Sector,* Artha Vijnana 53(1), 1-22.

Mitchell M.L., and Mulherin J.H., (1996) *The Impact of Industry Shocks on Takeover and Restructuring Activity,* Journal of Financial Economics, 41(2), 193-229.

Pagoulatos E., and Sorensen R., (1981) *A simultaneous equation analysis of advertising, concentration and profitability.* Southern Economic Journal, 47(3), 728-741.

Porter M. E., (1985) *Competitive strategy: Creating and sustaining superior performance.* New York: The free.

Sanjay S. K., Sunny S. K., and Shalini R., (2014) *Does Market Structure Matter? Evidence From The Indian Cement Industry,* Studies in Business and Economics, 9(3), 107-124.

Saraswathy B., (2015) *Production Efficiency of Firms with Mergers and Acquisitions in India,* (Working Paper 299). New Delhi: Indian Council for Research on International Economic Relations.

Scherer F. M., (1967) *Market Structure and the Employment of Scientists and Engineers,* American Economic Review, 57 (3), 524-531.

Scherer F.M., (1980) Industrial Market Structure and Economic Performance. (2ndEd). Chicago: Rand McNally College Publishing Company.

Schumpeter, J. A. (1949) *Economic Theory and Entrepreneurial History-Change and the Entrepreneur, Postulates and Patterns for Entrepreneurial History.* Cambridge, MA: Harvard University Press

Schumpeter J. A., (1942) *Capitalism, Socialism, and Democracy.* New York: Harper.

Shelton L. M., (1988) *Strategic Business Fits and Corporate Acquisitions: Empirical*

Evidence, Strategic Management Journal, 9(3), 279-287.

Shepherd W. G., (1982) *Causes of increased competition in the US economy, 1939-1980,* The Review of Economics and Statistics, 64(4), 613-626.

Singh S. P., (2013) *Assessment of competition in cement industry in India.* New Delhi: Competition Commission of India.

Steiner P. O., (1975) *Mergers: Motives, effects, policies.* Michigan: University of Michigan Press.

Tirole J., (1988) *The theory of industrial organization.* MIT press.

Trautwein F., (1990) *Merger motives and merger prescriptions,* Strategic management journal, 11(4), 283-295.

Venkiteswaran N., (1997) *Restructuring of corporate India: the emerging scenario.* Vikalpa, 22, 3-14.

Weiss C., (2005) *Retailer Concentration and Product Innovation in Food Manufacturing,* European Review of Agricultural Economics, 32 (2), 219-244.

Williamson O. E., (1965) *Innovation and Market Structure.* Journal of Political Economy, 73 (1), 67-73.

Chapter 5

Gender identity, perceived gender discrimination and stress among working professionals

Navya Jain[1] and Meena Osmany[2]

Abstract

Gender Identity is a concept of self with respect to social categories, the association of oneself with a particular gender - male or female. It can be linked to how employees perceive their treatment at work and may be associated with the perception of gender discrimination. The experience of discrimination and unfair treatment due to one's gender can have negative implications that may elevate stress levels at work. This quantitative study examines the relationship between gender identity, perceived gender discrimination and stress among employees working across different professions (males and females). The total sample consisted of 119 working professionals comprised of 50 males and 69 females. The data was analyzed using IBM SPSS. t-test results indicated significant differences between male and female working professionals on all dimensions of gender identity and the perception of gender discrimination. Among females, three dimensions of gender identity were found to be significantly correlated with perceived gender discrimination; two were significantly correlated with stress and perceived gender discrimination was significantly correlated with stress. Among males, one dimension of gender identity was found to be significantly correlated with

---

[1] Research Scholar, Department of Psychology, Jamia Millia Islamia, New Delhi-110025, navyajain66@gmail.com

[2] Assistant Professor, Department of Psychology, Jamia Millia Islamia, New Delhi-110025, meena.osmany@gmail.com

perceived gender discrimination and one with stress. For the total sample, three dimensions of gender identity significantly correlated with perceived gender discrimination, two dimensions with stress and perceived gender discrimination was significantly correlated with stress. Step-wise multiple regression analysis revealed that gender identity significantly predicts perceived gender discrimination (29.5% for total sample; 37.5% for females) and that gender identity and perceived gender discrimination together predict stress (20.5% for total sample; 31.3% for females; 11.4% for males)

Keywords: Gender Identity, Perceived Gender Discrimination, Stress, Gender, Social Identity

5.1. Introduction

The workplace comprises of various social situations and people are organized into groups, bound by shared visions, goals, responsibilities and aspirations. An individual's behaviour in social situations can be attributed to their group memberships and social identity that "reflect[s] the cognitive and emotional significance of such groupings" and plays a part in "shaping and changing people's minds, motivations and behaviours" (Reynolds, Haslam and Turner, 2012, pp.55). Social identity postulates group membership to be an important source of self-esteem and creates the tussle between in-group and out-group, each group trying to elevate its status (Tajfel and Turner, 1979). Group processes such as organization, cooperation, communication, coordination, cohesion and influence stem from social behaviours (Haslam, 2004 as cited in Reynolds, Haslam and Turner, 2012, pp. 58) and hence it is imperative to examine the role of social identities at work. This paper draws from the social identity theory to examine gender identity and how it relates to gender discrimination and stress at work.

Gender can be understood as a social construct that categorizes an individual as male or female and plays an important role in the daily lives of individuals as it has the ability to shape individuals' thoughts and behaviors. The incorporation of cultural meanings attached to being male or female, into the individual psyche leads to the formation of gender identity, evoking gendered responses and thought processes (Wood and Eagly, 2015).

Researchers have approached gender identity largely through gender stereotypical traits and interests and from the perspective of the social identity theory (Wood and Eagly, 2015). The need to study gender as a psychological construct, not just as a categorical variable and the importance of gender identity has been highlighted while examining gender discrimination (Leslie and Gefland, 2008). This approach is followed in this paper where the focus on gender is not just as a demographic variable but on gender identity of the individual.

Social identity theory provides a relevant contextual framework for the study of gender identity and gender discrimination in that, the social status of groups (gender in this case) will be such that one is advantaged and the other is relatively disadvantaged. Perceived gender discrimination may be understood as the individual perception of differential or unfair treatment due to one's gender (Sanchez and Brock, 1996). The literature on social identity and gender discrimination suggests that individuals (males and females) with relatively high levels of social identification may experience discrimination (Cameron, 2001). It has been demonstrated that perceptions of gender discrimination harm the psychological well-being of women, not men, and women may cope with negative well-being by increasing their identification with their group (women) whereas perceived discrimination was found to be unrelated to group identification among men (Schmitt and Branscombe, 2002; Schmitt, Branscombe, Postmes and Garcia, 2014).

In the Indian context where a patriarchal culture has been prevailing for years, males are considered the dominant, advantaged group, as compared to females. This has contributed to the differential treatment meted out to females in the Indian society which extends to women in the professional sphere in the form of gender discrimination, sexual harassment, gender bias, gender stereotypes, glass ceiling, etc. However, societal change, better education opportunities and a recent spurt in pro-women reforms in the industry (better maternity policies such as in the case of Flipkart, policies against sexual harassment driven through labour legislation, the statutory requirement of women in the boardroom, etc.) warrant a review of the current scenario at Indian workplaces.

Moreover, studies on gender discrimination have mostly focused on the disadvantaged group of women more than men. Though this is justifiable in order to promote an improvement in the conditions for women, it would be unfair to not examine the same for men. The age-old social structure where man is the primary breadwinner and woman is the primary caregiver, has perhaps propagated the lack of adequate paternity leaves or existence of such policies in organizations, an issue which is seeing voices from the likes of Mark Zuckerberg, Founder of Facebook.

Research so far indicates a difference in the strength of beliefs regarding gender discrimination among Indian men and women executives and significant difference in their demographics (age, education, job level, work experience, salary) and psychographics (the perception of organizational environment, managerial abilities, equality of opportunities and gender stereotypes) (Sandhu and Mehta, 2008). Women have shown a positive attitude towards the capabilities of women managers whereas men's opinion in this regard was found to be negative (Gulhati, 1990; Sandhu and Mehta, 2008). Women have reported higher levels of perceived gender discrimination as compared to men (Foley, Hang-Yue and Wong, 2005).

Perceived discrimination has been observed as a "culturally relevant work stressor", surpassing other work stressors in terms of impact on employee and organizational outcomes (Sanchez and Brock, 1996). It has also been seen that women who reported recent experiences of discrimination had higher levels of distress (Pavalko, Mossakwoski and Hamilton, 2003). Stress has also been reported as an outcome of gender discrimination (Shaffer, Joplin, Bell, Lau and Oguz, 2000). Perceived gender discrimination poses a threat to women's cognitive and emotional engagement at work (Sia, Sahoo and Duari, 2015) and their psychological well-being, especially when it is pervasive (Schmitt et al., 2014).

Research also indicates that social identity may be associated with psychological adjustment measures (Luhtanen and Crocker, 1991) and social identity may have a protective function, capable of reducing stress and depression (Haslam and Reicher, 2006).

Stress can be understood to be any "real or interpreted threat to the physical or psychological integrity of an individual that results in physiological and/or behavioral responses" (McEwen, 2000, as cited in Rajeswaran and Bennett, 2013, pp14). Stress was recently reported as the biggest workplace issue globally and second biggest workplace issue for India while reducing stress was reported as a top priority for organizations' health and productivity strategy for Indian workplaces (Willis Towers Watson, 2016). Research has shown significant differences (attributable to biology and socialization) between males and females with respect to stressors, strains and coping, making a strong case for examining gender in stress research (Gaur and Jain, 2013, pp.184).

Workplace attitudes, prejudices and perceptions of male and female executives comprise the corporate world and ultimately shape the organizational environment and corporate culture (Sandhu and Mehta, 2008).

In light of these findings, the following are the objectives of the study:

1. To study the self-concept of gender identity, perceived gender discrimination and stress levels among working male and female professionals.
2. To study the relationship between gender identity, perceived gender discrimination and stress levels among working male and female professionals.
3. To study whether gender identity predicts perceived gender discrimination.
4. To study whether gender identity and perceived gender discrimination predict stress among working male and female professionals.

Based on the above, the following hypotheses were formulated for the study:

Hypothesis 1: There will be significant difference between male and female working professionals on the measures of gender identity, perceived gender discrimination and stress.

Hypothesis 2: There will be significant correlation between gender identity, perceived gender discrimination and stress levels for working males, females and for the total sample.

Hypothesis 3: Perceived gender discrimination will be predicted by gender identity among male and female working professionals and for the total sample.

Hypothesis 4: Stress will be predicted by gender identity and perceived gender discrimination among male and female working professionals and for the total sample.

5.2. Methods

5.2.1. Participants and Sampling

The sample consisted of working professionals of varied age groups in India, engaged in private firms of the corporate sector, across different industries. Snowball sampling was used to identify potential respondents. During the data collection phase, a total of 129 responses were received. A total of 119 entries of working professionals were finally considered usable, of which 50 (42%) were males and 69 (58%) were females.

Measurement Tools:

a. 16 item Gender version of the Collective Self-esteem Scale (CSES) (Luhtanen and Crocker, 1992), adapted by Leslie and Gefland (2008) was used to measure gender identity (GI). The scale comprises of four dimensions (sub-scales) of collective self-esteem: Membership self-esteem (MSE), Private collective self-esteem (PRI), public collective self-esteem (PUB) and importance to identity (IID). Leslie and Gefland (2008) reported scale reliability of α=0.86 for the Gender version of CSES as against α=0.85-0.89 reported in other samples (Luhtanen and Crocker, 1992). Means and total of overall score were considered as each sub-scale represents different dimensions of GI and the same has been recommended by the authors. The 16 item Gender version of CSES was found to have α=0.718 for total sample, α=0.791 for males and α=0.623 for females.

b. 4 item Perceived Gender Discrimination Scale (Foley, Hang-Yue and Wong, 2005) adopted from Sanchez and Brock (1996) was used to measure perceived gender discrimination (PGD). The calculated scale reliability was α=0.868 (Foley, Hang-Yue and Wong, 2005). The PGD scale was found to have α=0.808 for total sample, α=0.789 for males and α=0.785 for females

c. 24 item Professional Life Stress Scale (PLSS) (Fontana, 1989) was used to measure stress level. The scale categorizes stress into 4 levels: non-problematic (scoring 1-15), moderate (scoring 16-30), problematic (scoring 31-45) and major (45-60). The scale reliability was reported to be α=0.74 (Fontana and Abouserie, 1993). The PLSS was found to have α=0.722 for total sample, α=0.677 for males and α=0.746 for females.

5.2.2. Procedure

The instruments were replicated in an online form and shared with potential respondents via social media. The first page of the online form provided a brief rationale for the study, relevant details on voluntary participation in the study and contact details of the researcher. Participant privacy and confidentiality of data was maintained during the course of the study. The responses so obtained were downloaded and collated through Microsoft Excel. Data analysis was conducted through SPSS software-Version 23.

5.2.3. Statistical Analysis

Descriptive and inferential statistics were applied for data analysis. Scale reliabilities for the research instruments were calculated for total sample and for each gender. Mean and standard deviations were calculated. t-test was conducted to check mean difference between male and female working professionals on GI, PGD and PLSS. Pearson Product Moment Correlation was conducted to identify and assess the relationship between the three measures. Stepwise, multiple regression analysis was conducted to test predictions of perceived gender discrimination and stress.

5.3. Results

The average age (in years) and work experience (in months) for the sample was 27 and 48 respectively. The majority (47%) of the sample had an educational degree at Masters level, were unmarried (54%) and earned between Rupees 40000-60000 per month (29%). Out of 119 participants, 64 (54%) exhibited non-problematic stress level, 49 (41%) exhibited moderate stress levels, 6 (5%) exhibited problematic stress levels and 0 exhibited major stress levels. Demographic details are given in Table 1.

An independent sample t-test was conducted to test Hypothesis 1, i.e., there will be significant differences in mean scores of male and female working professionals on the measures of GI (MSE, PRI, PUB, and IID), PGD and PLSS. Female working professionals reported higher mean scores as compared to males on MSE, PRI, IID, PGD and PLSS whereas males reported higher mean scores on PUB as compared to female working professionals. It was observed that male and female employees differed significantly on all dimensions of GI (MSE, PRI, PUB and IID) and on PGD at work. MSE $t(75.290) = -5.36$, $p<0.05$; PRI: $t(117) = -2.31$, $p<0.05$; PUB: $t(117) = 2.59$, $p<0.05$; IID: $t(117) = -3.82$, $p<0.05$; PGD: $t(117) = -3.97$, $p<0.05$. However, t-test results indicated that there were no significant differences between males and females in the experience of stress (PLSS). Thus, evidence for Hypothesis 1 was found, leaving out stress. Details are given in Table 2.

Table 5.1: Demographics

Demographic Variable	Males	Males (%)	Females	Females (%)	Total	Total (%)
Gender	50	42	69	58	119	100
Age (Years)						
21-25	8	16	14	20	22	18
26-30	33	66	47	68	80	67
31-35	8	16	5	7	13	11
36-40	1	2	3	4	4	3
Highest Education						
XIIth Standard	1	2	0	0	1	1
Bachelors Degree	16	32	8	12	24	20
Masters Degree	18	36	38	55	56	47
PG Diploma	14	28	22	32	36	30
Other	1	2	1	1	2	2
Marital Status						
Unmarried	24	48	40	58	64	54
Engaged	2	4	2	3	4	3
Married	24	48	23	33	47	39
Other	0	0	4	6	4	3
Monthly Income (In INR)						
0-20000	2	4	1	1	3	3
20000-40000	7	14	18	26	25	21
40000-60000	16	32	19	28	35	29
60000-80000	14	28	8	12	22	18
Greater than 80000	9	18	18	26	27	23
Work Experience (Years)						
1	13	26	12	17	25	21
1-2	2	4	7	10	9	8
2-3	1	2	8	12	9	8
3-4	12	24	15	22	27	23
4-5	9	18	14	20	23	19
Greater than 5	13	26	13	19	26	22

Table 5.2.: t-test between male and female working professionals on the measures of Gender Identity, Perceived Gender Discrimination and Stress (N=119)

Variable	Gender	N	Mean	Std. Deviation	p-value	t
Membership self-esteem (MSE)	Male	50	5.31	1.13	0.000	-5.36
	Female	69	6.27	.69		
Private self-esteem (PRI)	Male	50	5.62	.99	0.02	-2.31
	Female	69	6.04	.99		
Public self-esteem (PUB)	Male	50	4.81	1.20	0.01	2.59
	Female	69	4.22	1.25		
Importance to identity (IID)	Male	50	3.93	1.33	0.00	-3.82
	Female	69	4.86	1.31		
Perceived gender Discrimination (PGD)	Male	50	8.78	4.40	0.00	-3.97
	Female	69	12.37	5.19		
Professional life stress Score (PLSS)	Male	50	15.78	6.87	0.34	-0.94
	Female	69	17.13	8.26		

Degree of freedom (df =117)

Pearson Product Moment Correlation was conducted to test Hypothesis 2, i.e., there will be a significant correlation between GI, PGD and PLSS for working males, females and for the total sample. The analysis yielded significant correlations as follows. PRI was negatively correlated with PGD (r=-0.23) and PLSS (r=-0.26) for total sample. PRI was negatively correlated to PGD among females (r= -0.43). PRI and PLSS was negatively correlated for females (r= -0.41).PUB was negatively correlated with PGD (r= -0.44) and PLSS (r= -0.35) for total sample. PUB was negatively correlated with PGD among males (r= -0.31) and females (r= -0.44). PUB was negatively correlated with PLSS among males (r= -0.33) and females (r=-0.34). IID and PGD was positively correlated (r=0.19) for total sample and for females (r=0.29).PGD and PLSS was positively correlated (r=0.41) for total sample and for females (r=0.51).

Correlation analysis was conducted to test Hypothesis 2, i.e., there will be significant correlation between GI, PGD and PLSS for working males, females and for the total sample. The analysis yielded significant correlations as follows. PRI was negatively correlated with PGD (r= -0.23) and PLSS (r= -0.26) for total sample. PRI was negatively correlated to PGD among females (r= -0.43). PRI and PLSS was negatively correlated for females (r= -0.41). PUB was negatively correlated with PGD (r= -0.44) and PLSS (r= -0.35) for total sample. PUB was negatively correlated with PGD among males (r= -0.31) and females (r= -0.44). PUB was negatively correlated with PLSS among males (r= -0.33) and females (r= -0.34). IID and PGD was positively correlated (r=0.19) for total sample and for females (r=0.29). PGD and PLSS was positively correlated (r= 0.41) for total sample and for females (r= 0.51).

Thus, three (PRI, PUB and IID) out of four dimensions of GI were found to be correlated with PGD significantly and two (PRI and PUB) with PLSS for female working professionals. One (PUB) dimension of GI was found to be correlated with PGD and PLSS significantly among male working professionals. Three dimensions (PRI, PUB and IID) of GI were found to be significantly correlated with PGD for total sample. PGD was positively correlated with PLSS for total sample and for female working professionals significantly. These results provide evidence for Hypothesis 2.

Subscale correlations for the dimensions in the gender version of CSES were also observed. MSE was positively correlated with PRI (r= 0.62) and IID (r= 0.27) for total sample. MSE and PRI were also found to be correlated for males (r= 0.74) and females (r= 0.49). PRI was positively correlated with PUB (r= 0.36) for total sample as well as for males (r= 0.57) and females (r= 0.33). MSE and PUB was positively correlated for males (r= 0.47). Given below are the correlation matrices in Table 3, Table 4 and Table 5.

Table 5.3: Correlations Matrix for Total Sample (N=119)

Variables	MSE	PRI	PUB	IID	PGD
Private self-esteem (PRI)	0.62**				
Public self-esteem (PUB)	0.16	0.36**			
Importance to identity (IID)	0.27**	0.15	-0.11		
Perceived gender discrimination (PGD)	0.111	-0.23**	-.44**	0.19*	
Professional life stress score (PLSS)	-.09	-0.26**	-0.35**	0.12	0.41**
*p>0.05 level; **. p>0.01 level					

Table 5.4: Correlations Matrix for female working professionals (N=69)

Variables	MSE	PRI	PUB	IID	PGD
Private self-esteem (PRI)	0.49**				
Public self-esteem (PUB)	0.16	0.33**			
Importance to identity (IID)	0.20	-0.03	-0.15		
Perceived gender discrimination (PGD)	0.03	-0.43**	-0.44**	0.29*	
Professional life stress score (PLSS)	-0.16	-0.41**	-0.34**	0.17	0.51**
*p>0.05 level; **. p>0.01 level					

Table 5.5: Correlations Matrix for male working professionals (N=50)

Variables	MSE	PRI	PUB	IID	PGD
Private self-esteem (PRI)	0.74**				
Public self-esteem (PUB)	0.47**	0.57**			
Importance to identity (IID)	0.08	0.27	0.12		
Perceived gender discrimination (PGD)	-0.16	-0.18	-0.31*	-0.24	
Professional life stress score (PLSS)	-0.16	-0.07	-0.33*	-0.01	0.18
*p>0.05 level; **. p>0.01 level					

Stepwise multiple regression analysis on PGD was conducted to test Hypothesis 3, i.e., PGD will be predicted by GI among male and female working professionals and for the total sample. It was observed that PUB explained 19.7 % variance in PGD in Model 1. PUB and MSE explained 23.1% variance in PGD in Model 2. PUB, MSE and PRI together explained 29.5 % variance in PGD in Model 3. Additionally, the same was conducted for males and females separately. Results obtained for female working professionals indicated that PUB explained 20.2% variance in PGD in Model 1; PUB and PRI explained 29.4% variance in PGD in Model 2; PUB, PRI and MSE explained 37.5% variance in PGD in Model 3. Results obtained for male working professionals indicated that PUB explained 9.9% variance in PGD. These results provide evidence in support of Hypothesis 3. Given below are the regression models in Table 6, 7 and 8.

Table 5.6: Model Summary of regression analysis on Perceived Gender Discrimination (PGD) for Total Sample (N=119)

Model	Predictor Variable	R	R Square	Adjusted R Square	F	β	t	p-value
1	Public self-esteem (PUB)	0.444	0.197	0.190	28.707	-0.444	-5.358	0.000
2	Public self-esteem (PUB), Membership self-esteem (MSE)	0.481	0.231	0.218	17.461	-0.474 0.188	-5.751 2.278	0.000 0.025
3	Public self-esteem (PUB), Membership self-esteem (MSE), Private self-esteem (PRI)	0.543	0.295	0.276	16.014	-0.383 0.388 -0.343	-4.550 3.844 -3.212	0.000 0.000 0.002

Table 5.7: Model Summary of regression on Perceived Gender Discrimination (PGD) for Female working professionals (N=69)

Model	Predictor Variable	R	R Square	Adjusted R Square	F	β	t	p-value
1	Public self-esteem (PUB)	0.449	0.202	0.190	16.915	-0.449	-4.113	0.000
2	Public self-esteem (PUB), Private self-esteem (PRI)	0.542	0.294	0.272	13.715	-0.343 -0.321	-3.127 -2.932	0.003 0.005
3	Public self-esteem (PUB), Private self-esteem (PRI), Membership self-esteem (MSE)	0.613	0.375	0.346	13.014	-0.343 -0.483 0.328	-3.304 -4.101 2.915	0.002 0.000 0.005

Table 5.8: Model Summaryof regression on Perceived Gender Discrimination (PGD) for Male working professionals (N=50)

Model	Predictor Variable	R	R Square	Adjusted R Square	F	β	t	p-value
1	Public self-esteem (PUB)	0.314	0.099	0.080	5.267	-0.314	-2.295	0.026

Stepwise multiple regression analysis was conducted to test Hypothesis 4, i.e., PLSS will be predicted by GI and PGD among male and female working professionals and for the total sample. It was observed that PGD explains 16.9% variance in PLSS by in Model 1. It was observed that PGD and PUB explain 20.5 % variance in PLSS in Model 2. The procedure was repeated on males and females separately to check for predictors in male and female working professionals. Results for female working professionals indicated that 26.8% variance in PLSS was explained by PGD in Model 1; 31.3% variance in PLSS was explained by PGD and PRI. Results for male working professionals indicated that 11.4% variance in PLSS was explained by PUB in Model 1. Thus, for male working professionals, PGD did not predict PLSS. These results provide evidence in support of Hypothesis 4 partially. The regression tables are given below in Tables 9, 10 and 11.

Table 5.9: Model Summary of regression on Professional life stress (PLSS) for Total Sample (N=119)

Model	Predictor Variable	R	R Square	Adjusted R Square	F	β	t	p-value
1	Perceived gender discrimination (PGD)	0.411	0.169	0.161	23.715	0.411	4.870	0.000
2	Perceived gender discrimination (PGD), Public self-esteem (PUB)	0.453	0.205	0.191	14.938	0.316 -0.213	3.422 -2.300	0.001 0.023

Table 5.10: Model Summaryof regression on Professional life stress (PLSS) for Female working professionals (N=69)

Model	Predictor Variable	R	R Square	Adjusted R Square	F	β	t	p-value
1	Perceived gender Discrimination (PGD)	0.518	0.268	0.257	24.563	0.518	4.956	0.000
2	Perceived gender discrimination (PGD), Private self-esteem (PRI)	0.560	0.313	0.292	15.045	0.416 -0.235	3.670 -2.077	0.000 0.042

Table 5.11: Model Summaryof regression on Professional life stress (PLSS) for Male working professionals (N=50)

Model	Predictor Variable	R	R Square	Adjusted R Square	F	β	t	p-value
1	Public self-esteem (PUB)	0.338	0.114	0.096	6.191	-0.338	-2.488	0.16

5.4. Discussion

Results from t-test indicate that gender plays a significant role in the formation of gender identity and the experience of gender discrimination. It was seen that females derive greater collective self-esteem from their gender (MSE) than males. They perceive their gender to be more valuable (PRI) as compared to males and attach greater importance to their gender in the conceptualization of the self (IID) as compared to males. On the other hand, when it comes to others' opinions of their gender (PUB), females tend to believe that others view the female gender less favorably whereas males tend to believe that others view the male gender more favorably. Females were also found to perceive greater gender discrimination at work than their male counterparts as was also observed by Foley, Hang-Yue and Wong, 2005. There were no significant differences found between males and females in the perception of professional life stress.

Insignificant differences in the perception of stress at work may arise out of occupational factors. Studies have indicated that "stressors are a function of occupation and that within an occupational group the stressors for men and women would be more or less similar" and several meta-analytical studies have observed negligible gender differences in occupational stress (Gyllensten and Palmer, 2005 as cited in Gaur and Jain, 2013, pp.192). It may be that the said sample experiences similar stress levels as they come across similar stressors, inherent to the corporate sector, irrespective of gender.

The sub-scale correlations of gender version of CSES were mostly in line with past research on CSES. Highest, significant correlation was observed between membership self-esteem and private self-esteem on total sample and the same was reported by Luhtanen and Crocker, 1992 also. Notable differences from the results reported previously by Luhtanen and Crocker, 1992, is that this study reported significant correlation between membership self-esteem and importance to identity and no significant correlation was found between public self-esteem and membership self-esteem. These may be due to the context of gender; past research has explored CSES generically and with respect to race.

Among key observations, it was seen that public self-esteem and perceived gender discrimination were significantly, negatively correlated. This means that if others view one's gender favorably, then one may perceive lesser gender discrimination. Importance to identity was significantly, positively correlated with perceived gender discrimination, especially among females, i.e., as the importance of gender to one's identity increases, the more the likelihood of perceiving gender discrimination.

Private self-esteem for female working professionals was significantly, negatively correlated with perceived gender discrimination but the same was not observed for male counterparts. Private self-esteem measures individuals' judgements about the goodness of their gender and results suggest that as one starts to think more favorably about one's gender, one's perception of gender discrimination would start decreasing. Thus, private and public self-esteem may be a very important factor in addressing the problem of gender discrimination at work, especially among females.

Results from multiple regression analysis on perceived gender discrimination also support the findings of the correlational analysis for Hypothesis 2 as public, private and membership self-esteem were found to be significant predictors of perceived gender discrimination for the total sample and for female working professionals. Results also suggest that public self-esteem significantly predicts perceived gender discrimination among male working professionals. In support of Hypothesis 3, it was observed that gender identity can play an important role in the perception of gender discrimination at work.

Private self-esteem was significantly, negatively correlated with stress for female working professionals, i.e., the worthier a female considers her gender, the less likely she is to experience stress. Public self-esteem was also found to be significantly, negatively correlated with stress for total sample as well as among male and female working professionals. Perceived gender discrimination and stress were significantly, positively correlated for total sample and for female working professionals. This means that higher levels of perceived gender discrimination are associated with higher levels of stress, especially among female working professionals.

Supporting Hypothesis 4, results also suggest the importance of perceived gender discrimination in predicting stress, especially among female working professionals. It was observed that perceived gender discrimination and gender identity were significant predictors of stress. Gender identity exhibits a stress buffering capacity which can be utilized to reduce stress among working professionals.

5.5. Conclusion

The present study provides evidence from the Indian context that gender identity, perceived gender discrimination and stress are related constructs, especially among female working professionals. It was observed that perceived gender discrimination was significantly predicted by gender identity and that stress was significantly predicted by gender identity and perceived gender discrimination in part (as perceived gender discrimination did not predict stress among males).

Findings of the study indicate a stress buffering capability and a deterrent ability towards perceived gender discrimination for private and public self-esteem dimensions of gender identity. These findings have serious implications for organizations and can be particularly helpful for human resource practitioners and managers as they can use these inputs to create gender sensitive programmes that will help in cultivating favorable notions of one's own gender (private self-esteem) as well as improving others' opinions about one's gender (public self-esteem) thereby reducing the likelihood of perceived gender discrimination and stress at work. At the same time, organizations must be mindful of the importance to identity dimension of gender identity which is associated with higher perceived gender discrimination. The study also highlights that female working professionals tend to view themselves more positively as worthy members of their gender as compared to their male counterparts, which can be explored further. The findings contribute to the research area of gender identity at a dimensional level, in an Indian context where few studies were found on the same.

Research findings also present evidence that male and female working professionals differ significantly on gender identity and their perception of gender discrimination whereas no significant difference was found between the two genders on the experience of stress. This suggests that future studies on stress must be carried out on both genders for comprehensive results. Thus, the study adds to the knowledge on stress research and gender discrimination in a holistic manner by representing both male and female voices in the contemporary Indian workplace.

One of the limitations of the study is the possibility of misrepresentation of data by respondents as the research instruments were self-report measures. Western scales are used in the study so the application of these scales for an Indian sample may be questioned, however, overall scale reliability of the sample met acceptable limits and few Indian studies have used the said scales.

Bibliography

Cameron E. J., (2001) *Social identity, modern sexism, and perceptions of personal and group discrimination by women and men*, Sex Roles, 45 (11/12), 743-766.

Foley S., Hang-Yue N., and Wong A., (2005) *Perceptions of discrimination and justice: Are there gender differences in outcomes?* Group & Organization Management, 30 (4), 421-450. doi: 10.1177/1059601104265054

Fontana D., (1989) *Professional life stress scale adapted from Managing stress.* The British Psychological Society and Routledge Ltd. Retrieved from http://content.bandzoogle.com/users/the6thhouse/files/LifeStressScale.pdf(Accessed on 10.04.2016)

Fontana D., and Abouserie R., (1993) *Stress levels, gender and personality factors in teachers*, British Journal of Educational Psychology, 63, 261–270.

Gaur P. S., and Jain S.S., (2013) *Gender issues in work and stress. In D. M. Pestonjee & S. Pandey* (Eds.). *Stress and work: Perspectives on understanding and managing stress* (pp180-208). New Delhi, India: Sage Response.

Gulhati K., (1990) *Attitudes toward women managers: Comparison of attitudes of male and female managers in India*, Economic and Political Weekly, 25(7/8), M41-48. Retrieved from http://www.jstor.org/stable/4395962

Haslam S. A., and Reicher S. D., (2006) *Stressing the group: social identity and the unfolding dynamics of stress.* Journal of Applied Psychology, 91, 1037-52. doi: 10.1037/0021-9010.91.5.1037

Leslie M. L., and Gefland J. M., (2008) *The who and when of internal gender discrimination claims: An interactional model*, Organizational Behaviour and Human Decision Processes, 107, 123-140.

Luhtanen R., and Crocker J., (1992) *A collective self-esteem scale: Self-evaluation of one's social identity.* Personality and Social Psychology Bulletin, 18, 302-318. doi: 10.1177/0146167292183006

Major B., and Dover L. T., (2016) *Attributions to Discrimination Antecedents and Consequences. In Todd D. Nelson (Ed.), Handbook of Prejudice, Stereotyping, and Discrimination* (pp 213-234). New York, United States of America: Taylor & Francis.

Pavalko, K. E., Mossakowski N. K., and Hamilton J. V., (2003) *Does perceived discrimination affect health? Longitudinal relationships between work discrimination and women's physical and emotional health*, Journal of Health and Social Behaviour, 44(1), 18-33. doi: 10.2307/1519813

Rajeswaran J., and Bennet N. C., (2013) *The Neuropsychology of Stress. In D. M. Pestonjee & S. Pandey (Eds.), Stress and work: Perspectives on understanding and managing stress* (pp 13- 30). New Delhi, India: Sage Response.

Reynolds J. K., Haslam A. S., and Turner C. J., (2012) *Prejudice, social identity and social change: resolving the Allportian problematic. In J. Dixon & M. Levine (Eds.), Beyond Prejudice: Extending the social psychology of conflict, inequality and social change* (pp 48-69). New York, Unites States of America: Cambridge University Press

Sanchez I. J., and Brock P., (1996) *Outcomes of perceived discrimination among Hispanic employees: Is diversity management a luxury or a necessity?,* Academy of Management Journal, 39(3), 704-719.

Sandhu S. H., and Mehta R., (2008) *Using psychographic dimensions to discriminate between men and women executives: An empirical analysis,* Journal of Services Research, 8(1), 139-153.

Schmitt T. M., and Branscombe R. N., ((2002) *Perceiving discrimination against one's gender group has different implications for well-being in women and men,* Personality and Social Psychology Bulletin, 28(2), 197-210. doi: 10.1177/0146167202282006

Schmitt T. M., Branscombe R. N., Postmes T., and Garcia A., (2014) *The consequences of perceived discrimination for psychological well-being: A meta-analytic review* Psychological Bulletin, 140(4), 921-948. doi: 10.1037/a0035754

Shaffer A. M., Joplin W.R.J., Bell P. M., Lau T., and Oguz C., (2000) *Gender discrimination and job-related outcomes: A cross-cultural comparison of working women in the United States and China,* Journal of Vocational Behaviour, 57, (395-427). doi: 10.1006/jvbe.1999.1748

Sia K. S., Sahoo C. B., and Duari P., (2015) *Gender discrimination and work engagement: Moderating role of future time perspective,* South Asian Journal of Human Resources Management, 2(1),58-84. doi: 10.1177/2322093715577443

Tajfel H., and Turner J.C., (1979) *An integrative theory of intergroup conflict. In W. Austin & S. Worchel (Eds.), The social psychology of intergroup relations,* 33-48. Pacific Grove, CA: Brooks/Cole

Willis Towers Watson. (2016). *Staying at work Asia findings.* Retrieved from https://www.willistowerswatson.com/en/insights/2016/03/2015-2016-Staying-at-Work-Asia-findings (Accessed on 14.07.2016)

Wood W., and Eagly A. H., (2015) *Two traditions of research on gender identity.* Sex Roles, *73*(11-12), 461-473. DOI:10.1007/s11199-015-0480-2

Chapter 6

Modelling drivers of Financial Inclusion in India to aid policy-makers – an AHP approach

Syed Hameedur Rahman Zaini[1], and Asif Akhtar[2]

Abstract

The importance of Financial Inclusion for the development of a nation has been well documented in recent times. It has been widely accepted that the adoption of financial inclusion policies is key to the overall development of India as a nation. Policy-makers over the years have consistently proposed reforms to make financial services accessible for one and all. The implementation of such reforms has improved the situation to some extent, but certain hindrances need to be overcome in order to make access to financial services more wholesome. This paper aims to highlight the drivers of financial inclusion in India as evidenced from literature. The role of these actors is analysed and categorised using an empirical technique known as Analytic Hierarchy Process (AHP). The AHP method applied in this paper is a structured technique for organizing and analysing complex decisions. This method has proven to be effective in various group decision-making applications. It thus finds application in the present study to create a hierarchy among the identified study variables by assigning weights. The drivers of financial inclusion in the Indian context identified upon reviewing the relevant literature sources comprise the input variables for the study. The study would be relevant for policy-makers as a tool highlighting the key variables that would need to

[1] Research Scholar, Department of Business Administration, Aligarh Muslim University, Aligarh – 202002, hameedzaini@yahoo.com

[2] Assistant Professor, Department of Business Administration, Aligarh Muslim University, Aligarh – 202002, asifakh@gmail.com

be emphasized for the wider outreach of future financial inclusion programs. It would also help in the identification of factors which have driven and inhibited financial inclusion programs and this knowledge will help in framing a future course of action.

Keywords: Financial Inclusion, Analytic Hierarchy Process, Policy, India, MCDM

6.1. Introduction

Financial development is widely seen as a facilitator of economic growth. It has been empirically shown that development of the financial system contributes to economic growth (Rajan and Zingales, 2003). The positive association between financial development and economic growth has been highlighted in various researches (Abu-Bader and Abu-Qarn, 2008; Bittencourt, 2012; Yang and Yi, 2008).

The attainment of financial inclusion, which broadly refers to the delivery of affordable formal financial services for access and use by disadvantaged and low-income members of society, is imperative if development is meant to be all-encompassing. The challenge lies in the fact that despite the tremendous progress shown in recent times by the banking sector in terms of financial viability, profitability and competitiveness, necessary banking services have not reached underprivileged groups. In this realization, efforts at financial inclusion for the uplift of living standards of the poor and disadvantaged have been recommended.

In India, the regular formation of task-forces to report on the status of financial inclusion in the country has been carried out by the various authorities irrespective of their political allegiance. Notable work has been done by these committees by way of recommendations provided to improve upon the number of 'unbanked' individuals. Das (2013) has discussed the recommendations of Rangarajan Committee Report (2008) instituted by the National Bank for Agriculture and Rural Development (NABARD), Raghuram Rajan Committee Report set up by Planning Commission (2009), Malegam Committee Report (2011) commissioned by the Reserve Bank of India (RBI) to study issues and concerns in the Microfinance Institutions (MFIs), and Microfinance Institutions (Development and Regulations) Bill (2012) instituted by the Finance Department, Government of India.

Rangarajan Committee Report (2008) recommended that financial inclusion can be enhanced by concentrating on the supply side to improve the delivery aspects of financial services. Additionally, looking at the limited or weak demand for financial services from certain sections of the population and sub-sections of the economy, the report called for demand side efforts to be undertaken to improve their level of inclusion. The efforts proposed included improvement of human and physical endowments, increasing productivity, mitigating risk and strengthening market linkages. A more significant role for NABARD was formulated for identifying new initiatives to contribute effectively for reaching the poor through Self-help Groups (SHGs) and Microfinance Institutions (MFIs). Raghuram Rajan Committee Report of the Planning Commission (2009) titled *'A Hundred Small Steps'*, states that the justified role of the government today is to improve the financial sector, infrastructure and regulation of the same. This report places inclusion, growth and stability as three objectives of any reform process. Malegam Committee Report (2011) gives special importance to outreach through the Non-banking Financial Companies (NBFC) and Microfinance Institutions (MFI). It recommends that a separate category is created for NBFCs operating in the microfinance sector and regulations for this category should be specified. Mohanty Committee Report (2015) on the mid-term path on financial inclusion has reviewed the policy on financial inclusion and based on the learnings from cross-sectional experiences offered recommendations for implementation on a mid-term (Five years) basis. Among the key recommendations is the call for linkage of credit accounts to the unique identification number (Aadhaar) of citizens aimed at a more efficient delivery system. The committee also recommends that the bank's traditional business model should be augmented with greater reliance on mobile technology to improve 'last mile' service delivery.

In order to frame an action plan for financial inclusion, policy makers need information on the current state of affairs regarding inclusiveness. The availability of reliable indicators that measure the level of accessibility of financial services in a country are beneficial towards determining the extent of financial inclusion. In order to measure the state of financial inclusion in the country, researches carried out periodically have considered various factors and methods for determining the level of inclusiveness. Kumar (2013) has determined from a panel study conducted on data pertaining to 29 major Indian states from 1995 to 2008 that supply side of inclusion efforts through have resulted in intended impact of improved banking activity. Ambarkhane et al. (2016) have computed a financial inclusion index for 21 Indian states using data for indicators of three dimensions namely supply, demand and infrastructure. The dimensions of the study have been identified from various government reports on financial inclusion.

In their preparation of a Financial Inclusion Index (FII), Beck et al. (2007), have incorporated the use of banking services as an indicator in addition to the outreach dimension. Honohan (2005) deliberated both demand and supply considerations. He suggested indicators like payments, savings mobilization, monitoring of users of funds, and transferring risk for measuring financial inclusion. The Consultative Group to Assist the Poor (C-GAP, 2009) survey on financial inclusion also considered savings and payments, along with credit provisions and the delivery of financial services as factors for measuring access. The survey indicates considerable variation in the availability of financial access points (such as financial institutions' branches, ATMs, and point-of-sale terminals) across different regions of the world. Sarma (2008) calculated FII for 49 countries of the world and considered penetration, availability and usage as parameters of financial inclusion. Barring a few exceptions, most of the low income countries depict low scores on FII. Also, the high income countries mostly figure on the higher side of the FII. The Global Findex Database by Demirguc-Kunt and Klapper (2012) measured financial inclusion in 148 countries on the basis of savings, borrowings, payments, and insurance. The results have shown that only 50% of adults worldwide have an account at a formal financial institution. The account penetration varies widely across regions, income groups and individual characteristics. Fungacova and Weill (2015) used data from the World Bank Global Findex database considering dimensions of account ownership, account use and the use of formal credit to analyze financial inclusion in China, making comparisons with the other BRICS countries. Arora (2010) measured financial access across two groups, developing and developed countries of the world, considering outreach, ease and cost and taking into account banking as well as non-banking financial institutions. The article thus developed a unique socio-economic index which includes financial access index by incorporating indicators from the Human Development Index. Chakravarty and Pal (2012) improve upon the FII model of Sarma (2008) by employing the axiomatic measurement approach which helps to determine the percentage contributions of the considered factors towards financial inclusion.

6.2. Variables for the study

6.2.1. No-frills account

As a policy-measure, many governments have stipulated banks to offer more financially suitable product offerings, such as basic accounts that entail little to no fees or minimum balance requirements along with same additional banking benefits. Aggarwal and Klapper (2013) highlight the example of the South African Mzansi Account, a transactional bank account that targets low income customers, to improve banking penetration.

The Reserve Bank of India, in 2005, initiated for such no-frills accounts to widen outreach of financial services to vast unbanked sections of the

Indian population. In such accounts, provisions for ATM facility and small overdrafts have been advised.

6.2.2. Use of Regional Languages

The RBI has directed banks to make available all account opening material in the concerned regional languages, apart from English and Hindi (Agarwal, 2007; Agrawal, 2008).

6.2.3. Simplification of KYC norms

Certain relaxations in KYC (Know-your-customer) requirements for opening small bank accounts were initiated as early as August 2005 whereby any evidence regarding identity and address of the prospective customer would be admitted as required documentation. KYC norms have recently been simplified further by the acceptance of documents issued by Unique Identification Authority of India (UIDAI) containing details like name, address and Aadhaar number (Gupte et al., 2012).

6.2.4. Role of Rural Intermediaries

Agrawal (2008) points out that banks were permitted in January 2006, to use other rural organisations like Non-governmental organizations (NGOs), Self-help Groups (SHGs), Micro-finance Institutions (MFIs) etc. for the wider penetration of financial access.

6.2.5. Mobile Banking

In the mid-term report of the committee on financial inclusion, Mohanty (2015) references empirical evidence that suggests the low-cost delivery of basic banking services through mobile technology with the security of transactions enhanced through biometric identification.

The increased affordability of mobile phones along with increasing network coverage, make cell phones a vital means of increasing financial access (Aggarwal and Klapper, 2013).

According to Global Findex data, millions of people who do not have access to formal financial services, are enabled through mobile money to perform transactions such as paying bills and sending or receiving money (Demirguc-Kunt and Klapper, 2012).

6.2.6. Role of ICT (Information and Communication Technology)

Thorat (2006) has pointed out to a few projects initiated to test how leveraging of technology can lead to increased levels of financial inclusion: linking the opening of bank accounts with biometric identification enabled with smart cards, mobile or hand held connectivity devices that record the transactions in the bank's books on real time basis, routing of social security payments through smart cards etc. Delivery of other financial services like low-cost remittances and insurance can be provided effectively with the help of similar technology enabled channels. The use of ICT has enabled banks to handle the enormous increase in the volume of transactions for millions of households for processing, credit scoring, credit record and follow up.

Gwalani and Parkhi (2014) have highlighted the role of technology as an enabler for improving the reach of banks to the unbanked at an affordable price.

6.2.7. Electronic Benefit Transfer

To overcome issues related to the delivery of government benefits and subsidies, the government of India launched Direct Benefit Transfers (DBT) program in January 2013. Through this initiative, residents receive benefits and subsidies electronically in their accounts linked to biometric based identification system (Aadhaar). The transfer of liquefied petroleum gas (LPG) subsidy is a prominent example from the 35 DBT schemes currently in place. Such a system that comprises electronic benefit transfer helps in speeding up payments, removing leakages and intermediaries, thereby improving financial inclusion (Larquemin, 2016).

6.2.8. Financial Education

Atkinson and Messy (2013) have shown how low levels of financial inclusion are associated with lower levels of financial literacy. Findings from different surveys conducted in both developed and developing countries show that low financial education is significantly correlated with fewer retirement savings, higher interest rate borrowing, and lower formal financial sector participation (Lusardi and Mitchell, 2008; Stango and Zinman,2014; Alessie et al., 2011).

The Mohanty Committee Report (2015) recommends a wider financial literacy drive that exploits all possible communication channels to educate customers.

6.2.9. Overdraft facility

Access to credit has been widely identified as a contributor to financial inclusion policies. The provision of small overdrafts on savings account would encourage the unbanked to engage in formal banking activity. This facility can be effectively administered with the help of bank correspondents and other rural intermediaries.

6.2.10. Kisan Credit Cards

The Kisan Credit Cards (KCC) scheme was initiated towards providing adequate and timely credit for the requirements of farmers under the single window for their agricultural needs. The KCC scheme provides a short-term credit limit with simplified renewal every year up to the fifth year, after which a maximum permissible limit is arrived at. This scheme has witnessed wide acceptance and has helped in increasing the accessibility of financial services in the country.

6.2.11. General Credit Cards

General Credit Cards (GCC) scheme was put in place to extend hassle-free credit for non-agrarian activities to bank customers in rural and semi-urban areas. The guidelines on General Credit Card (GCC) schemes were simplified to enable customers' access credit on simplified terms and conditions, without insistence on security, purpose or end-use of credit (Agarwal, 2007).

6.3. Method

The different drivers of financial inclusion have been identified from the literature. The role of these actors is analysed and categorised using an empirical technique known as Analytic Hierarchy Process (AHP).

The Analytic Hierarchy Process (AHP) was developed at the Wharton School of Business by Thomas Saaty in the 1970s. The method has found application for making complex policy decisions in areas involving multiple criteria. AHP helps in capturing subjective and objective information (Manning et al., 2011) by identifying and weighting the criteria considered essential to these decisions. The method also incorporates a check for consistency of the various weights employed to overcome bias in the overall decision-making process (Saaty, 1994). While other Multi Criteria Decision Making (MCDM) methods could have been selected for application to our problem, these methods do not have ready provisions for testing of key parameters using sensitivity analysis, or checking for inconsistency to enable correction of results should the selected participants in the study generate inconsistent rankings of alternatives. One of the other main benefits of the AHP is that it gives coherence to, and allows the ranking of experts' knowledge about competing alternatives with multiple attributes. It is less useful in areas where knowledge is limited.

Since its formulation, AHP has been applied for a vast number of areas, but its application for the problem that has been taken up in this paper is unprecedented. The method has previously been applied in wide-ranging disciplines such as the health sector (Saaty, 1994), as well as the education sector (Alexander & Saaty, 1977). It has also witnessed applications in the areas of finance (Saaty, 1990) and engineering (Triantaphyllou & Mann, 1995). The AHP procedure involves six essential steps (Lee et al., 2008),

1. Definition of the unstructured problem
2. Development of the AHP hierarchy
3. Pair-wise comparisons
4. Estimation of the relative weights
5. Check for consistency
6. Establishment of overall rating

These steps are briefly explained as follows:

Step 1: Define the unstructured problem

In this step the unstructured problem and its determinants should be recognized and the objectives and outcomes stated clearly.

Step 2: Developing the AHP hierarchy

This step involves the decomposition of the decision problem into a hierarchy that consists of the most important elements of the decision problem (Boroushaki and Malczewski, 2008). In this step the complex problem is decomposed into a hierarchical structure with decision elements.

Figure 6.1.: Triangular membership function

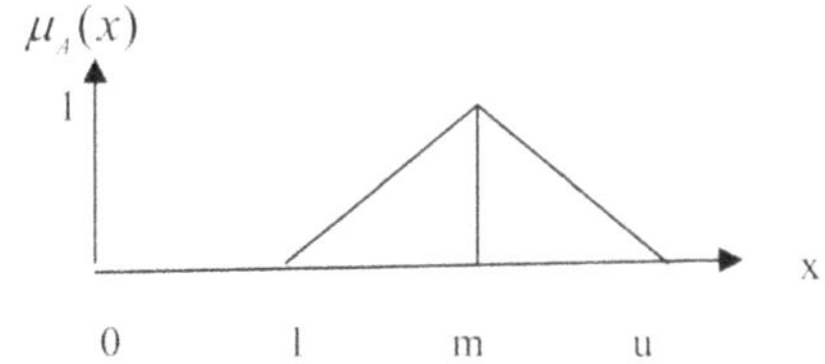

Step 3: Pair-wise comparison

For each element of the hierarchy structure, pair wise comparison of all the associated elements is carried out in pair-wise comparison matrices as follows:

$$A = \begin{matrix} 1 & \frac{w_1}{w_2} & \cdots \frac{w_1}{w_n} \\ \frac{w_2}{w_1} & 1 & \cdots \frac{w_2}{w_n} \\ \frac{w_n}{w_1} & \frac{w_n}{w_2} & 1 \end{matrix}$$

Where: A = comparison pair-wise matrix,

w_1= weight of element 1,

w_2= weight of element 2,

w_n= weight of element n.

In order to determine the relative preferences for two elements of the hierarchy in matrix A, an underlying semantic scale is employed with values ranging from 1 to 9 to rate relative importance (Table 6.1).

Table 6.1.: Scales for pair-wise comparison (Saaty, 1980)

Preferences expressed in linguistic variables	Preferences expressed in numeric variables	Reciprocal (decimal)
Extreme Importance	9	1/9 (0.111)
Very strong to extremely	8	1/8 (0.125)
Very strong Importance	7	1/7 (0.143)
Strongly to very strong	6	1/6 (0.167)
Strong Importance	5	1/5 (0.200)
Moderately to Strong	4	1/4 (0.250)
Moderate Importance	3	1/3 (0.333)
Equally to Moderately	2	1/2 (0.500)
Equal Importance	1	1 (1.000)

Step 4: Estimate the relative weights

Some methods like eigenvalue method are used to calculate the relative weights of elements in each pair-wise comparison matrix. The relative weights (W) of matrix A is calculated from following equation:

$$A \times W = \lambda_{max} \times W$$

Where λ_{max} = the biggest eigenvalue of matrix A, I = unit matrix.

Step 5: Check the consistency

In this step the consistency property of matrices is checked to ensure that the judgments of decision makers are consistent. For this end some pre-parameter is needed. Consistency Index (CI) is calculated as:

$$CI = \frac{\lambda_{max} - n}{n - 1}$$

The consistency index of a randomly generated reciprocal matrix shall be called to the random index (*RI*), with reciprocals forced. An average *RI* for the matrices of order 1–15 was generated by using a sample size of 100 (Nobre et al., 1999). The table of random indexes of the matrices of order 1–15 can be seen in Saaty (1980). The last ratio that has to be calculated is *CR* (Consistency Ratio). Generally, if *CR* is less than 0.1, the judgments are consistent, so the derived weights can be used. The formulation of *CR* is:

$$CR = \frac{CI}{RI}$$

Step 6: Obtain the overall rating

In last step the relative weights of decision elements are aggregated to obtain an overall rating for the alternatives as follows:

$$w_i^s = \sum_{j=1}^{m} w_{ij}^s w_j \qquad ,i=1,2.....n$$

Where *s*

w_i^s= total weight of alternative i,

w_{ij}^s= weight of alternative i associated to attribute j,

w_j= weight of attribute j,

m = number of attributes,

n= number of alternatives

6.4. Results and Discussion

For the construct of the proposed model, the following 11 drivers which comprise the various dimensions of financial inclusion viz. access to accounts, use of accounts, and access to formal credit are considered,

Table 6.2.: Drivers of Financial Inclusion

S. No.	Criteria
1	No-frills Account
2	Use of Regional Languages
3	Simplification of KYC Norms
4	Rural Intermediaries
5	Mobile Banking
6	Role of ICT
7	Electronic Benefit Transfer
8	Financial Education
9	Overdraft Facility
10	Kisan Credit Cards
11	General Credit Cards

Having identified the various drivers which affect financial inclusion, the next step in the AHP method is formulation of Criteria Comparison Matrix.

Table 6.3.: Criteria Comparison Matrix

Criteria		Account Ownership					Account Usage			Access to Credit		
		No-frills account	Regional languages	Simplification of KYC Norms	Rural Intermediaries	Mobile Banking	Role of ICT	Electronic Benefit Transfer	Financial Education	Overdraft Facility	Kisan Credit Cards	General Credit Cards
Account Ownership	No-frills account	1.000	3.000	0.333	0.333	3.000	0.333	5.000	1.000	3.000	3.000	1.000
	Regional languages	0.333	1.000	0.200	0.143	0.333	0.143	0.200	0.333	1.000	0.333	0.200
	Simplification of KYC Norms	3.000	5.000	1.000	0.333	7.000	1.000	1.000	3.000	5.000	5.000	3.000
	Rural Intermediaries	3.000	7.000	3.000	1.000	7.000	3.000	7.000	5.000	7.000	5.000	5.000
	Mobile Banking	0.333	3.000	0.143	0.143	1.000	0.200	1.000	0.333	0.333	0.200	0.333
Account Usage	Role of ICT	3.000	7.000	1.000	0.333	5.000	1.000	3.000	1.000	5.000	5.000	3.000
	Electronic Benefit Transfer	0.200	5.000	1.000	0.143	1.000	0.333	1.000	0.333	5.000	0.333	0.333
	Financial Education	1.000	3.000	0.333	0.200	3.000	1.000	3.000	1.000	5.000	3.000	5.000
Access to Credit	Overdraft Facility	0.333	1.000	0.200	0.143	3.000	0.200	0.200	0.111	1.000	0.333	0.333
	Kisan Credit Cards	0.333	3.000	0.200	0.200	5.000	0.200	3.000	0.333	3.000	1.000	1.000
	General Credit Cards	1.000	5.000	0.333	0.200	3.000	0.333	3.000	0.200	3.000	1.000	1.000
Sum		13.533	43.000	7.743	3.171	38.333	7.743	27.400	12.644	38.333	24.200	20.200

The next step is normalization of Criteria Comparison Matrix.

Normalization of Comparison Matrix: Normalization of matrix is made by dividing each criteria with sum of the respective column.

Table 6.4.: Normalized Criteria Matrix

Criteria		Account Ownership					Account Usage			Access to Credit		
		No-frills account	Regional languages	Simplification of KYC Norms	Rural Intermediaries	Mobile Banking	Role of ICT	Electronic Benefit Transfer	Financial Education	Overdraft Facility	Kisan Credit Cards	General Credit Cards
Account Ownership	No-frills account	0.074	0.070	0.043	0.105	0.078	0.043	0.182	0.079	0.078	0.124	0.050
	Regional languages	0.025	0.023	0.026	0.045	0.009	0.018	0.007	0.026	0.026	0.014	0.010
	Simplification of KYC Norms	0.222	0.116	0.129	0.105	0.183	0.129	0.036	0.237	0.130	0.207	0.149
	Rural Intermediaries	0.222	0.163	0.387	0.315	0.183	0.387	0.255	0.395	0.183	0.207	0.248
Account Usage	Mobile Banking	0.025	0.070	0.018	0.045	0.026	0.026	0.036	0.026	0.009	0.008	0.017
	Role of ICT	0.222	0.163	0.129	0.105	0.130	0.129	0.109	0.079	0.130	0.207	0.149
	Electronic Benefit Transfer	0.015	0.116	0.129	0.045	0.026	0.043	0.036	0.026	0.130	0.014	0.017
Access to Credit	Financial Education	0.074	0.070	0.043	0.063	0.078	0.129	0.109	0.079	0.130	0.124	0.248
	Overdraft Facility	0.025	0.023	0.026	0.045	0.078	0.026	0.007	0.009	0.026	0.014	0.017
	Kisan Credit Cards	0.025	0.070	0.026	0.063	0.130	0.026	0.109	0.026	0.078	0.041	0.050
	General Credit Cards	0.074	0.116	0.043	0.063	0.078	0.043	0.109	0.016	0.078	0.041	0.050

After arriving at Normalized matrix, a Criteria Weight matrix is to be calculated

Criteria Weight {W}: It can be found out by taking average of each row which is shown as follows:

$$\{Ws\} = \begin{bmatrix} 0.084 \\ 0.021 \\ 0.149 \\ 0.268 \\ 0.028 \\ 0.141 \\ 0.054 \\ 0.104 \\ 0.027 \\ 0.059 \\ 0.065 \end{bmatrix}$$

Now the consistency of the criteria matrix is to be checked. The check for consistency ascertains that the ranking that emerges is practically feasible.

For consistency check, the consistency ratio is to be calculated.

If the consistency Ratio<0.1 then the rankings are consistent and practically possible.

If the consistency Ratio>0.1 then the pair-wise comparisons should be recalculated.

6.5. Checking for Consistency

The procedure in checking for consistency is:

1) Determine the weight sum vector, $\mathbf{W_s}$

$$\{W_s\} = [C]\{W\}$$

$$\{Ws\} = \begin{bmatrix} 1.114 \\ 0.251 \\ 1.920 \\ 3.172 \\ 0.338 \\ 1.806 \\ 0.648 \\ 1.376 \\ 0.319 \\ 0.743 \\ 0.810 \end{bmatrix}$$

2) Find the Consistency Vector

$$\{\text{Consistency Vector}\} = \{W_s\}.\{\frac{1}{W}\}$$

$$\{\text{Consistency Vector}\} = \begin{bmatrix} 13.221 \\ 12.061 \\ 12.854 \\ 11.847 \\ 12.132 \\ 12.799 \\ 11.922 \\ 13.186 \\ 11.889 \\ 12.683 \\ 12.516 \end{bmatrix}$$

3) Determine the average of the elements of {Consistency Vector}, Call this λ

$$\text{Average}(\lambda) = 12.465$$

4) Determine the Consistency Index, CI

$$CI = \frac{\lambda - n}{n - 1}$$

$$CI = 0.146$$

Now Consistency Ratio,

$$CR = \frac{CI}{RI}$$

Here, for n=11, average Random Index, RI = 1.51

$$CR = \frac{0.146}{1.51}$$

$$CR = .097$$

The value of CR is less than 0.1, which is in the acceptable range.

The emergence that the consistency ratio falls within acceptable limits means that the pair-wise comparisons deliver practically possible results. The weights assigned to the different criteria are thus acceptable and may be used to define a hierarchical order among them.

The priorities of the different drivers considered for the study are assigned on the basis of their calculated weights. This helps to rank all the drivers of financial inclusion starting from most effective to least effective.

Table 6.5.: Ranking of Factors

Criteria	Criteria Weight(W)	Rank
No-frills account	0.084	5
Regional languages	0.021	11
Simplification of KYC Norms	0.149	2
Rural Intermediaries	0.268	1
Mobile Banking	0.028	9
Role of ICT	0.141	3
Electronic Benefit Transfer	0.054	8
Financial Education	0.104	4
Overdraft Facility	0.027	10
Kisan Credit Cards	0.059	7
General Credit Cards	0.065	6

Using the ranking based on the calculated criteria weights, a hierarchical model is developed.

Figure 6. 2.: AHP Model

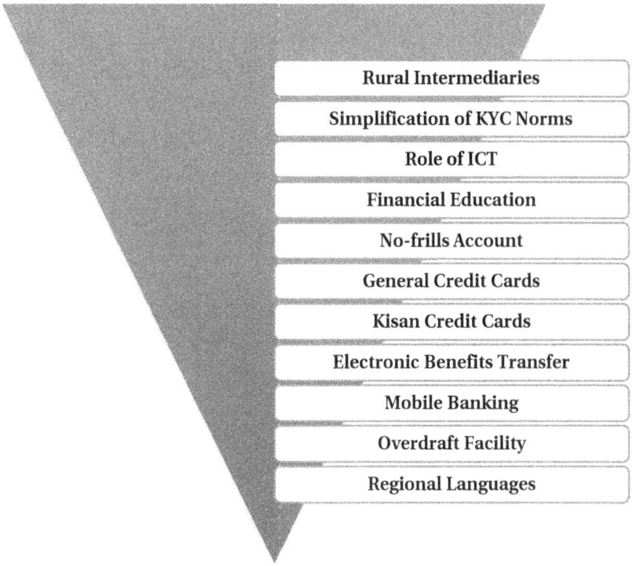

The above figure signifies that the importance of different factors decreases as we move down the inverted pyramid.

Among the drivers of financial inclusion considered for the study, it emerges from the developed AHP model that the role of rural intermediaries is primarily important for increasing financial access in India. The channels adopted previously in this aspect have included outreach efforts through intermediaries including business correspondents, self-help groups and microfinance institutions. Regulators may frame future policy to emphasize the role of rural intermediaries on the basis of results from this study. Simplification of KYC norms figures next in the hierarchy that emerges in our model. Stringent KYC requirements are in place to counter money-laundering and terrorism funding, but this also proves to be a big hindrance in the way of financial inclusion of the unbanked especially in rural areas. It may be considered that certain relaxations towards KYC requirements may be admitted in policy measures for the inclusion of such members in rural and semi-urban areas. Further, it is seen that Information and Communication Technology needs to be tapped for making financial access available to all members of society. The effective implementation of ICT would also enable banks to track the delivery of services.Financial education and financial literacy are the buzzwords for policy-makers working in the area of financial inclusion. The importance of financial education is seen as one of the key drivers to increase levels of financial access since a large number of self-excluded individuals are unaware of the benefits associated with formal banking services. The provision of no-frills or basic bank accounts has resulted in a substantial increase in the subscription of banking services throughout the country. Credit instruments like General credit cards, Kisan credit cards and overdraft facility feature towards the lower end of our model.

6.6. Conclusion

The present study demonstrates that Analytic Hierarchy Process can be applied to help decision makers to design a regulatory framework to improve upon the state of financial inclusion. It is unique in the sense that the application of AHP as a tool to determine the drivers of financial inclusion has not previously been undertaken. Here, AHP has been applied to assign weights to the various drivers of financial inclusion. The study is relevant for use as a tool highlighting the key variables that would need to be emphasized for the wider outreach of future financial inclusion programs. The hierarchy determined by the application of the AHP method ranks the role of rural intermediaries at the top of the order. Various other identified drivers follow in the hierarchy depicting their lower levels of importance towards the overall goal of financial inclusion.

The successful application of AHP to aid decisions regarding financial inclusion parameters paves the way for further application in this domain. Future research may be conducted in other countries by considering variables suitable in the respective contexts. Also, the present study may be expanded by the identification of more variables for hierarchical modelling.

Bibliography

Abu-Bader, S., & Abu-Qarn, A. S. (2008). Financial development and economic growth: The Egyptian experience. *Journal of Policy Modeling, 30*(5), 887-898.

Agarwal, R. (2007). 100% Financial Inclusion: A challenging task ahead. Jaipuria Institute of Management, Lucknow, Conference on Global Competition & Competitiveness of Indian Corporate, New Delhi.

Aggarwal, S., & Klapper, L. (2013). Designing government policies to expand financial inclusion: Evidence from around the world. *Retrieved July, 27,* 2016.

Agrawal, A. (2008). The need for financial inclusion with an Indian perspective. *Economic Research,* 3, 1-10.

Alessie, R. J., Van Rooij, M., & Lusardi, A. (2011). *Financial literacy, retirement preparation and pension expectations in the Netherlands* (No. w17109). National Bureau of Economic Research.

Alexander, J. M., & Saaty, T. L. (1977). The forward and backward processes of conflict analysis. *Behavioral Science, 22*(2), 87-98.

Ambarkhane, D., Singh, A. S., & Venkataramani, B. (2016). Measuring Financial Inclusion of Indian States. *International Journal of Rural Management,* 12(1), 72-100

Arora, R. U. (2010). Measuring financial access. *Griffith University, Discussion Paper in Economics, (7),* 1-21.

Atkinson, A., & Messy, F. A. (2013). Promoting financial inclusion through financial education. *OECD Working Papers on Finance, Insurance and Private Pensions,* 34 (1).

Beck, T., Demirguc-Kunt, A., & Peria, M. S. M. (2007). Reaching out: Access to and use of banking services across countries. *Journal of Financial Economics, 85*(1), 234-266.

Bittencourt, M. (2012). Financial development and economic growth in Latin America: Is

Schumpeter right? *Journal of Policy Modeling, 34*(3), 341-355.

Boroushaki, S., & Malczewski, J. (2008). Implementing an extension of the analytical hierarchy process using ordered weighted averaging operators with fuzzy quantifiers in ArcGIS. *Computers & Geosciences, 34*(4), 399-410.

Chakravarty, S. R., & Pal, R. (2012). Measuring financial inclusion: an axiomatic approach. *Indira Gandhi Institute of Development Research, Mumbai Working Papers.*

Das, T. K. (2013). Financial Inclusion and Regulation in India. *Available at SSRN 2287414.*

Demirguc-Kunt, A., & Klapper, L. F. (2012). Measuring financial inclusion: The global findex database. *World Bank Policy Research Working Paper,* (6025).

Fungacova, Z., & Weill, L. (2015). Understanding financial inclusion in China. *China Economic Review, 34,* 196-206.

Gupte, R., Venkataramani, B., & Gupta, D. (2012). Computation of financial inclusion index for India. *Procedia-Social and Behavioral Sciences, 37,* 133-149.

Gwalani, H., & Parkhi, S. (2014). Financial Inclusion–Building a success model in the Indian context. *Procedia-Social and Behavioral Sciences, 133,* 372-378.

Honohan, P. (2005). Measuring microfinance access: Building on existing cross-country data. *World Bank Policy Research Working Paper,* (3606).

Kumar, N. (2013). Financial inclusion and its determinants: evidence from India. *Journal of Financial Economic Policy, 5*(1), 4-19.

Larquemin, A. (2016). The difficult assessment of the financial inclusion policies in India. *International Journal of Social Sciences and Management,3*(1), 31-37.

Lee, A. H., Chen, W. C., & Chang, C. J. (2008). A fuzzy AHP and BSC approach for evaluating performance of IT department in the manufacturing industry in Taiwan. *Expert systems with applications, 34*(1), 96-107.

Lusardi, A., & Mitchell, O. S. (2008). *Planning and financial literacy: How do women fare?* (No. w13750). National Bureau of Economic Research.

Malegam, Y. H. (2011), Report of the Sub-Committee of the Central Board of Directors of Reserve Bank of India to Study Issues and Concerns in the MFI Sector, Reserve Bank of India, Mumbai, January.

Manning, M., Homel, R., & Smith, C. (2011). An economic method for formulating better policies for positive child development. *Australian Review of Public Affairs, 10*(1), 61-77.

Ministry of Finance (2012), The Microfinance Institutions (Development and Regulation) Bill, Bill No. 62 of 2012, Government of India, New Delhi.

Mohanty, D. (2015), Report of the Committee on Medium-term Path on Financial Inclusion, Reserve Bank of India, Mumbai, December.

Nobre, F. F., Trotta, L. T. F., & Gomes, L. F. A. M. (1999). Multi-criteria decision making–an approach to setting priorities in health care. *Statistics in medicine, 18*(23), 3345-3354.

Planning Commission. (2009). 'A Hundred Small Steps: Report of the Committee on FinancialSector Reforms'. Government of India. Retrieved from http://planningcommission.nic.in/reports/genrep/rep_fr/cfsr_all.pdf (accessed on July 27, 2016).

Rajan, R., & Zingales, L. (2003). *Saving capitalism from the capitalists* (Vol. 2121). New York: Crown Business.

Rangarajan, C. (2008), Report of the Committee on Financial Inclusion, National Bank for Agriculture and Rural Development (NABARD), Mumbai, January.

Saaty, T.L., (1980). "The Analytic Hierarchy Process." McGraw-Hill, New York.

Saaty, T. L. (1990). Multicriteria decision making: The Analytical Hierarchy Process. Pittsburgh, USA: RWS Publications.

Saaty, T. L. (1994). How to make a decision: the analytic hierarchy process. *Interfaces, 24*(6), 19-43.

Sharma, M. (2008). *Index of financial inclusion.* Indian Council for Research on International Economics Relations.

Stango, V., & Zinman, J. (2014). Limited and varying consumer attention evidence from shocks to the salience of bank overdraft fees. *Review of Financial Studies*, hhu008.

The Consultative Group to Assist the Poor (C-GAP). 2009. 'Financial Access 2009: Measuring Access to Financial Services Around the World'. World Bank. Retrieved from www.gsma.com/mobilefordevelopment/wp-content/uploads/2012/06/fa2009_6.pdf (accessed on July 27, 2016).

Thorat, U. (2006). Financial Inclusion for Sustainable Development: Role of IT and intermediaries. *Reserve Bank of India, Speeches published on Financial Inclusion and Related Topics in its following, Monthly Bulletins.*

Triantaphyllou, E., & Mann, S. H. (1995). Using the analytic hierarchy process for decision making in engineering applications: some challenges. *International Journal of Industrial Engineering: Applications and Practice, 2*(1), 35-44.

Yang, Y. Y., & Yi, M. H. (2008). Does financial development cause economic growth? Implication for policy in Korea. *Journal of Policy Modeling, 30*(5), 827-840.

Chapter 7

What drives level of Financial Inclusion: Study with reference to India?

Ravindra Tripathi[1], Priyanka Tandon[2], and Nikhil Yadav[3]

Abstract

Financial Inclusion is becoming the buzzword amongst the policy makers and academicians. Financial inclusion is one of the important strategies for reaching the inclusive growth of any economy. Past studies reveal that there are a number of factors that drive the level of inclusion in an economy such as level of income, occupation, gender, education level, financial literacy and so on. These factors vary with the cross-country studies. The objective of the present study is to find out the significant factors that determine the level of financial inclusion with reference to India. The determinants include the per capita income as a representative for the overall wellbeing, domestic credit to the private sector as a percentage of GDP as an indicator of financial depth, number of commercial bank branches per 1,00,000 adult population as an indicator of financial infrastructure and internet usage per 100 adults as indicator technological penetration. The data collected is secondary in nature which spans over the period 2007-2014 and collected through GLOBAL FINDEX data of World Bank. The study employs the OLS Regression to assess the dimensions of financial inclusion. The study finds that the number of commercial bank branches, internet usage and per capita income are the significant indicators of the level of financial inclusion but are highly

[1] Associate Professor, Department of Humanities and Social Sciences, Motilal Nehru National Institute of Technology, Allahabad, Uttar Pradesh.

[2] Research Scholar, Department of Humanities and Social Sciences, Motilal Nehru National Institute of Technology, Allahabad, Uttar Pradesh.

Corresponding Email: neha.tandon886@gmail.com

[3] Research Scholar, Department of Humanities and Social Sciences, Motilal Nehru National Institute of Technology, Allahabad, Uttar Pradesh.

correlated to each other. So, we introduced the interaction term of the number of bank branches per 1 lakh adults and internet usage to see the interaction effect and variable found to be significant. Finally, it can be concluded that in order to increase the penetration of the financial services in the country banks and other formal financial institutions should world diligently in the areas of technology, physical access and overall wellbeing.

Keywords: Financial Inclusion, Per Capita Income, Technology, Access, Usage, Financial depth

7.1. Introduction

With the growth of the Indian economy, especially focusing on the achievement of sustainable development there must be maximum involvement of all the sections of the society. But the lack of awareness and financial literacy among the Indian population is hindering the growth of the country. Since, a significant proportion of the Indian population is unbanked or do not have access to a formal financial system (Report on financial Inclusion, 2008), the economy is unable to achieve the targeted growth and development. This is a matter of great concern amongst the policy makers, regulating authority and government of India. The issue of financial Inclusion is on the top priority for the RBI and government of India evidence being the launch of various schemes recently and one amongst them is Pradhan Mantri Jan DhanYojana (PMJDY). This step also shows the serious concern of the government towards achieving the inclusive growth financially. Every step taken by the central bank, a regulator of economy and monetary policy framer, is guided to towards sustainable economic development and balancing of the economy.

Conceptually, financial inclusion is the process of enhancing the access to financial services to those who are deprived of it such as weaker sections, underprivileged sections or low income group sections. Financial Inclusion basically focuses on two things namely, access to financial services which may be proxied to transactions and finance or money. Hence, it is an economic activity comprising of money and its transactions.

7.1.1. Financial inclusion–conceptual framework

There are number factors which affect the financial inclusion. From demand side, it is lack of awareness and illiteracy (Thorat, 2007) and from the supply side, it is the lack of avenues for investment such as branch network. But apart from these there are several other factors such as income of consumers, cost beared by banks and inefficiency by banks. Sinclair (2001) defines financial inclusion as an inability to access necessary financial services in an appropriate form. Carbo et al. (2005) defined financial exclusion as the inability of some societal groups to access the financial system. Various authorities in India defined financial inclusion. The comprehensive definition of financial inclusion as given by Reserve Bank of India is as follows:

"The process of ensuring access to appropriate financial products and services needed by all sections of the society in general and vulnerable groups such as weaker sections and low income groups in particular at an affordable cost in fair and transparent manner by mainstream institutional players".

7.1.2. Review of literature

Research on financial inclusion had always been a priority for researchers and policy makers due to its very nature. The ample research and survey studies have been conducted on financial inclusion worldwide. Many important committees had been formulated in India to overlook the status of financial inclusion. World Bank and International Monetary Fund are the key agencies that collect the cross-country data on level of inclusion based on demand and supply factors respectively. In India, Reserve Bank of India is the key agency and policy framer for the financial inclusion. Some of the literature on financial inclusion are discussed here as under.

Report on financial Inclusion (2008) reported that both the demand and supply factors responsible for the financial exclusion of households in India. The report revealed various demand side factors such as level of poverty, resource endowment issues which includes social, financial, natural and physical, lower level of literacy, increasing dropouts, inadequate access to natural capita and productivity issues such as low productivity, poor market linkage. The demand side factors depict the household's perspectives regarding exclusion from financial services. While, supply-side factors include barriers to physical access to banks, lower penetration of bank branches in the rural area, poor functioning of banks, poor attitude of bank employees etc. the report highlighted both factors as the root cause for the increased level of financial exclusion. Report on Medium Term Path (2015) report various recommendations for enhancing the level of financial inclusion in India. The report highlighted that banking penetration has taken a significant leap in rural and urban areas. BSBD accounts have increased six-fold and nearly half of these accounts were opened by BCs. Eastern, Northern-eastern and central regions lag behind the banking penetration. States such as Bihar, Jharkhand, Uttar Pradesh, West Bengal and Madhya Pradesh are less penetrated in terms of banking penetration in relation to population. Gender remains the serious concern in exclusion. The report also mention important determinants of financial inclusion in India namely, income level, adult literacy, urbanization, inequality, physical and electronic connectivity, information availability, voluntary exclusion, financial literacy and governance.

UNDP (2012) conducted a survey in various states of India regarding financial literacy. The study checked the impact of various policies of financial literacy on households. The findings of the study revealed that various policies on financial literacy had enhanced the level of awareness of households in Uttar Pradesh, Bihar, and Rajasthan more than in Chhattisgarh, Jharkhand, Madhya Pradesh and Odisha. While it has not helped in initiating the use of savings accounts in Uttar Pradesh and Bihar, the usage result was positive in Rajasthan. Sarma (2008) has proposed an index of financial inclusion by using three indicators bank penetration, availability of banking services and usage of banking services. Bhanot, Bapat & Bera (2012) in their study explored various determinants which are important in explaining the level of financial inclusion in financially remote areas. The study was conducted in Assam and Meghalaya. Logistic Regression was used to identify the significant factors explaining the financial inclusion. Level of financial inclusion in north-east India remains very low. Income, financial information from various channels and awareness of self help groups (SHGs), and education are influential factors leading to inclusion. Nearness to post office banks increases the likelihood of inclusion. Factors like area terrain and receipt of government benefit individually do not facilitate inclusion. However, recipients of government benefits in plain areas show an increased level of inclusion. Ghosh (2011) studied 14 major Indian states during 1973-2004. In his paper, the author tries to find out the solution behind the question that financial outreach affects economic growth. The study employs various univariate test and panel regression techniques. The analysis suggests that improvements in financial outreach led to a noticeable rise in per capita growth. In terms of degrees, the surge in demographic outreach by 10 percent increases state per capita growth by 0.3 percent; in the case of geographic outreach, the increase is lower. Finally, the analysis supports the hypotheses that states with higher manufacturing share tend to grow faster and the quality of state-level institutions and infrastructure employ a significant bearing on growth. Bruntha & Indirapriyadharshini (2015) in their study analyzes the income level and banking habits of street hawkers in Pollachi, Tamil Nadu to find out whether the measures taken by the government and banks regarding inclusive growth have reached the street hawkers. Chi-square test is employed to test the association between the selected variables and the level of awareness. The findings reveal that there is no significant association between the selected variables and level of awareness on financial inclusion measures taken by banks. Unnikrishnan & Jagannathan (2015) in their study tries to analyze the role of technology in facilitating financial inclusion at the bottom of the pyramid (BoP). The study compares the financial inclusion of BRICS Nations. By using the t-test and the ANOVA study, it proves that there is a significant difference between the ownership of bank accounts and inclusion between the bottom of pyramids (BoP) and the mainstream population of BRICS nations. The study quantifies the financial level using the index of financial inclusion as proposed by Sarma (2008). In their study, Ghosh & Vinod (2016) analyse the interface between gender and financial inclusion. The study uses a multivariate regression model to empirically assess. When the dependent variable is access to finance, the Tobit model is used and when the dependent variable is the use of finance, the double-hurdle model is used. The results of the study revealed that female-headed households are less likely to have access to formal finance as compare to men. The study also revealed that female households are prone to access informal finance.

At international level as well number of studies conducted on access to finance on cross-country data (Beck & Kunt, 2008); access to and use of banking services(Beck, Kunt &Peria; 2005; Kunt & Klapper, 2013), impact and review of access to financial services (Beck, Kunt & Hanohan, 2009; Classens, 2006), an Islamic banking increase financial inclusion (Naceur, Barajas &Massara, 2015), variation in household access to financial services in 160 countries (Patrick, 2007), impact of financial innovation on economic growth(Hao, 1997), financial inclusion with reference to post office in Britain(Midgley, 2005),financial inclusion in liquidity constraint environment in Zimbabwe (Laurine & Patrick, 2012).

7.1.3. Research Objective

The objectives of the study are:

1. To analyze which factors significantly influence the level of financial inclusion in India.
2. To establish the empirical relationship between financial inclusion and financial infrastructure, financial depth, and technological penetration.

7.2. Research methodology

7.2.1. Sampling

The sample consists of India for the period which spans over 2007-2014. The sampling technique is purposive sampling.

7.2.2. Data collection and technique

The data is secondary in nature. The data is collected from the database of World Bank (Global FINDEX). It is an official database of World Bank which collects data on demand side factors of financial inclusion of world economies. Another source of data is International Monetary Fund data on financial inclusion which is known as IMF Financial Access Survey. IMF collects data on supply side factors.

Table 7.1.: Variables Studied and Statistical technique

S. No	Variables	Code used in Study	Dimension and Level of Financial Inclusion (Hypothesized)	Source
1	Number of Deposits account	LogDEP*	Financial Inclusion	Basic Statistical Returns of Banks in India, RBI
2	Domestic Credit to Private sector as percentage of GDP	DCr	**Level I**: Financial depth	World Bank FINDEX
3	Number of commercial bank branches per 1,00,000 adult population	Br	**Level II**: Financial Infrastructure	IMF Financial Access Survey
4	Internet usage per 100 adults	InT	**Level II**: Technological Penetration	World Bank FINDEX
5	Per Capita Income	LogPCI*	**Level III**: Overall wellbeing	World Bank FINDEX

Table 7.2.: Data Summary of Variables over the period 2007-2014

Year	Number of Deposits account (Log)	Domestic Credit to Private sector as percentage of GDP	Number of commercial bank branches per 1,00,000 adult population	Per Capita Income (Log)	Internet usage per 100 adults
2007	20.0677982	44.8	9.075937866	6.591948043	3.95
2008	20.18139322	48.5	9.391850958	6.604025122	4.3
2009	20.31123281	47.2	9.691121565	6.697404549	5.12
2010	20.415203	49.5	10.14111383	6.766306915	7.5
2011	20.51270449	50.7	10.62802996	6.813774216	10.07
2012	20.62145486	51.7	11.31489156	6.853299093	12.58
2013	20.76738281	51.9	12.00239847	6.904550148	15.1
2014	20.92760177	51.6	13.03529379	6.962148763	18

Source: Basic Statistical Returns of Banks in India, RBI
World Bank FINDEX, IMF Financial Access Survey

The relationship between the above variable is been analyzed by employing multiple regression through OLS estimation method.

7.2.3. Hypothesis and model specification

On the basis of the objectives of the study following hypothesis has been formulated:

Level I

H_{0a}: There is significant relationship between financial inclusion and financial depth (Domestic Credit to Private sector as percentage of GDP).

Level II

H_{0b}: There is significant relationship between financial inclusion and financial infrastructure (Number of commercial bank branches per 1,00,000 adult population).

H_{0c}: There is significant relationship between financial inclusion and technological penetration (Internet usage per 100 adults).

Level III

H_{0d} There is significant relationship between financial inclusion and overall well-being (Per Capita Income).

Based on the above hypothesis, model has been specified:

$$LogDEP_t = LogPCI_t + DCr_t + Br_t + InT_t + e$$

Where,

$LogDEP_t$ is log of number of deposits account

$LogPCI_t$ is log of Per capita income of the country

DCr_t is the Domestic Credit to Private sector as percentage of GDP

Br_t is the number of bank branches per 1, 00, 000 adults

Int_t is the internet usage per 100 adults

7.2.4. Data analysis and interpretation

Table 7.3.: Correlation Matrix

	Deposits Accounts	Domestic Credit To Private Sector as % of GDP	Internet Usage Per 100 People	No of Branches Per 1 lakh adults	Per Capita Income
Deposits Accounts		0.843415	0.989402	0.998218	0.980740
Domestic Credit To Private Sector as % of GDP	0.843415		0.858216	0.844967	0.880782
Internet Usage Per 100 People	0.989402	0.858216		0.994438	0.980374
No of Branches Per 1 lakh adults	0.998218	0.844967	0.994438		0.976812
Per Capita Income	0.980740	0.880782	0.980374	0.976812	

Table 7.4.: Results of OLS Estimation

Dependent Variable: LOG_DEP				
Method: Least Squares				
Date: 07/01/16 Time: 11:29				
Sample: 2007 2014				
Included observations: 8				
Variable	**Coefficient**	**Std. Error**	**t-Statistic**	**Prob.**
C	10.66621	1.045784	10.19925	0.0020
Per Capita Income	1.084714	0.168280	6.445878	0.0076*
Domestic Credit to private sector	0.011611	0.004339	2.676077	0.0753**
No. of Branches per 1 lakh adults	0.204211	0.034704	5.884411	0.0098*
Internet Usage per 100 adults	-0.030294	0.009731	-3.113030	0.0528**
R-squared	0.999140			
Adjusted R-squared	0.997994			
S.E. of regression	0.013063			
Sum squared resid	0.000512			
Log likelihood	27.27531			
F-statistic	871.8034			
Prob(F-statistic)	0.000063			
Durbin-Watson stat	3.177110			

The R square value for the model is 0.99 which is a good indicator for the fitness of the model. As we can see that coefficient for the variable per capita income is 1.084714 which is having positive sign while the p-value is 0.0076 which is significant at 1% level of significance. Hence, it implies that there is positive significant relationship between per capita income and level of financial inclusion. In other words, per capita income has positive significant impact over the level of financial inclusion. A unit increase in per capita income will lead to a 10.8% increase in the level of financial inclusion. Hence, it can be concluded that per capita income is significant variable for explaining financial inclusion. Similarly, p-value for the domestic credit for the private sector as % of GDP is 0.753, the number of branches for 1 lakh adults is 0.0098 and for internet usage is 0.0528 which is significant at 10%, 1% and 5% level of significance. Hence, all the independent variables are significant in explaining the financial inclusion. The signs for the coefficient are as per expectation except for internet usage per 100 adults which is negative. It implies that more and more increase in internet penetration lesser will be the financial inclusion. It signifies that there is technological penetration has an adverse impact on financial inclusion. This may be due to the less trust of households on the technology for the use of the banking services.

By looking over the correlation matrix, it clear that there is a very high correlation among the variables. It is also signified by VIF value which is an indicator of the presence of multicollinearity in the model. The VIF value is 93.15, 21.28 and 107.87 for the variables number of branches per 1 lakh adults, log per capita income and internet usage per 100 adults respectively. Hence, it is clear that there is a problem of multicollinearity in the model. Hence, the model is not appropriate for conclusion. The problem of log per capita income is omitted from the model since it is highly correlated where an interaction of two variables (number of bank branches per 1 lakh adults and internet usage per 100 adult is introduced) in the model.

$$LogDEP_t = DCr_t + + (InT_t * Br_t) + e$$

Table 7.5.: Results of OLS estimation after introducing Interaction Effect

Dependent Variable: LOG_DEPOSITS_ACCOUNTS				
Method: Least Squares				
Variable	**Coefficient**	**Std. Error**	**t-Statistic**	**Prob.**
C	18.59476	0.655029	28.38769	0.0000
Domestic Credit To Private Sector % Of GDP	0.031382	0.014104	2.225008	0.0766**
No Of Branches Per 10000*Internet Usage Per 100_Persons	0.003024	0.000492	6.142178	0.0017*
R-squared	0.975870	Mean dependent var		20.47560
Adjusted R-squared	0.966217	S.D. dependent var		0.291699
S.E. of regression	0.053614	Akaike info criterion		-2.734001
Sum squared resid	0.014373	Schwarz criterion		-2.704210
Log likelihood	13.93600	Hannan-Quinn criter.		-2.934926
F-statistic	101.1034	Durbin-Watson stat		1.775008
Prob(F-statistic)	0.000090			

*Significant at 1% level of significance
**Significant at 10% level of significance

The results here signify that domestic credit to the private sector is significantly influencing the level of financial inclusion. While the interaction effect of the variable number of branches per 10000 and internet usage per 100 persons together significantly influences the level of financial inclusion in India. It means that nowadays with the advent of technology and implementing the internet in banking sector technology plays a vital role and hence influences the financial inclusion level to a great extent.

In order, to run OLS estimation for a model it is important that model must fulfill certain assumptions.

- First, there should be no serial correlation among the error terms. If there will be problem of autocorrelation in the model, then OLS estimators will still be biased. Table 4 presents the results of Breusch-Godfrey Serial Correlation LM Test which is done to check the presence of serial correlation. The Durbin Watson statistic is 1.77 (refer table 3) which is less than 1 and Prob chi-square is 0.3885 which is insignificant. Both the value signifies that there is no serial correlation exists in the model.
- Second, there must be homoscedasticity present in the model. To check this, Breusch-Pagan-Godfrey test is conducted. The results show that Prob. Chi-Square is 0.1891 which is more than level of significance. Hence, it concludes that there is presence of homoscedasticity (constant variances).

Table 6: Breusch-Godfrey Serial Correlation LM Test

F-statistic	0.464350	Prob. F(2,3)	0.6673
Obs*R-squared	1.891108	Prob. Chi Square(2)	0.3885

Table 7: Heteroskedasticity Test: Breusch-Pagan-Godfrey

F-statistic	1.783501	Prob. F(2,5)	0.2602
Obs*R-squared	3.330923	Prob. Chi-Square(2)	0.1891
Scaled explained SS	1.084089	Prob. Chi-Square(2)	0.5816

7.3. Findings and discussion

The findings from the above study depict that when there established the relationship between the independent variable and level of financial inclusion, though all the variables turned out to be significant at 1%, 5% and 10% level of significance, there was a problem of multicollinearity in the model. So, in order to remove the problem of multicollinearity, we have introduced the interaction effect of number of bank branches per 1 lakh adults and internet usage (financial infrastructure and technological penetration). The findings of the study are as follows:

- **H_{0a}**: There is significant relationship between financial inclusion and financial depth (Domestic Credit to Private sector as percentage of GDP).

Table 5 shows that coefficient of the variable is 0.031382 which is positive depicting the positive relationship with the dependent variable. While the p-value is 0.076 which is significant at 10% level of significance. Hence, there comes out to be positive significant relationship between financial depth and financial inclusion. It implies that more and more lending to private sector will influence the financial inclusion.

- **H_{0b}**: There is significant relationship between financial inclusion and financial infrastructure (Number of commercial bank branches per 1, 00,000 adult population).
- **H_{0c}**: There is significant relationship between financial inclusion and technological penetration (Internet usage per 100 adults).

In our study we have introduced the interaction effect of the two variables (number of bank branches and internet connectivity), then the results turned out to be significant with no autocorrelation presence in the model. The coefficient value is 0.003024 and p-value is 0.0017 which is significant at 1% level of significance. Hence there exists a relationship between the financial inclusion and financial infrastructure and technological penetration jointly.

H_{0d} There is significant relationship between financial inclusion and overall well-being (Per Capita Income).

We have also dropped variable per capita since it has highly correlated with all other variables. Before the interaction effect, this variable was highly significant but suffering from the problem of multicollinearity. Hence it is being dropped from the model.

7.4. Conclusion

Financial Inclusion is one of the public policies by the government of India since it is related to the economic growth of the country. Thus, in this study, we have undertaken the factors which are crucial in explaining the level of financial inclusion in any economy. The results of the study indicate that there is a positive and significant relationship between the domestic credit to private sector and the interaction effect of the number of bank branches and internet connectivity with financial inclusion. The literature on finance and growth suggest that financial inclusion is one of the major determinants of economic growth (RBI, 2008). Thus, it is imperative that in infrastructure must be developed in line with the financial inclusion to attain the ultimate objective of the economic growth.

Bibliography

Beck et al., (2007) Reaching *out: Access to and use of banking services across countries,* Journal of Financial Economics (Elsevier), 234-266.

Beck T., and Kunt A., (2008) *Access to finance: An unfinished Agenda,* The World Bank Economic Review. 22(3), pp: 383-396.

Beck T., and Kunt A.D., (2008) *Access to Finance: An Unfinished Agenda,* The World Economic Review, 22(3), pp: 383-396.

Beck T., Kunt A.D., and Peria M.S.M., (2005) *Access to and Use of Banking Services across countries.* Retry from https://pure.uvt.nl/portal/files/1023776/Reaching_out_Access_to_and_use_of_Banking_Services.pdf.

Beck T., Kunt A.D, and Patrick H., (2009) *Access to Financial Services: Measurement, Impact, and Policies,* The World Bank Research Observer, 24 (1), pp: 119-145.

Bhanot D., Bapat V., and Bera, (2012) *Studying Financial Inclusion in North-East India,* International Journal of Bank Marketing (Emerald), 30 (6), 465-484.

Bruntha P., and Indirapriyadharshini *B., (2015) An Enquiry into Financial Inclusion with Special Reference to Street Hawkers of Pollachi, Tamil Nadu,* The IUP Journal of Marketing Management, Vol. XIV, No. 4, pp: 56-70.

Carbo S., Gardener E.P., and Molyneux P., (2005) *Financial Exclusion.* Palgrave MacMillan.

Classens P. (2006) *Access to Financial Services: A Review of the Issues and Public Policy Objective,* The Review of World Bank Research Observer, 21 (2), pp: 207-240.

Ghosh S. and Vinod D., (2016) *How important is gender? Furthering Financial Inclusion Agenda in India,* Economic and Political Weekly, 15 (12).

Ghosh S., (2011) *Does Financial Inclusion engender Economic growth?,* Journal of Indian Business Research, 3(2), pp: 74-97.

Hanohan P., (2008) Cross-country variation in household access to financial services. Journal of Banking and Finance (Elsevier), 32 (11), 2493-2500.

Kunt D. A., and Klapper L., (2013) *Measuring Financial Inclusion: Explaining Variation in Use of Financial Services across and within Countries,* Brookings Papers on Economic Activity, World Bank, 279-321.

Laurine C. and Patrick M., (2012) *Financial inclusion by Zimbabwean commercial banks in a liquidity constrained environment,* Journal of Economics and International Finance, Vol. 4(10), pp. 252-259.

Midgley J., (2005) *Financial Inclusion, Universal Banking and Post Offices in Britain,* Area, 37 (3), pp: 277-285.

Naceur S. B., Barajas A., and Massara A., (2015) *Can Islamic Banking increase financial inclusion?* IMF Working Paper. WP/15/31.

Rangarajan C., (2008) *Report of the Committee on Financial Inclusion.* Retrieved from https://www.nabard.org/pdf/Full_Report.pdf.

Reserve Bank of India. (2008) *Financial Inclusion* (Chapter VII), Report on Currency and Finance Volume I, Retrieved from https://rbidocs.rbi.org.in/rdocs/Publications/PDFs/86722.pdf

Reserve Bank of India. (2015) *Report of the Committee on Medium Term Path on Financial Inclusion. Retrieved from* https://rbidocs.rbi.org.in/rdocs/PublicationReport/Pdfs/FFIRA27F4530706A41A0BC394D01CB4892CC.PDF.

Sharma M., (2008) *Index of Financial Inclusion. Indian Council for Research on International Economic Relations,* Working Paper No. 215.

Sinclair S. P., (2001) *Financial exclusion: An introductory survey,* Report of Centre for Research in Socially Inclusive Services, Edinburgh. Heriot-Watt University.

Thorat U., (2006) *Financial Inclusion and Millenium Development Goals.* Mumbai: RBI Publication.

UNDP. (2012) *Financial Literacy as a tool for financial Inclusion and client protection,* Financial Inclusion project of UNDP, Retrieved from http://www.in.undp.org/content/dam/india/docs/poverty/financial-literacy-as-a-tool-for-financial-inclusion-and-client.pdf.

Unnikrishnan J., and Jagannathan L., (2015) *Unearthing Global Financial Inclusion Levels And Analysis of Financial Inclusion as A Mediating Factor in Global Human Development,* Serbian Journal of Management, 10 (1), pp: 19-32.

Chapter 8

Need for institutional arbitration in construction contracts in India

Mohana Raje[1], Kavita Kalyandurgmath[2], and Jagdish Raje[3]

Abstract

Indian Arbitration and Conciliation Act1 1996, was enacted by the Parliament based on the model UNCITRAL Law so as to facilitate Indian trade and commerce in the global economy. The act was seen as a panacea by the Indian industry and professionals. All the stakeholders expected a faster resolution of disputes and verdicts consistent with the industry norms at lesser costs. However soon it was discovered that the process of Arbitration was controlled by the legal community, judicial interventions were frequent and disrupting, resulting in uncontrollable costs. The verdicts were found to be legally correct but inconsistent with industry practices. The sector that suffered the most was the construction sector.

Almost every construction work has disputes. The money under dispute either directly or as a compensation may be in crores. Though the present arbitration act, allows different kinds of arbitration, there is almost a norm to use ad-hoc arbitration and appoint non-technical but legally qualified personnel as arbitrators. It has been found that such appointments tend to delay the process of dispute resolution due to the time taken by such arbitrators to understand technical issues and many times the arbitral award though consistent with legal requirements is found wanting in consistency with industry practices. The resolution of such disputes needs

---

[1] Director and Head Contracts, GEM Engserv Pvt Ltd, Email: raje.mohana@gmail.com

[2] Prof. Operations, Welingkar Institute of Management Development and Research, Mumbai, Email:kavita.kalyandurgmath@welingkar.org

[3] M. Tech, MRICS, M.ASCE, Director GEMENGSERV Pvt. Ltd, Email: jagdish.raje@gemengserv.com

a deep understanding of the industry practices, the sequence of events and the cascading effects of the causes.

This study identifies and examines the factors influencing the resolution of construction disputes in the construction industry due to ad-hoc dispute resolution. A survey was conducted by the Researcher to find the reasons that contribute to the delays in the Alternative Dispute Resolution process through a questionnaire with engineers, lawyers and arbitrators as respondents.

Keywords: Dispute Resolution, Arbitration, Construction, Technical personnel, ad-hoc dispute resolution.

8.1. Introduction

Arbitration is one of the alternative ways to solve construction disputes. This chapter recognizes the need for Institutional Arbitration as a method to resolve disputes in the construction industry. The chapter discusses the effect of the quick settlement of disputes on the disputants as well as on the economy of the country. This will help the construction professionals and lawyers with an insight into dealing with construction disputes, at all stages, using principles that are applicable internationally.

Written by a team of qualified professionals and academicians who are a professional consulting engineer, a lawyer and a statistician. This includes the complete range of dispute resolution expertise required by construction professionals including advice on how to avoid potential disputes.

Alternative Dispute Resolution is the method to resolve disputes without taking the traditional litigation recourse of the Indian Court system. This study will help the disputing parties in construction disputes to make effective use of the procedures available, selecting the right methods and the best strategy for satisfactory resolution of disputes when they arise to minimize the time and costs expended.

This chapter has included the opinions of practicing construction and legal professionals of the industry and includes practical solutions to avoid delays in the completion of construction projects. When the construction industry is functioning smoothly the quick resolution of disputes through Institutional Arbitration will help boost the economy of the country. Written in an easy-to-read style, it is an essential and informative read for both professionals and students in the field of construction, law and engineering.

8.1.1. The Indian judicial system

As political philosopher, Charles de Montesquieu said; "In the state of nature...all men are born equal, but they cannot continue in this equality. Society makes them lose it, and they recover it only by the protection of the law (Montesquieu, 2000)."[4]

The Constitution of India was adopted and enacted, *inter alia*, to secure to all citizens of this country, through Preamble, which is the basic structure of the Constitution, JUSTICE – Social, Economic and Political. This golden goal set out in the Preamble of the Constitution is to be achieved through sustained and productive efforts and to secure to its citizen, social, economic and political justice. Article 14 of the Constitution makes it clear that the State shall not deny any person equality before the law or the equal protection of the laws within the territory of India. The aim of Article 14 is to ensure equal justice.[5]Thus the State through the Constitution of India guarantees to establish a social order in which the legal system of the country provides justice to all the citizens. All the citizens irrespective of social, economic and political barriers have been ensured access to justice. (Menon, n.d)[6]The litigation mode of access to justice in India is based on the adversarial legalism. In this mode of justice, the State plays a neutral role and it is the parties who are responsible for initiating and conducting litigation. This system is generally followed in common law countries.[7]

The noted jurist Mr. N.A. Palkhivala, attributing this cause to legal profession inter-alia, observed: “The fault is mainly of legal professionals. We ask for adjournments on the most flimsy grounds. If the Judge does not readily grant an adjournment, he is deemed highly unpopular; I think it is the duty of the legal profession to make sure that it co-operates with the judiciary in ensuring that justice is administered speedily and expeditiously, it is a duty of which we are totally oblivious”.[8]

---

[4] Montesquieu, C. d. S. b. d., 2000. Montesquieu's Science of Politics: Essays on the Spirit of Laws. s.l.:Rowman & Littlefield Publishers, 2000.

[5] Anon., n.d.
https://www.india.gov.in/sites/upload_files/npi/files/coi_part_full.pdf.
[Online] [Accessed 25 11 2016].

[6] ibid

[7] (Menon, n.d.). http://rajasthanjudicialacademy.nic.in/docs/1_s5.pdf, Social Context Education for Social Justice Adjudication

[8] Tribute to Nani Palkhiwala by the Bar Council of India says that Nanabhoy

Litigation in the Indian courts suffers from severely backlogged dockets Sourjya Bhowmick[9] "Justice has a Mountain to Climb of 31.3 million pending cases," dated 4 September 2014, "and it may take up to 15 years to obtain a decision says Ministry of Law and Justice. National Legal Mission to Reduce Average Pendency Time from 15 Years to 3 Years," dated 23 June 2010.

The procedural safeguards and natural principles of justice when enforced by the state resulted in severe problems in resolving the litigation.[10] They are: 1. Inordinate delay, 2. Escalating costs, and 3. Mounting arrears, 4. Pervasive corruption. Absence of procedural delays would change the economics as disputes will be decided faster and progress would be achieved.[11]In India, it was an attempt made by the legislators and judiciary alike to achieve the "Constitutional goal" of achieving Complete Justice. Alternative Dispute Resolution in India was founded on the Constitutional basis of Articles 14 and 21 which deal with Equality before Law and Right to life and personal liberty respectively.[12]

8.1.2. Arbitration in India

The modern system of Alternative Dispute Resolution mechanisms evolved to provide complete justice to persons in conflicts and legal disputes. The need for Alternative Dispute Resolution mechanism such as mediation, conciliation, arbitration, Lok Adalats etc. as a feasible

("Nani") Ardeshir Palkhivala's achievements in the field of public policy and Constitutional law are significant and enviable even to a seasoned policy-maker.

[9] National Legal Mission to Reduce Average Pendency Time from 15 Years to 3 Years (2010). Available at:
http://pib.nic.in/newsite/erelcontent.aspx?relid=62745 (Accessed: 25 July 2016)

[10] Rani, Bittoo, 2015. Justice at Cross Roads – A Critical Analysis of the Functioning of the Indian Judicial System and the Need for an Alternative. Global Journal of HUMAN-SOCIAL SCIENCE: A Arts & Humanities - Psychology, [Online]. 15(6), 1-13. Available at:
https://globaljournals.org/GJHSS_Volume15/1-Justice-at-Cross-Roads-A-Critical.pdf [Accessed 30 July 2016].

[11] Department of Administrative Reforms & Public Grievances. 2007. Fifth report: Second Administrative Reforms Commission. [ONLINE] Available at:
https://www.darpg.gov.in/sites/default/files/public_order5_0.pdf. [Accessed 26 July 2016].

[12] Justice A.P. Shah, Chief Justice High Court of Delhi, the inaugural address delivered at the conference on international (commercial arbitration and sale of goods UNCITRAL perspective) highlighted the issues.

substitute to the conventional court litigation.[13] Having first started as a mission to find solutions to the problem of the ever-growing burden on the courts, Alternative Dispute Resolution is at present is a movement all over the commercial world to find an answer to never-ending litigation and never reaching solutions.[14] There was much delay in the settlement of disputes between parties in law courts, which prevented the investment of money in India by other countries. India has undertaken major reforms in its arbitration law in recent years as part of the initial economic reforms in 1991. The Arbitration and Conciliation Act of 1996 was thus enacted by the Parliament bringing in substantial reforms in arbitration, regarding domestic and international disputes[15] indicating that the Civil Procedure Code which is the adversarial system of procedural law for civil litigation in the judicial system may not be followed. It is the prerogative of the parties to decide the procedure. This was envisaged to make it easier for the parties to resolve a dispute which may take a number of years in the adversarial judicial system where valuable time is not lost.

The Law Commission published its first set of recommendations to reform the arbitration law in 2001.

Arbitration in India has suffered from some of the same efficiency issues as litigation and has been plagued by "high costs and delays.[16] It has emerged that Arbitration is particularly important in India because it can offer a partial solution to the problems of high cost and delays in the formal judicial system and can benefit the formal system by reducing its caseload. The evolution of law has not been unfortunately matched by an evolution in the judicial approach to arbitration. The 1996 Act makes provision for the supervisory role of courts, for the review of the arbitral award only to ensure fairness.[17]

---

[13] Subhan, Jelis, 2010, Arbitration Conciliation and Mediation- Conflict between Formal and Informal Setups (September 3, 2010). Available at SSRN:
https://ssrn.com/abstract=2145187 or http://dx.doi.org/10.2139/ssrn.2145187

[14] Love, I. (2011). Settling Out of Court: How effective is alternative dispute resolution? [online] Siteresources.worldbank.org. Available at:

http://siteresources.worldbank.org/FINANCIALSECTOR/Resources/282044-1307652042357/VP329-Setting-out-of-court.pdf (Accessed 27 Jul. 2016).

[15] Government of India. 2009. LAW COMMISSION OF INDIA. [ONLINE] Available at: http://lawcommissionofindia.nic.in/reports/report222.pdf. [Accessed 28 July 2016].

[16] Sharma, D. and Bhatnagar, P. (2014). Risk Allocation & Subsequent Legal Issues in Construction Contracts.

[17] Anon, 2013. Corporate Attitudes & Practices towards Arbitration in India. Price

8.1.3. Essence of amicable settlement

Amicable settlement of a dispute involves the following steps:

(a) bringing the parties to the negotiating table;
(b) identifying the problems;
(c) establishing the facts;
(d) clarifying the issues;
(e) developing the options for settlement; and
(f) ultimately reaching agreement.

Advantages of amicable settlement

Advantages of amicable settlement are:

i. enables the parties themselves to resolve the dispute and to bury the past;
ii. preserves the present relationship; and also
iii. paves a better future.[18]

8.1.4. Institutional Arbitration

Alternative Dispute Resolution if properly institutionalized, as an adjunct to judiciary would prove to be a vital tool for easy and early settlement of disputes. Institutional arbitration shall be promoted in India to make India an important venue of both domestic and international arbitration. Institutional arbitration and mediation shall be promoted in cases of settlement outside the court. Only accredited Institutions registered with the Government may be entrusted with the task of appointment of arbitrators, mediators etc.[19]These decisions are significant especially coming from courts in India since litigants choose arbitration specifically to avoid the long-drawn litigations before the courts, emphasizing the need for institutional arbitration, coupled. Ministry of Law and Justice proposed in a 2010 consultation paper to make institutional arbitration mandatory for all disputes valued at over 5 crores make a strong case for institutional arbitration in India. In a country where arbitration is such an

---

Watherhouse Coopers. Available at: https://www.pwc.in/assets/pdfs/publications/2013/corporate-attributes-and-practices-towards-arbitration-in-india.pdf [Accessed July 28, 2016].

[18] Allison, J. R., 1990. Five Ways to Keep Disputes Out of Court. Harvard Business Review, Jan-Feb.Issue Jan-Feb.

[19] National Legal Mission to Reduce Average Pendency Time from 15 Years to 3 Years (2010). Available at: http://pib.nic.in/newsite/erelcontent.aspx?relid=62745 [Accessed: 25 July 2016]

important form of commercial dispute resolution due to the time taken in judicial proceedings, it is crucial that clients make an informed decision with regard to the type of arbitration while negotiating the arbitration clause. The structure and procedural predictability that is provided by institutional arbitration may have great advantages in the Indian context.

Among the recommendations of the Law Commission in the 246th Report on the "Amendment to the Arbitration and Conciliation Act, 1996," the establishment of able and efficient institutions across the nation while recommending support from the government in terms of initial funds and land for the establishment of such institutions has been encouraged. It has discussed a novel idea of having an Arbitral Commission of India which would encourage the spreading of institutional arbitration in India. The Commission has suggested the promotion of institutional arbitration by recommending suitable proposals which it hopes will be used by the Supreme Court and the High Courts to promote institutional arbitration. It further proposes to accord legislative sanction to the institutions such as ICC and SIAC providing for "Emergency arbitrator" by expanding the definition of "arbitral tribunal."[20]

All these are provided for transparency, reliability and familiarity to the arbitration and quicken its process in India. There are several advantages of institutional arbitration. For instance:

i. Availability of pre-determined rules and procedures which assure that arbitration will get off the ground and proceed to conclusion;
ii. Managerial and secretarial assistance from institutions providing a secretariat or a court of arbitration;
iii. Names of qualified arbitrators;
iv. Appointment of arbitrators by the institution, if required;
v. Facilities and support service for arbitration; and
vi. A1n established format with a proven record.

There is a need to evolve a method in India for commercial matters so that costs do not escalate owing to delay.

[20] 'Law Commission's Report to Revamp the Indian Arbitration Experience' (2014) Kluwer Arbitration Blog, 23 August. Available at: http://arbitrationblog.kluwerarbitration.com/2014/08/23/law-commissions-report-to-revamp-the-indian-arbitration-experience/ (Accessed: 30 July 2016).

8.1.5. Research objectives:

1. To study the factors influencing the delays caused in ad-hoc arbitration in Construction Projects with respect to time and the method/procedure to resolve the delays.
2. To study the existing methods of solving delay in construction-related disputes.
3. To study the required skills set required by dispute resolution professionals to solve construction disputes.

8.2. Construction disputes and arbitration

Ideally, Construction Disputes need to be resolved through Institutional Arbitration.

Justice A.P. Shah, Chief Justice High Court of Delhi, the inaugural address delivered at the conference on international commercial arbitration enumerated that Arbitration is particularly important in India because it can offer a partial solution to the problems of high cost and delays in the formal judicial system and can benefit the formal system by reducing its caseload. The need of the hour is the institutionalization of arbitration in India, along with the lines suggested by the Parliamentary Standing Committee Report, which is now long overdue and can help to revitalize commercial arbitration in India.[21]

According to Prof. (Dr.) A.K. Garg, Head Research, NICMAR, the present Alternative Dispute Resolution mechanisms have provided insufficient relief to the affected agencies. But it is necessary to have an effective institutional arbitration mechanism of international standards to provide an institutional mechanism for the resolution of construction related disputes. In his view, in today's modern and complex commercial world, for disputes involving smaller scale claims ad hoc arbitration is appropriate. In the context and setting of international commercial disputes and owing to globalization and intricacies and complexities of construction projects, institutional arbitration is more suitable than ad hoc arbitration.[22]

---

[21] Rastogi, N. & Trivedi, M., 2016. PESTLE TECHNIQUE – A TOOL TO IDENTIFY EXTERNAL RISKS IN CONSTRUCTION PROJECTS. International Research Journal of Engineering and Technology, 3(1). Available at: https://www.irjet.net/archives/V3/i1/IRJET-V3I165.pdf [Accessed July 21, 2016].

[22] Donald R., Sweet & Maxwell, Index to Legal Citations and Abbreviations 3rd edition, 2008, 560 pages, £99, ISBN 9781847036049

In the year 2013 a survey conducted by PWC in India, showed that parties are increasingly choosing to resolve disputes away from the courts through arbitration. The survey as per PWC is a pioneering effort at exploring the level of knowledge, current practices and perceptions regarding arbitration among companies in India. The growth in domestic and international trade and commerce has spurred competition, provided new opportunities and imputed risks. Commercial arbitration in India is witnessing a steady transition and resolution of domestic and cross-border disputes is becoming more sophisticated. In-house counsels are leveraging the advantages offered by this mechanism including speed of resolution, flexible processes and confidentiality of proceedings while overcoming the hurdles of undue delay in proceedings and lack of institutional arbitration infrastructure. The survey about the future of arbitration appears guardedly positive due to numerous advantages and disadvantages that arbitration makes available in India.[23]

8.2.1. Qualifications of Arbitrators

Among the challenges faced in Arbitration, is the challenge that the arbitrator is not properly qualified to take on the task and the challenges concerning the performance of the arbitrator while conducting the arbitration. The arbitrator finds these issues sensitive. To Arbitral Institutions like International Centre for Dispute Resolution (ICDR), Stockholm Chamber of Commerce (SCC), Singapore International Arbitration Centre (SIAC), or Hong Kong International Arbitration Centre (HKIAC), challenges can be made arbitrations on grounds that an arbitrator lacks relevant professional experience, knowledge of relevant law, linguistic skills or other necessary qualifications.[24]At RICS (Royal Institute of Chartered Surveyors) the training for dispute resolution professionals is focused specifically on property, the built environment and related sectors. [25]

---

[23] National Legal Mission to Reduce Average Pendency Time from 15 Years to 3 Years (2010). Available at:
http://pib.nic.in/newsite/erelcontent.aspx?relid=62745 (Accessed: 25 July 2016

[24] Vidya R, Darshan P., 2013. Corporate Attitudes & Practices towards Arbitration in India. Price Watherhouse Coopers. Available at:
https://www.pwc.in/assets/pdfs/publications/2013/corporate-attributes-and-practices-towards-arbitration-in-india.pdf [Accessed July 28, 2016]

[25] Anon, Royal Institution of Chartered Surveyors. Available at:
http://www.rics.org/in/join/member-accreditations-list/dispute-resolution-service/diploma-qualifications-in-dispute-resolution/, [Accessed July 30, 2016]

8.2.2. Construction activity through construction contracts

The nature of contracts done for the construction projects are quite complex and distinguished from other types of contracts. There are a number of different specific aspects of a construction project such as size and length of the project, a high degree of complexities, a huge amount of investment made in the project, and the fluctuations in the price agreed and amount of work done in the project with the progress of the project. These differentiated aspects of construction projects signify that the nature of conduction projects can be different from that of other types of contracts.

Institutional arbitration for construction with the custom-made administration of the proceedings, set rules and procedures of the institute, no interference from the country's legal system and arbitration friendly infrastructure in the developed countries, is a preferred type of arbitration owing to the presence of a variety of institutions. Need is felt for a strong institutional arbitration infrastructure to overcome challenges concerning selection and availability of arbitrators to save consequent time and cost of the proceedings to come to an informed decision and receive benefits from the seat of arbitration.[26]In the United States where Alternative Dispute Resolution is frequently used to ensure effective arbitration and to increase the general credibility of the arbitral process, arbitrators sit as a panel of three consisting of an expert in the legal area within which the dispute falls (such as contract law in the case of a dispute over the terms and conditions of a contract), an expert in the industry within which the dispute falls (such as the construction industry, in the case of a dispute between a homeowner and his general contractor), and an experienced arbitrator.[27]

Contracts for the construction of roads, buildings and other works present certain special features from the legal perspective. Having regard to the importance of these contracts in the economic life of the country, it is proper that their legal significance is examined in some detail.[28]

---

[26] Kanchi, 2015. Institutional Arbitration – The Dawn of Expeditious Justice System. Akademike, 12 January, Issue January 12, 2015.

[27] Global Arbitration Review -GAR. Available at: http://www.globalarbitrationreview.com/ (Accessed: 30 July 2016).

[28] Mason, J. (2017) Intelligent contracts and the construction industry. Journal of Legal Affairs and Dispute Resolution in Engineering and Construction, 9 (3). ISSN 1943-4162 Available from: http://eprints.uwe.ac.uk/30522

A good deal of construction activity has been going on in the country, for the last four decades. Both the public sector and the private sector have been engaged in projects of varying magnitude. One feature common to most construction activities is that they involve a good deal of "contracting." There may be only one contract if the work is small in magnitude. Or, there may be a number of contracts, where the project is a large one - a case of "horizontal multiplicity." If the contract is a complex one, then there may be a hierarchy of contractors, involving several "sub-contractors." That can be called an instance of "vertical multiplicity." But, whatever the nature and magnitude of the contract involved, it is obvious that the transaction is a consensual one, intended to have "defined legal consequences." In terms of the Arbitration and Conciliation Act, 1996, it is a "defined legal relationship," which is contractual in nature. It is in this respect that the law of contracts becomes very relevant.[29]

8.2.3. Nature of construction projects and problems involved

The special features of the construction industry can be thus enumerated:

(a) The industry itself is a specialized one, with its own patterns and practices.

(b) Planning and execution of a construction project involves several parties and organizations, who must work in harmony. A small deviation (real or alleged) affects the various parties.

(c) A construction project is a continuous one, usually spread over a number of years. A dispute that operates as an impediment at any single stage may upset the entire timetable unless the dispute is speedily resolved.

(d) Some of the problems that arise in the working of the project are not predictable or, even if they are predictable, their magnitude may not be imaginable. The tension created by the development of various problems may increase than resolve if litigation is resorted to.

In a construction contract, there are several diverse parties involved having their stakes in the contracts. They have different interests, roles and responsibilities in the construction contracts. Some of the main parties in the construction contract are:

---

[29] (Anon, 2016). A Guide to Construction Contracts, Bowmans, Available at: http://www.bowmanslaw.com/wp-content/uploads/2016/12/Guide-Construction-Contracts.pdf

Employer or owner of a project: An employer is a juristic person owning all rights and the ownership of a construction site and project. Contractor: Contractor is the person under the contract with the employer to perform different activities linked with the construction project to build the project. Subcontractor: subcontractors are the party who contracts with main contractor or employer to perform different supportive construction related activities. Subcontracts apart from helping the contractor also help in providing different supplies, services, or engineering and specified construction works.

Tenderer: Tenderer is a person who submits a tender offer for the purpose of completing different the project and the construction associated activities. Agent: Agent is the party who is not the employer or employee but acts on behalf of the employer of the project.[30] These are some of the prominent parties involved in a construction contract who are responsible for the different activities and practices included within a construction project. In the risk allocation process, these parties mitigate different types of risks involved in the construction project. Types of risks in a construction contract; risk is one of the most essential and integral aspects of practices undertaken within construction projects. In this aspect, Abrahamson Principles of risk allocation in different construction projects can be considered quite effective. As per the principle, different parties involved in the construction contract face different types of risks in large or small sized construction project. Some of the risks are common for all the parties involved within the contract, while some risks are specifically born by a specific party. Risks for the owner of the project according to Abrahamson Principles, the owner of the project is known as the principal party.[31]In this context, the principal party of the construction contract bears some critical risks which can be elaborated as below:

1. Resources: among the resources to be made available: Land Acquisition risk: This is the prime risk for the principal of the project. It is required that the owner of the project has proper and legal acquisition of the land for his construction project. In the absence of proper acquisition of land, due to different legal obligations the entire project can be stalled. Deficiency in critical

---

[30] Allison, J. R., 1990. Five Ways to Keep Disputes Out of Court. Harvard Business Review, Jan-Feb.Issue Jan-Feb.

[31] Mead, P., 2007. Current Trends in Risk Allocation in Construction Projects and Their implications for Industry Participants. (2007) 23 Const. L.J. No. 1 • Sweet & Maxwell Ltd and Contributors, Volume 1, p. 23.

resources like land, finance, human power can prove to be a critical risk for a construction project. Construction projects have a longer period of time, adequate resources for a contingent situation is fairly essential for the owner.

2. Delay in the project completion: The completion of the project on time can be considered as one of the main factors for the successful completion of a construction project. Delay in the completion of the project due to natural or manmade reasons, can cost significantly for the owner of the project as he invests a substantial amount of money and time in such types of projects.
3. Increased cost of the project: Generally, construction projects are carried out over a long period of time, variations in the cost and prices of raw material and labor over a long period of time are natural occurrences.[32]These fluctuations may lead to the increase in the projected cost of the entire project. Although, principals generally undertake contingency reserves for such type of fluctuations, yet still these increments in the cost of the project can be quite a critical risk for the project owner.
4. Deficiencies in infrastructure or services can lead to making the project unsuccessful.
5. Design and construction defects: Defects in the design and construction of the project can affect efficiency of the internal operations and quality of the output of the project. The project owner should have proper monitoring and effective evaluation of the outcome of the project.
6. Political risk
7. Market risks: In addition to other risks, risk related to market physiognomies as well as movements can also be considered some of the critical risks. In order to mitigate risks involved in a construction project, there is a need for some crucial and effective contractual agreements and norms which can govern different construction related practices and norms. The legal agreement among different parties involved in a construction project is known as a construction contract. The primary reason

[32] Hendrickson, C., 2000. Project Management for Construction. First Edition originally printed by Prentice Hall, ISBN 0-13-731266-0, 1989 with co-author Tung Au. ed. s.l.: Department of Civil and Environmental Engineering, Carnegie Mellon University, Pittsburgh, PA 15213 Copyright C. Hendrickson 1998.

purpose of such contracts is to regulate the entire construction project and mitigate different types of risks.[33]

Any legal issue which can arise under any contract, in general, is likely to arise in a construction contract too. These include problems relating to the formation, legal validity and performance of the contract. Effect of force majeure, assignment of the contract, damages and other issues are also included. Nevertheless, in the case of construction contracts, some of these issues, arising as in a contract of some a higher value or complication, need special attention as there arise a few odd features. These legal issues are related to the risks in the construction projects.[34]

Litigation: the psychological aspect of litigation– it is based on the essence of contest which highlights the dissimilarities and keeps the parties insulated from each other. There is a "forced" decision, which the losing party may not find emotionally acceptable. At the cost of goodwill of the losing party, the winning party succeeds.

As goodwill is essential in a construction contract during its duration, this facet assumes considerable importance.

As per a World Bank Report in Alternative Dispute Resolution, the proof for parties in a dispute is growing on the cost and time savings. Methods such as binding arbitration offer final solutions, whereas, there is a risk with the others that cases can go back to court, mounting up the total cost and time. Thus, for policy makers seeking to improve the efficiency of court systems should be a priority, maximizing success resolution of Alternative Dispute Resolution cases.[35] It could be deliberated that cost and time savings could be just the tip of the iceberg. Potentially even more significant and vital to the complete contribution of Alternative Dispute Resolution to the economic development will depend on the secondary and indirect impacts with respect to improvements in court effectiveness, the business environment, and faith in the legal system. The result would be an increase in the overall economy and development of the country. Due to the slow court systems, Alternative Dispute Resolution programs appear to be an

---

[33] Global Arbitration Review -GAR. Available at: http://www.globalarbitrationreview.com/ (Accessed: 30 July 2016).

[34] (Ellis B, Luke, R, 2). Allocation of Risk in Construction Contracts, The Guide to Construction Arbitration, Available at: https://globalarbitrationreview.com/chapter/1145082/allocation-of-risk-in-construction-contracts

[35] Anon, Supreme Court of India. Available at: http://www.sci.nic.in/ncmspap.pdf [Accessed July 21, 2016].

attractive option in many developing countries. Easing out the courts' case backlogs and improve their effectiveness could be the result of Alternative Dispute Resolution.[36]Improving the quality of the legal system and increasing trust in the just and impartial resolution of conflicts is another unnoticeable advantage of Alternative Dispute Resolution. Another connection between improvements in court speed in India and Alternative Dispute Resolution is outcomes for firms in terms of augmented investment and improved access to finance.[37] According to the International Financial Corporation, World Bank Group study of Balkan countries (2006) reports among clients who used mediation; the survey shows evidence of greater trust in the legal system.[38] Alternative Dispute Resolution may also affect investors' perceptions of investment in a country. Weaknesses in the judicial system are regularly referred to as a restriction on foreign investment in emerging markets.[39] Alternative Dispute Resolution can improve foreign investors' perceptions of the business environment in a country, which may result in the growth of foreign investment.[40]Foreign investors in India prefer Alternative Dispute Resolution mechanisms to transnational litigation.[41]156 parties have ratified the Convention on the Recognition and Enforcement of Foreign Arbitral Awards (also known as the New York Convention) United Nations Convention on International Trade Law (UNCITRAL), Status: 1958 Convention on the Recognition and Enforcement of Foreign Arbitral Awards.[42]

---

[36] Ibid 11

[37] Chemin (2010) 'Does Court Speed Shape Economic Activity? Evidence from a Court Reform in India', Journal of Law, Economics, and Organization Advance, (), pp. [Online]. Available at: (Accessed: 11th November 2010).

[38] Anon, 2010. Alternative Dispute Resolution Program (ADR) in THE Western Balkans: Giving Mediation a Chance. Available at:

https://www.ifc.org/wps/wcm/connect/991f510047e98d59a52ebd6f97fe9d91/PublicationBalkansGivingMediationaChanceADRStory.pdf?MOD=AJPERES [Accessed July 27, 2016].

[39] Anon., 2007. WORLD BANK. [Online], Available at:

http://siteresources.worldbank.org/FINANCIALSECTOR/Resources/2820441307652042357/VP329-Setting-out-court.pdf, [Accessed 21 6 2016].

[40] POUGET, S., 2013. Arbitrating and Mediating Disputes, s.l.: World Bank Group.

[41] Anon., 2013. CHALLENGES OF ARBITRATION IN INDIA. Corporate Disputes, Oct-Dec.

[42] Convention on the Recognition and Enforcement of Foreign Arbitral Awards (1958). Available at: http://www.uncitral.org/uncitral/en/uncitral_texts/arbitration/NYConvention_status.html (Accessed: 30 July 2016).

8.3. Research methods

The research design was crafted for this study to achieve the objectives below. It is a working paper of academic research for a Doctor of philosophy. The researcher collected Data both primary and secondary sources. An exploratory survey was carried out to identify factors that are mainly responsible for disputes in the field of construction of Civil engineering/construction projects and the methods of dispute resolution. The study emphasizes identifying the most important factors of those causing disputes leading to claims along with the most appropriate method to resolve the disputes. The different causes of disputes and subsequent claims, resolution of the disputes and the best method for dispute resolution were gathered through a comprehensive literature review. The exploratory survey has consolidated all the factors in a construction project, and thus some factors are grouped into:

1) Delay with respect to dispute resolution method/process (Delay): The time factor taken to resolve a dispute: Since disputes are the major reasons of delay, and since delay due to a dispute resolution causes considerable loss to the owner of the project, the reasons for the delays in dispute resolution has been considered a major factor for research.
2) Method/Procedure of the dispute resolution (Method): Factors like roles and responsibilities of different personnel, appropriate form/method like litigation or Alternative Dispute Resolution process affect the timely and successful completion of the project.
3) Skillsets of the Alternative Dispute Resolution Professionals (Skillset): The study aims to identify the most appropriate method for Alternative Dispute Resolution process. Therefore, the skillset of the professionals conducting the process is studied and therefore this factor is considered.

A Primary survey was conducted using different approaches for primary data collection namely questionnaire, and few expert opinions of civil engineers working in the relevant field, focus group to the respondents who were lawyers, engineers, and arbitrators. The area of study considered is India. Population size considering India for the study is 2500 and the required sample size of 153 respondents was determined by using statistical methods. The sampling techniques used to collect the primary data are Purposive Sampling, Quota sampling and Snowball Sampling. The study emphasis is construction, so nearly 75% of the respondents were divided into civil engineers, and the remaining 25% are lawyers who acted as arbitrators. The Likert five-point scale (Strongly Agree to Strongly Disagree) was used for measuring the data. Also, a brainstorming session was conducted including various experts in the field of construction to get the most important factors among 14 factors related to Institutional arbitration. The pilot survey was conducted using scheduled interviews. The questions of the questionnaire were drafted to conduct the structured online survey. Research scholar being a lawyer could collect the primary data from lawyers.

Analysis of Data was carried out using Statistical Software namely IBM SPSS and Microsoft Excel. Reliability of data was tested using Cronbach alpha and was turned out to be more than 0.7 Validity of the data was ensured asking and correcting the questions during the pilot survey. Advanced Multivariate Statistical technique viz., factor Analysis was used to extract the prominent factors and the ranks due to which the disputes arise majorly.

Researchers collected the necessary primary data and later coded the data using Microsoft Excel and IBM SPSS Version 20. The following analysis was carried out to satisfy the study objectives.

Table 8.1 represents the satisfaction level of the respondents towards the facilitation of the adoption of the Institutional Arbitration mode

The 1996 Arbitration and Conciliation Act has facilitated the adoption of the Institutional Arbitration mode and has taken some bold initiatives in attempting to provide an effective framework for the resolution of disputes without depending on the overburdened judicial system of the country.							
Answer Options	Totally disagree	Disagree	Neutral-Neither agree or Disagree	Agree	Strongly Agree	Rating Average	Response Count
	2	9	39	83	20	3.72	153

67% of the respondents agree that the 1996 Arbitration and Conciliation Act has facilitated the adoption of the Institutional Arbitration mode and has taken some bold initiatives in attempting to provide an effective framework for the resolution of disputes without depending on the overburdened judicial system of the country.

8. 4. Results and Discussion

Figure 8.1 depicts the level of effectiveness of the Arbitration process

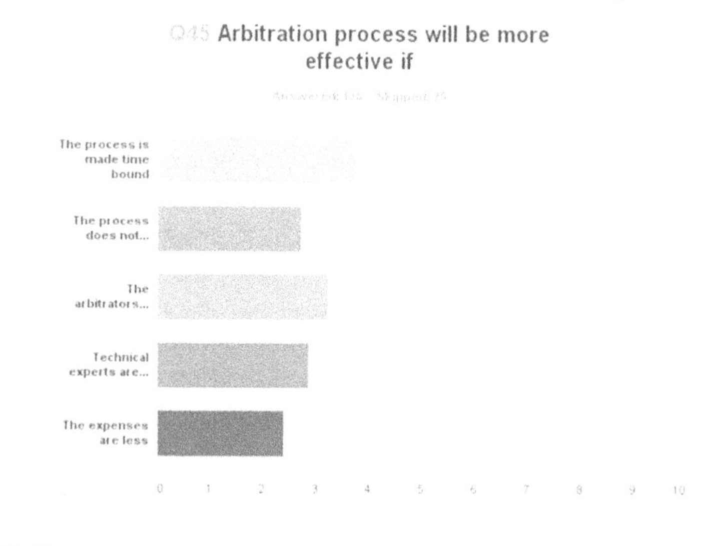

Figure 8.2 depicts the respondents 100% satisfaction for adopting Institutional Arbitration framework

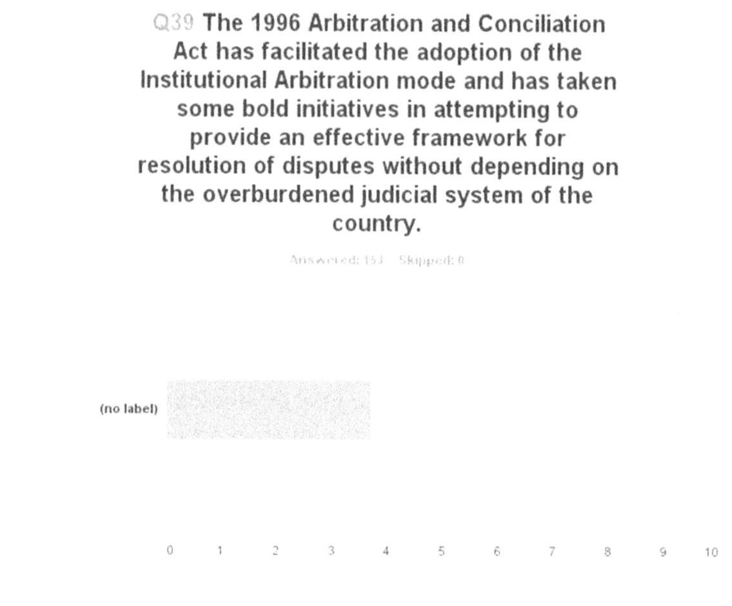

The figures show that respondents were asked to rate the following parameters. The respondents strongly agreed to:

1. The process for Arbitration is long and tedious and should be made time bound.
2. Since the Arbitration process does not follow court procedures it is more effective
3. The respondents expect that the arbitrators have experience in projects of a similar nature. However, the assumption made here is the arbitrators are exclusively working on construction projects, unlike litigation judges who follow the court procedures like affidavits etc.
4. Conduction of the Arbitration by technical experts who define the arbitration process will result in an effective arbitration.
5. Arbitration expenses are less in comparison to court expenses.

The researcher carried out advanced Statistical Multivariate Analysis using Factor Analysis, and the following 22 factors out of 49 factors are found to be prominent in the order level mentioned below:

1. The 1996 Arbitration and Conciliation Act has facilitated the adoption of the Institutional Arbitration mode and has taken some bold initiatives in attempting to provide an effective framework for the resolution of disputes without depending on the overburdened judicial system of the country.
2. Specialized firms or organizations are more promising and reliable in this sphere and people choose to consult them and engage their services for dispute resolution.
3. If the adversarial relationship between the client and the contractor changes then the number of disputes will be reduced.
4. The third party mediator should be a civil engineer.
5. A standard form of contract fixing duties, responsibilities, and remedies will reduce the number of disputes.
6. Parties do not transparently share difficulties which lead to disputes.
7. To make mediation work the site teams of both the client and the contractor should be made to discuss the issues in the presence of their respective top managements and then

the top managements shall take balanced decisions with the help of a third party mediator.
8. Institutional arbitration should be made compulsory.
9. The mediator should be trained in mediation.
10. An arbitrator must be a civil engineer with sufficient experience in the handling dispute resolution.
11. The best way to resolve a dispute is to through mediation.
12. Site Management does not have authority in the contract to help the contractor if he apprises them of his difficulties.
13. Though the arbitration act does not require following the civil procedure code, in practice it is followed.
14. Awards made by the arbitrators are generally biased towards the contractor.
15. Risk allocation and identification is as important as project management
16. Civil engineering issues are too complicated to be understood by an arbitrator without any technical background.
17. Arbitrators should be selected randomly from a panel by a lucky draw system
18. Risk allocation in the contract is very important
19. Identification of risks is important for all contracts
20. A major reason of disputes is incompatible personalities of the personnel of the Client and Contractor.
21. Arbitration takes nearly as long as a civil suit in the courts of law.
22. Considering the effort required and benefits achieved, filing a civil suit is better than going into arbitration.

The above 22 prominent factors can be categorized mainly as per the research objectives broadly into:

1. Delay
2. Method
3. Skillsets

Among the above Factors 1, 7, 15, 21and 22 are classified under Delay Factor.

Factors 1, 2, 3, 4, 5,6,7,8,13,14,17,18,19,22 are classified as Method related Factor.

And Factors 2, 3,9,10,11,16,20 are related to the Skill set Factor.

8.5. Conclusion

After analysing the above data, the following conclusions are made:

Institutional Arbitration with its rules and procedures and time taken to resolve the disputes in the field of construction is considered the best among all forms of alternative dispute resolution.

A civil engineer holding a specified technical skillset is better qualified as a mediator in order to solve the disputes in the field of construction.

The mediation has emerged as one of the best practices for dispute resolution.

The results also highlighted that the relationship between the client and the contractor should be strongly positive in order to resolve the possible conflicts that would arise between different incompatible personnel in the field of construction.

Authorship contributions:

Conception and design of study: Jagdish Raje, Consulting Engineer, Mohana Raje, PhD

Acquisition of data: Mohana Raje, PhD, Jagdish Raje, Consulting Engineer

Analysis and interpretation of data: Kavita Kalyandurgmath, PhD, Mohana Raje, PhD

Category 2

Drafting the manuscript: Mohana Raje, PhD, Kavita Kalyandurgmath, PhD

Revising the manuscript critically for important intellectual content:

Category 3

Approval of the version of the manuscript to be published: Mohana Raje, PhD, Kavita Kalyandurgmath, PhD, Jagdish Raje, Consulting Engineer

Acknowledgements: Special thanks to Prof. Chitralekha Kumar for encouraging to participate in this Unique conference on Law, Technology and Management, and Dr. Sandeep Bhavsar for helping in referencing the chapter.

Bibliography

Allison, J. R., (1990) Five Ways to Keep Disputes Out of Court. Harvard Business Review, 66 (1), 166-8,172-4, 176-7. Online. Available at https://www.ncbi.nlm.nih.gov/pubmed/10106402 (Accessed October 16, 2018)

Anon., (2007) WORLD BANK. Online. Available at: http://siteresources.worldbank.org/FINANCIALSECTOR/Resources/282

0441307652042357/VP329-Setting-out-court.pdf, [Accessed June 21, 2016].

Anon, (2010) Alternative Dispute Resolution Program (ADR) in The Western Balkans: Giving Mediation a Chance. Online. Available at: https://www.ifc.org/wps/wcm/connect/991f510047e98d59a52ebd6f97fe9d91/PublicationBalkansGivingMediationaChanceADRStory.pdf?MOD=AJPERES [Accessed July 27, 2016].

Anon, (2013) *Corporate Attitudes & Practices towards Arbitration in India.* Price Watherhouse Coopers. Online. Available at: https://www.pwc.in/assets/pdfs/publications/2013/corporate-attributes-and-practices-towards-arbitration-in-india.pdf [Accessed July 28, 2016].

Anon, (2013) *Corporate Attitudes & Practices towards Arbitration in India. Price Watherhouse Coopers. Oct-Dec 2013,* Available at: https://www.pwc.in/assets/pdfs/publications/2013/corporate-attributes-and-practices-towards-arbitration-in-india.pdf [Accessed July 28, 2016].

Anon, (2016) *A Guide to Construction Contracts,* Bowmans, Online. Available at: http://www.bowmanslaw.com/wp-content/uploads/2016/12/Guide-Construction-Contracts.pdf (Accessed November 25, 2016).

Anon, Royal Institution of Chartered Surveyors.: 2018, Online. Available at: http://www.rics.org/in/join/member-accreditations-list/dispute-resolution-service/diploma-qualifications-in-dispute-resolution/, [Accessed July 30, 2016]

UNCITRAL Secretaria, (2016) Convention on the Recognition and Enforcement of Foreign Arbitral Awards (1958). Online. Available at: http://www.uncitral.org/uncitral/en/uncitral_texts/arbitration/NYConvention_status.html (Accessed July 30, 2016). Department of Administrative Reforms & Public Grievances. (2007) *Second Administrative Reforms Commission.* Fifth report, Online. Available at: https://www.darpg.gov.in/sites/default/files/public_order5_0.pdf. [Accessed July 26, 2016].

Donald R., (2013) Index to Legal Citations and Abbreviations, London: Sweet & Maxwell, 4th edition.

Ellis B, Luke, R,. (2017) Allocation of Risk in Construction Contracts. White & Case LLP 1996-2018, Available at: https://www.whitecase.com/sites/whitecase/files/files/download/publications/allocation-of-risk-in-construction-contracts.pdf (Accessed October 16, 2018).

Global Arbitration Review-GAR, (2016) Online. Available at: https://globalarbitrationreview.com/chapter/1145220/documents-in-construction-disputes (Accessed: 30 July 2016).

Government of India. (2009) *Law Commission of India,* Online. Available at: http://lawcommissionofindia.nic.in/reports/report222.pdf. (Accessed July 28, 2016).

Hendrickson, C., (2000). Project Management for Construction: Fundamental Concepts for Owners, Engineers, Architects and Builders, Online. World Wide Web Publication. Available at https://www.cmu.edu/cee/projects/PMbook/ (Accessed October 16, 2018)

Kanchi, (2015) *Institutional Arbitration – The Dawn of Expeditious Justice System, Akademike,* 12 January, Issue January 12th.

Law Commission of India. (2014) *Report to Revamp the Indian Arbitration Experience,* Kluwer Arbitration Blog, Online. Available at: http://arbitrationblog.kluwerarbitration.com/2014/08/23/law-commissions-report-to-revamp-the-indian-arbitration-experience/ (Accessed: July 30, 2016).

Love I., (2011) *Settling Out of Court: How effective is alternative dispute resolution?,* Online. Siteresources.worldbank.org. Available at:http://siteresources.worldbank.org/FINANCIALSECTOR/Resources/282044-1307652042357/VP329-Setting-out-of-court.pdf (Accessed July 27, 2016).

Mason J., (2017) *Intelligent contracts and the construction industry,* Journal of Legal Affairs and Dispute Resolution in Engineering and Construction, 9 (3). ISSN 1943-4162 Available from: http://eprints.uwe.ac.uk/30522. (Accessed October 16, 2018).

Mead, P., (2007). *Current Trends in Risk Allocation in Construction Projects and Their implications for Industry Participants.* 23 Const. L.J. No. 1, Sweet & Maxwell Ltd and Contributors, p. 23.

Madhava Meanon N. R., (2005) *Social Context Education for Social Justice Adjudication.* Journal of the National Judicial Academy, Vol. 1, 241. Online. Available at http://rajasthanjudicialacademy.nic.in/docs/1_s5.pdf (Accessed October 16, 2018).

Montesquieu, C. d. S. b. d., (2000) *Montesquieu's Science of Politics: Essays on the Spirit of Laws.* s.l.: Rowman & Littlefield Publishers.

Ministry of Law and Justice, (2010) National Litigation Policy, Government of India. Online. Available at: http://pib.nic.in/newsite/erelcontent.aspx?relid=62745 (Accessed July 25,2016)

Pouget, S., (2013) Arbitrating and Mediating Disputes: Benchmarking Arbitration and Mediation Regimes for Commercial Disputes Related to Foreign Direct Investment. Policy Research Working Paper; No. 6632. World Bank, Washington, DC. © World Bank. https://openknowledge.worldbank.org/handle/10986/16849 License: CC BY 3.0 IGO.

Rani B., (2015) *Justice at Cross Roads – A Critical Analysis of the Functioning of the Indian Judicial System and the Need for an Alternative,* Global Journal of Human- Social Science: A Arts & Humanities - Psychology, Online. 15(6), 1-13. Available at:https://globaljournals.org/GJHSS_Volume15/1-Justice-at-Cross-Roads-A-Critical.pdf [Accessed July 30, 2016]

Science: A Arts & Humanities - Psychology, Online. 15(6), 1-13. Available at:https://globaljournals.org/GJHSS_Volume15/1-Justice-at-Cross-Roads-A-Critical.pdf [Accessed July 30, 2016].

Rastogi N.I.T.A.N.K., and Trivedi M.K., (2016) *Pestle Technique – A Tool to Identify External Risks in Construction Projects.* International Research Journal of Engineering and Technology, 3(1). Online. Available at: https://www.irjet.net/archives/V3/i1/IRJET-V3I165.pdf (Accessed July 21, 2016).

Sharma, D. and Bhatnagar, P. (2014) Risk Allocation & Subsequent Legal Issues in Construction Contracts. Online. Available at https://papers.ssrn.com/sol3/papers.cfm?abstract_id=2403045 (Accessed October 16, 2018).

Subhan J., (2010) *Arbitration Conciliation and Mediation- Conflict between Formal and Informal Setups* (September 3). Online. Available at SSRN: https://ssrn.com/abstract=2145187 or http://dx.doi.org/10.2139/ssrn.2145187. (Accessed October 16, 2018)

Vidya R., and Darshan P., (2013) *Corporate Attitudes & Practices towards Arbitration in India,* Price Watherhouse Coopers. Online. Available at: https://www.pwc.in/assets/pdfs/publications/2013/corporate-attributes-and-practices-towards-arbitration-in-india.pdf [Accessed July 28, 2016].

Chapter 9

Economic analysis of Pharmaceutical Patent regime in India: A study in light of pre and post TRIPS regime

Dr. Hardik H. Parikh[1]

Abstract

Pharmaceutical patents are the most important aspects of the intellectual property regime driven economy. India is always recognized as a pharmaceutical industry hub in the world. However, with the implementation of TRIPS agreement in the year 2005 especially in the field of patents, the said industry faced some fear of international aspects of a strict patent regime. The fear was visible in the form of various patent infringement claims and shutdown of various generic pharmaceutical industries which were governed and progressed under the process patent regime. The adaption of international aspects is always measured through the economic aspects, and after 2005, the evaluation of pharmaceutical industries has become very crucial. The post TRIPS regime emphasized the product patent regime and due to the same, many pharmaceutical units are facing trouble in operation especially those which are included in the generic drugs industries. Also, the price increasing aspects are not apart. This research paper will focus on various economic aspects of pre and post TRIPS pharmaceutical patent regime. The basic economic concept cannot be discussed in the absence of constitutional mandates and judicial decisions. Thus, the researchers want to justify the concept of economic analysis of pharmaceutical patent regime in view of international aspects as well as the interest of people and genuine requirement of medicines. Finally, this research will also consider the new

[1] Assistant Professor of Law, Gujarat National Law University, Gandhinagar, Gujarat. E – Mail hparikh@gnlu.ac.in

IPR policy introduced by the government recently, and it will also justify the futuristic aspects of the implementation of the policy by virtue of suitable amendments.

Keywords: Pharmaceutical, Patents, TRIPS

9.1 Introduction

The legal protection and identification to intellectual property has been available in India since British rule. The British law regarding protection of intellectual property was enacted while considering the legal requirement of British Rule in India and it provided the highest degree of protection to the pharmaceutical industry. On the other side, it also led to very high prices of medicines in India. To provide cheap medicine and to promote the Indian pharmaceutical industry, the Indian Patent Act 1970 was implemented which allowed the process of patent changes in law to cause a paradigm shift in the business of Indian pharmaceutical industry. The Patent Act of 1970 had not only brought about the development of the Indian pharmaceutical industry but also has contributed to the improvement of health and welfare in India. However, after 1994 the Indian pharmaceutical industry faced new challenges due to the existence of the WTO-TRIPS Agreement. It was presumed that the initiation of the system to grant product patent to the pharmaceuticals would have a negative impact on the Indian pharmaceutical industry and its growth would be hampered. It is quite evident that due to the new system, the industry shall not be able to manufacture various pharmaceutical products by reverse engineering or export drugs whose product patents are in effect. However, contrary to such presumptions or speculations, the Indian pharmaceutical industry has been growing in the post-TRIPS period which is visible in various studies. On the other hand, there are still concerns that the new patent act might reduce generic drug supplies and lower access to medicines in India. Ensuring access to medicines at affordable prices is one of the most important tasks of the Indian government. Taking into consideration that India is the major supplier of affordable generic drugs, the issue of access to medicines is crucial not only for India but also for other poor developing countries. Thus, the Indian government should seek an appropriate balance between the development of the Indian pharmaceutical industry and the improvement of public health. In other words, the government should balance intellectual property protection with the right to health aspects and economic development of the country, in particular, in pharmaceuticals.

9.2 Patent system in India

The patent system is not new in India. The first patent law was enacted in the year 1858. A comprehensive law was enacted by the British rulers in the year 1911. This act was designed to serve foreign interests and for the control over markets for finished goods by multi-national corporations. In so far as pharmaceutical products are concerned, over a period almost 85 percent of medicines were supplied by multi-national corporations. Kefauver Committee of the USA, which deliberated extensively on the availability of medicines worldwide and the role of the multi-nationals, pointed out that the prices of antibiotics and other medicines in India were the highest in the world. The Indian people were virtually fleeced on the availability and affordability of medicines.

Immediately after the independence in the year 1947, our leaders were concerned about the enactment of a national patent system which may or may not be suitable to the system and our stage of development. The basic objectives for the system were that there should be faster industrialization of the country and law should be designed to serve the public interest in a balanced manner. Therefore, two important committees headed by Justice Bakshi Tek Chand and Justice Rajgopal Iyenger carried out a study with regard to the patent law issues relevant to our country which got reflected in their reports. Based on the recommendations in these reports, a comprehensive Patents Bill was framed and placed for the debate extensively in parliamentary committees and both the Houses of Parliament. Finally, the Indian Patent Act was enacted in the year 1970. This law served the objectives which were required at the development phase of our country and our leaders had visualized. With the passage of time, the Indian pharmaceutical companies grew at a fast speed and their share of the market in the availability of medicines went up to about 85 percent. Moreover, due to quite a competitive market environment in India as a result of the new patent system, the prices of medicines became the lowest in the world. Apart from that, the Indian industry also developed enough surplus capacity to meet export demands from the developed and developing countries.[2] The main features of the Patents Act 1970 were (1) Absence of product patent for pharmaceuticals, food and chemical based products. These industrial sectors were covered by process patent only (2) The term of the patent was 7 years from the date of application or 5 years from the date of sealing of patent whichever period was lower (3) In order to ensure pronounced role of the domestic

---

[2] Keayla B. K. 'India and The Patent Regime Amended Patents Act 1970: A Critique', Combat Law Vol. 4 Issue 4 June-July 2005

enterprises in the patented product, a system of licensing of right was also provided for the sectors covered by the process patents (4) No constrained on exports (5) The patent holder was under the obligation of working of the patent (6) There was also provision for revocation of patent for non-working (7) For licenses of right, the royalty ceiling was stipulated at 4 percent.[3]

The patent system in India is governed by the Patents Act 1970 as amended by the Patents (Amendment) Act 2005 along with the Patent Rules 2003 as amended by the Patents (Amendment) Rules 2006. The patent is a statutory right granted for an invention for a limited period of time to the patentee by the government in exchange of full disclosure of his invention for excluding others, from making, selling, importing the patented product or process for producing that product for those purposes without his consent. Patent protection is territorial right and therefore, it is effective only within the territory of India. However, filing an application in India enables the applicant to file a corresponding application for the same invention in convention countries, no later than twelve months from the filing date in India. Therefore, separate patents should be obtained in each country where the applicant requires the protection of his invention in those countries. There is no worldwide patent system available.

After enactment of the Patents Act 1970 but before TRIPs, when Indian Government was granting Process Patents only but not the product patents, this policy made new drugs cheaply available and promoted import substitution by encouraging the local firms to make copies of the drugs by developing their own processes. This resulted in bulk drug production and the large development of pharmaceutical industries in India. But after TRIPS in 1994, it became mandatory for every country to comply with it. India also amended their Patents Act so that TRIPS provisions could be satisfied and from 2005, India enforced TRIPS provisions by granting product patent for pharmaceutical products. Thus, after granting the product patent, the drug cannot be copied by using another process. Therefore, product patent is a much more stringent restriction than process patent.

Thus, it is apprehended that the implementation of the TRIPS Agreements will give rise to the factors that can put access to medicines out of reach for millions of people in the developing countries. At present, Indian Patent Law is in full compliance of TRIPS agreement, and because

---

[3] ibid

of that the pharmaceutical companies have to struggle more in developing new pharmaceutical inventions which can be patented rather than simply copying the drug by the usage of a different product.

9.3 Significance of Patents

Patents have the primary function of serving as devices for society to measure an invention's value, thus allowing the patentee to stipulate competitive prices for inventions and, consequently, on the products and services that embody them. Patents are, therefore, primarily neutral social mechanisms that contribute to an adequate allocation of private resources to the creation of technology. Promotion of the invention and innovation is accomplished by allowing inventors to obtain rents from the results of their activities. That can be done in two different ways. The first is, to require users of the inventions to pay for them directly. For this, it is essential to establish a proper legal mechanism that allows inventors to decide the price of their inventions. That is exactly the role that patents and trade secrets perform. The second way to obtain rents is to provide inventors with public funds or other privileges. In this case, the government allocates rents to the inventor. Users of the inventions will still pay for them, but in an indirect manner, through taxes. For that matter, so will tax-paying non-users.[4]

Social welfare and economic growth depend on technological innovations which not only facilitate a more efficient utilization of available scarce resources, but also provide access to new resources. Therefore, society needs a continued flow of inventions should be developed and made generally available. However, that is not true. Patents are not strictly necessary to promote inventive activities. History shows that societies around the world have lived and evolved technologically without a patent system, i.e. without a system of private property rights whereby owners have the right to exclude others from using their technical creations. For thousands of years, governments have relied on public awards to promote and encourage invention and in technological fields where the awards did not reach or were not granted, economic interests in inventions have been protected through trade secrets. The function of the patent system has thus far been explained in two different ways. The most common and accepted view is that patents are rewards granted to individuals who contribute to economic and technological progress by inventing and disclosing the inventions. This is the reward

---

4 Nuno Pires de Carvalho, 'The TRIPS Regime of Patent Rights', Kluwer Law International (2002) p. 1

doctrine in a nutshell. A second theory challenges the reward doctrine on the ground that when patents are granted, the inventors may not yet be aware of the usefulness of their inventions. Patents, therefore, operate as titles of legal security that permit the inventors to prospect the market for commercial opportunities, very much like concessions granted to gold prospectors. This is the prospect theory by Edmund Kitch.[5]

The next paragraphs show that both theories fail to give a complete any systematic explanation for the patent system as a whole. Some patents can indeed be viewed by inventors as awards. Other patents can actually permit some inventors to seek practical applications for their inventions, applications that might not have been obvious while they were developing them. These theories rely on the secondary effects of the patent system and therefore, they do not have a general validity and cannot provide an overall explanation of the system.[6]

It has been suggested that there must be a balance between the patentee's capacity to extract monopoly income from the invention and the invention's intrinsic value. Ultimately, the reward should be tantamount to the inventions' worth. But it is precisely this kind of comparison that the U.S. Supreme Court deemed unacceptable when it stated that patents are not certificates of merit. What the Court intended to emphasize is that the legal value of a patent does not maintain any equivalence with the inventions' technical or economic value. With regard to the legal dimension of patentees' rights, the owner of a patent for a toy has precisely the same rights as the owner of a patent for a drug that cures cancer. Actually, if the merit if the invention were to be taken into account for purposes of rights enforcement, courts might take two different and opposite approaches. On the one hand, an important invention might induce courts to yield a benevolent treatment to the patentee such as in cases involving misuse, on the other hand, if courts leaned towards the public interest, they might feel compelled to impose a sticker standard of behavior upon the patentee. It is not practical to try to detect whether the externalities arising from the patentee's conduct are equivalent to or exceed the value of the patentee's contribution to knowledge. An objective comparison between such factors is just not feasible for lack of reliable figures.

---

[5] Kitch Edmund W., (1977) '*The Nature and Functions of the Patent system*', Journal of Law and Economics, University of Chicago Press, Vol. 20, No. 2 (Oct., 1977) pp. 265-290 [online] Available at http://www.law.nyu.edu/sites/default/files/upload_documents/Kitch.pdf [Accessed 20 August 2016]

[6] Supra Note 4

At the beginning of this century, in particular after 2000, developing countries have realized that social and economic development requires policies which are consistent with integration into the global economy. The question of intellectual property rights protection has attracted much attention in recent years. The World Bank Report has also highlighted the role of knowledge and the contributions of intellectual property rights in the social and economic progress.[7] Even among the developing countries, greater attention is clearly paid to the protection and enforcement of intellectual property rights. There is an enhanced and more widespread awareness of the importance of intellectual property in general. Nevertheless, intellectual property policies have been a source of dissension between developed and developing countries, as well as within the developed countries themselves.[8]

9.4. Patents and the Pharmaceutical industry

Many countries are quite receptive to the introduction of multinational pharmaceutical firms as a method of increasing the flow of foreign capital and foreign direct investment into their domestic markets.[9] FDI has helped in seeking benefits such as increased efficiency in resource allocation, transfers of technology and knowledge, infrastructural improvements and the countries having a developing economy have a strong desire of this in order to increase capital inflows in the country that would cultivate domestic industries of the country. On the other hand, motivated efforts to draw in FDI are often found to be linked with high prices of drugs in relative markets and result in an inadequate provision of medicine to poorer demographics which means that there is often a trade-off between the ability of a country to attract FDI and the price of drugs to levels conducive for widespread distribution. Furthermore, there are additional concerns about the impact of FDI on indigenous industries relative to the displacement of domestically held enquiry as foreign firms enter the marketplace.

---

[7] World Bank, World Bank Development Report – Knowledge for Development, New York, Oxford University Press 1999

[8] World Intellectual Property Organization (WIPO) Annual Report 2000, p.23, www.wipo.org

[9] Feinberg Susan E and Majumdar Sumit K.,, 'Technology Spillovers from Foreign Direct Investment in the Indian Pharmaceutical Industry', Journal of International Business Studies (Palgrave Macmillan Journals) 32 No. 3, Quarter 3, 2001, p. 421-437

With regard to the industrial firms, the policies accepted by a particular nation create high influence on the lucrativeness of marketing and production in the country. Moreover, due to the change of laws between various nations, dissimilar policy regimes may have effect on the trading of pharmaceuticals globally. The World Trade Organization has a high interest in the relative policy structures of member nations and focuses its efforts to support the trading of pharmaceuticals by reducing barriers in its trading and standardizing regulatory practices that may otherwise serve as hindrances.[10] For pharmaceutical companies, the treatment of intellectual property rights is one of the major concerns faced by various firms in the country. Accordingly, the TRIPS agreement shows an attempt to address those concerns by attempting to reduce the variability of intellectual property rights protection between two or more countries' policy regimes. Conceived as a part of the Uruguay round, the goal of the TRIPS Agreement is: "Reduce distortions and impediments to international trade and talking into account the necessity to promote effective and adequate protection of intellectual property rights and to ensure that measures and procedures to enforce intellectual property rights do not themselves become barriers to legitimate trade".[11]

In the same way, the safeguarding of intellectual assets is the main component in attracting foreign investment because it creates the incentive for such property to be developed in a particular country. For pharmaceuticals, such safety is often given in the form of patents whereby the patent holder retains the sole rights to produce market and thus earn profit from his invention. While on the other hand, a lack of patent protection provides a distinctive for pharmaceutical innovations and creations to be developed in a certain country due to the constant risk of that property being generically developed and marketed by other parties, thereby abducting the creator from profiting or possibly even recouping the costs of developing the product.[12] In other words, IPR is the fundamental driving forces behind the pharmaceutical industry. Apart from that, the additional implication of patent protection for the

---

[10] Lanoszka Anna, 'The Global Politics of Intellectual Property Rights and Pharmaceutical Drug Policies in Developing Countries', International Political Science Review, Sage Publications, 24 No. 2, April 2003, p. 181-197

[11] Agreement on Trade-Related Aspects of Intellectual Property rights (TRIPS) 1994, Appendix 1A

[12] Chaudhary Shubham, Pinelopi K. Godberg, and Panle J., (2006) *'Estimating the effects of Global Patent Protection in Pharmaceuticals: A Case Study of Quinolones in India'*, The American Economic Review 96, No. 5.

pharmaceutical-related patents and intellectual property is the monopoly granted to the patentee for a certain period of time in a particular market economy. Such kind of exclusive right given to the entity to develop, produce and market a particular product results in the absence of competitors which directly results in the profit of the firm.

The pharmaceutical industry is a very important industry, which is ranked as one of the top three profitable industries. In spite of various market fluctuations, it has remained continuously robust and profitable. As discussed earlier, until 1970 the major consumption of pharmaceutical products was managed by importation and production on a small scale. Due to this, such products were costly for the pockets of consumers. Therefore, the Government of India introduced a new Patents Act in the year 1970. This new act provided only the process for a patent, which was important for curbing the absolute monopoly by prohibiting similar processes. Yet, the possibility of creating similar products by using different processes remained open and available for the manufacturers. This method was adopted by many companies, and in addition to that, the term for the patents was reduced because many foreign manufacturing companies left the Indian market due to insufficient protection. This action widely benefitted various domestic pharmaceutical manufacturers, and by 1991 Indian firms accounted for 70% of the bulk drugs and 80% of formulations produced in the country.[13] However, India was subject to global pressure in regards to the product patent system and this international movement became very successful due to the establishment of the World Trade Organization and TRIPS Agreement. India was a founding member of WTO, and due to its significance for global trade, most countries became members of it. Thereafter, TRIPS was introduced which made it mandatory for all members of the WTO to introduce product patents. The clear implication for this was that the Indian drug companies could no longer produce copies of blockbuster drugs via a different process. However, being in the category of developing nations, India had a transition period of 10 years in order to implement the new system. This meant that the Indian pharma industry had about 10 years before the global pharma Companies could begin to enforce their IP rights in India. In the year 2005, the Indian Patents Act had been amended and implemented.

---

[13] Tirunagari Shreyas, 'What is the future of the Indian ph*arma industry?' Available at https://www.quora.com/What-is-future-of-the-Indian-pharma-industry accessed on 10th August 2016*

9.5. Impact of TRIPS agreement

As it is discussed above, the commitment of India to comply with the TRIPS Agreement required three sets of amendments to the country's Patents Act. Developing countries, in general, were allowed to make their patent laws TRIPS compliant through an amendment by January 1, 2000. Countries like India, which had process patent regime instead of product patent protection covering pharmaceuticals and agricultural chemicals, would enjoy a longer transition period before they were required to introduce product patents from January 1, 2005 as follows from Article 65(4) TRIPS Agreement. However, the longer transition period came with a set of conditions. In the first place, India was required by the WTO Panel in India – Patent Protection for Pharmaceutical and Agricultural Chemical Products case to provide "a means" by which product patent applications can be filed from January 1, 1995 (better known as the "mail-box" provision) following from Article 70.8(a)TRIPS Agreement. If the products figuring in these applications were granted a patent in any WTO member country and the products had obtained marketing approval in any WTO Member country, then exclusive marketing rights (EMRs) for five years had to be granted by India until the patent on the product was either granted or rejected in India. The first amendment of the Patents Act, 1970, notified in 1999, introduced these amendments. In 2002, a second amendment was introduced for bringing the Patents Act in conformity with all the substantive provisions of the TRIPS Agreement, with the exception of product patent protection for pharmaceuticals as an additional transition period of five years was applicable. The main issues included in the Second Amendment were, re-defining patentable subject matter, an extension of the term of patent protection to 20 years and amending the compulsory licensing system. A third amendment was introduced in 2005 to extend product patent protection to areas of technology not so protectable in its territory. Initially, it came into effect following the lapse of the transition period under the TRIPS Agreement.[14]

Thus, India included product patent protection for pharmaceuticals that were hitherto only covered by process patents. Although the third

---

[14] Dhar Biswajit & K. M Gopakumar., (2006) *'Post 2005 TRIPS scenario in patent protection in the pharmaceutical sector: The case of the generic pharmaceutical industry in India',* UNCTAD/ICTSD Project on Intellectual Property Rights and Sustainable Development [online] Available at https://unctad.org/en/PublicationsLibrary/ictsd-idrc2006d2_en.pdf [Accessed 16 August 2016]

amendment had a narrow remit, the Government used the opportunity to carry out the Patents Act. Among the major issues included in the third amendment were provisions relating to opposition to the grant of patents. From the perspective of the generic pharmaceutical industry in India, the TRIPS consistent patent law addresses three sets of issues that could have an immediate impact. First, the adoption of a new definition for "pharmaceutical substance", which should be a "new entity involving one or more inventive steps". The second is the exclusion of "mere discovery of a new form of a known substance" and "new use for a known substance" from the ambit of patenting, which could prevent the grant of patents on formulations. And the third, protecting the interests of producers who are already producing the products that may be granted patent protection in the new regime. The last-mentioned issue assumed importance given that India was required to accept "mail-box" applications from January 1, 1995, which were being examined after the product patent regime was introduced in 2005. Detailed provisions for the grant of compulsory licences are among the features of the Indian Patents Act, as amended. The Act provides that an application for the grant of compulsory licence can only be made after three years from the date of grant of the patent unless exceptional circumstances like a national emergency or an extreme emergency can be used to justify the grant of a licence on an earlier date. Three broad grounds for the grant of the compulsory licences have been provided. Firstly, reasonable requirements of the public with respect to the patented invention have not been satisfied, secondly, the patented invention is not available to the public at a reasonably affordable price, and thirdly, the patented invention is not worked in the territory of India. However, a compulsory licence can be granted only when the patentee is paid adequate remuneration by taking into account the economic value of the authorization. [15] Thus, the major post TRIPs changes in the Indian Patents Act 1970 are:

- Increase in Patent term i.e. the life of Patents to 20 years from the date of filing which is known as the priority date. Earlier this term was for only 7 years for pharmaceutical products, food and chemicals and for other inventions 14 years.
- Publication of all complete patent application on or after 18 months.
- Request for examination to be filed in all cases with fees. Patent gets automatically abandoned if no request is filed within 48 months of priority date.

---

[15] *Supra Note 3*

- o Provisions for filing Patent Co-Operation Treaty (PCT) applications from India.
- o Patentability for microorganisms to Budapest Treaty by which sample of the organism to be deposited in accredited Depository prior to filing the patent application.
- o License of Right provision was deleted which was equivalent to an automatic Compulsory License. However, third parties could apply for a compulsory license after 3 years of the grant of patent subject to certain conditions.
- o By virtue of this amendment, the onus or responsibility of proving infringement or non-infringement is shifted on the shoulder of Infringer – Defendant.
- o Penalties for violation of the provisions of the Act have been substantially increased.

The definition of the patentable invention is simplified. The invention is required to be Novel, Non-Obvious and Useful. The test to determine Novelty is any single prior art. For Non-Obviousness i.e. inventive step, any prior disclosure of any sort, such as patent publication, research article, prior public use or knowledge etc. is required to be tested. Industrial Applicability requires that the invention being patented must have at least one use which can be practically demonstrated. In brief, every invention which is originating from idea must be capable of reducing in practice.

9.6. Implications of the DOHA declaration

It is quite important to note that two of the three amendments of its Patents Act that India had undertaken were adopted in the backdrop of significant global developments. Growing concerns in developing countries with regard to the access to medicines at prices that their citizens could afford led to a considerable discussion amongst the WTO members. The outcome of this process of discussion was the Ministerial Declaration adopted at the conclusion of the Doha Ministerial Conference held in 2001 on TRIPS Agreement and Public Health.

Post TRIPS, a major milestone for the pharmaceutical industry is the Doha Declaration. Important paragraphs from the Doha Declaration relevant to pharmaceutical products industries are as under:

Para 1: *We recognize the gravity of the public health problems afflicting many developing and least developed countries especially those resulting from HIV / AIDS, tuberculosis, malaria and other epidemics.*

Para 3: *We recognize that intellectual property protection is important for the development of new medicines. We also recognize the concerns about its effects on prices.*
Para 4: *We agree that the TRIPS Agreement does not and should not prevent Members from taking measures to protect public health. Accordingly, while reiterating our commitment to the TRIPS Agreement, we affirm that the Agreement can and should be interpreted and implemented in a manner supportive of WTO Member's right to protect public health and in particular, to promote access to medicines for all. In this connection, we reaffirm the right of WTO Members to use, to the full, the provisions in the TRIPS Agreement, which provide flexibility for this purpose.*

In this way, Doha Declaration can be considered as one of the provisions to protect the health rights of the citizens against the product patents of pharmaceutical inventions. It has been emphasized that the WTO Members have the right to use the provisions in the TRIPS Agreement, which provide flexibility for this purpose. Two critical issues have been particularly emphasized in the Doha Declaration. The first was that the provisions of the TRIPS Agreement should be read in the light of the object and purpose of the Agreement as expressed, in particular, in its objectives and principles. The objectives of the Agreement on TRIPS provided in Article 7 states that the protection and enforcement of intellectual property rights should among other things be conducive to social and economic welfare, and to a balance of rights and obligations. Moreover, Article 8 of the Agreement directs WTO Members to adopt measures necessary to protect public health and nutrition while formulating or amending their laws and regulations relating to intellectual property. Thus, Articles 7 and 8 of the TRIPS Agreement require that WTO Members must ensure that the laws relating to all forms of intellectual property rights covered by the Agreement give due consideration to issues like protection of public health and nutrition and do not merely serve the interests of the owners of intellectual property.[16]

The second area of focus of the Doha Declaration was compulsory licences, the instrument that could have a vital role to play in determining the future prospects of the Indian pharmaceutical industry. It was mentioned in an earlier discussion that over the past few decades, India has witnessed the development of a strong pharmaceutical industry largely because of the absence of the product patent regime. However, with the product patent regime after the adoption of a TRIPS provisions by

[16] Supra Note 3, p.13

India, the future of the pharmaceutical industry in India would critically hinge on the ability of the producers to obtain licences from the owners of proprietary technologies. For obtaining the licences, these producers would have to depend on compulsory licences, an instrument that has been embedded in the patent system for preventing abuse of patent monopoly. The grounds for the grant of compulsory licences include the refusal of the patent holder to exploit the patent commercially in the country.

9.7. Landmark judicial pronouncements on Pharmaceutical Patents

In the very short span after the new TRIPS based product patent regime came into effect, there have been many landmark judgments pronounced by the Indian Judiciary which are interpreting various provisions of the Indian Patents Act along with various amendments. In spite of this, a large number of product patents are granted in India, and the infringement suits are limited to the few blockbuster molecules. Some of the landmark cases which changed the Indian scenario are discussed here.

In the case of *Novartis v. Union of India*[17] the issue was with regard to whether Novartis should be granted patent for Gleevec, an anti-leukemia drug. A patent application was filed by Novartis AG, a pharmaceutical company based in Switzerland in 1997 before the Controller of Patents, Madras for its beta crystalline form of '*Imatinib mesylate*'. The application was rejected by the Assistant Controller of Patents and Designs on the ground that it failed to satisfy the requirement of novelty and non-obviousness as per the Indian Patent Act 1970.

Thereafter, Novartis filed an appeal in the Madras High Court in 2006 and meanwhile, the Intellectual Property Appellate Board was formed and the case was transferred to it. The board held that Novartis met the requirements of novelty and non-obviousness as per the provisions of the Patents Act but rejected the appeal on the grounds that it was merely a discovery of a known substance and the component could not prove any significant efficacy of the drug as per the requirement of section 3(d) of the Act.

Aggrieved by the judgment, Novartis decided to approach Madras High Court by challenging section 3(d) of the act being it's violative of article 14 of the Indian Constitution. In 2007, the high court held that the objective of section 3 (d) was to prevent intellectual property monopoly and accordingly, the appeal was dismissed.

---

[17] (2013) 6 Supreme Court Cases 1

Finally, in the year 2009, Novartis approached the Supreme Court of India through a special leave petition under the provisions of article 136 of the Constitution of India. In the petition, the main contention made by the company was that the company had met the required criteria of novelty and inventive step. The compound in its beta crystalline form had enhanced efficacy over other variants of the same compound such as imatinib or imatinib mesylate and thereby all requirements of section 3(d) stands fulfilled. Moreover, it was also submitted that sufficient research was carried out to selectively prepare the beta crystalline form of imatinib mesylate and it was worthy of being granted patent rights.

The contention of the Additional Solicitor General of India was that the beta crystalline form of the compound is neither novel nor non-obvious owing to the publication about it in 'Cancer Research and Nature' in the year 1996 and various other disclosures in Zimmerman patents and by Food and Drug Administration, USA. Moreover, it was also contended that the requirement of efficacy as stated in section 3(d) of the act should be held to be interpreted on lines of therapeutic efficacy and not merely one of physical efficacy.

The Supreme Court held that Novartis failed to meet with the requirement of novelty thereby filing to qualify for the test of the invention as provided for under section 2(1)(j) of the Patents Act 1970. Further, the court decided to interpret efficacy as laid down in section 3(d) of the Act on lines of therapeutic efficacy and not merely physical efficacy. It was held that though the physical efficacy of imatinib mesylate in beta crystalline form is enhanced in comparison to other forms, there was no substantive and conclusive material and evidence to prove that beta crystalline form of imatinib mesylate will produce an enhanced of superior therapeutic efficacy. Thus, Novartis failed to meet with the requirement under section 3(d) of the act. In this way, the decision given by the Supreme Court upheld the rejection of the patent application filed by Novartis for Gleevec in the year 1998 before the Patent office.

This case is considered very important for India because there are a number of cases reported in India for leukaemia and Gleevec is considered to be a very important drug which costs about Rs. 1.2 lakh a month and that should be taken permanently by the patient under treatment. On the other hand, Indian companies were providing the medicine at a price of about Rs. 8000. If the patent would have been granted to Novartis, it would have prevented all other generic pharmaceutical companies who are providing cheaper drugs to patients. Because of this, a number of people could not afford the treatment.

In case of *Natco Pharma Limited v. Bayer Corporation* (2012), India allowed the first compulsory license of Bayer's anticancer drug nexavar to

Natco Pharma. In this case, the Bayer Corporation was the patent holder of an internationally renowned inventive drug called 'Sorafenib'. The drug was useful in the treatment of advanced stage liver and kidney cancer. It was patented in the USA and thereafter in India in 2008. Thereafter, a new drug was invented and launched under the trade name Nexavar and got approval also.

Natco Pharma was an Indian Generic Drug Manufacturer in India. They had developed a process to manufacture this drug. The patented drug was curing cancer and because of its dose, the life of a patient may be extended for 6 to 8 years. However, the cost of the drug was Rs. 2,80,428/- per month and it was required to be taken for the remainder of their life. In this way, per year cost of the drug was about Rs. 33,65,136/- In the year 2011, application for compulsory license filed by Natco Pharma. Earlier they applied for a voluntary license, but the deal could not materialize. The applicant proposed to sell the drug at Rs. 8800/- per month.

After hearing the case, a compulsory license was granted on 9th March 2012. The major grounds for the grant of such compulsory license were that Bayer supplied the drug to only 2% of the patient population and that the reasonable requirements of the public were not met. Bayer's pricing of the drug was excessive and did not constitute a "reasonably affordable" price. Bayer was not sufficiently "working" the patent in India. The order interpreted 'worked in the territory of India" under Section 84 of the Patents Act to mean manufactured to a reasonable extent in India.

Thus, it can be said that Indian patent litigations are very important and they are drawing global attention. Innovators and Corporations possessing patents have been successfully obtaining injunctions in the infringement suits except when the courts extended the balance of convenience to the third parties. While extensive patent litigations are in progress in India, there have been mixed reactions from various countries of the world and the Indian Patents Act and its provisions are being appreciated and adopted across the world.

9.8. Economic analysis of Pharmaceutical Patents

The offices under the administrative control of Controller General of Patent, Designs and Trademarks have witnessed an overall increase of around 4.40% in the filing of intellectual property applications during the year 2014-15 which is 262638 compared to the previous year which was 251564.

Table: 9.1: The trend of the last five years for intellectual property applications[18]

Type of Intellectual Property	2010-11	2011-12	2012-13	2013-14	2014-15
Patents	39400	43197	43674	42951	42763
Design	7589	8373	8337	8533	9327
Trade mark	179317	183588	194216	200005	210501
Geographical Indication	27	148	24	75	47
Total	226333	235306	246251	251564	262638

Table: 9.2: Recent Trend in Patent Applications[19]

Year	Application Filed	Application Examined	Application Granted
1992-1993	3467	2347	1272
1993-1994	3869	2590	1746
1994-1995	5330	2745	1759
1995-1996	7036	2862	1533
1996-1997	8562	3042	907
1997-1998	10155	2688	1844
1998-1999	8954	2931	1800
1999-2000	4824	2824	1881
2000-2001	8503	4264	1318
2001-2002	10592	5104	1591
2002-2003	11466	9538	1379
2003-2004	12613	10709	2469
2004-2005	17466	14813	1911
2005-2006	24505	11569	4320
2006-2007	28940	14119	7539
2007-2008	42951	18615	4227
2008-2009	36812	10296	16061
2009-2010	34287	6069	6168
2010-2011	39400	11208	7509
2011-2012	43197	11031	4381
2012-2013	43674	12268	4126
2013-2014	42951	18615	4227
2014-2015	42763	22631	5978

[18] Source: Annual Report 2014-15, The Office of Controller General of Patents, Trademarks, Designs and Geographical Indications, Government of India

[19] ibid

Based on the abovementioned figures, it is very clear that patent filing is quite significant in India. It is important for India to achieve a scenario that will provide for its industrial and residents to receive simultaneous benefit and it is a key to enable healthy and long term economic growth. On the other hand, India's need for foreign capital makes it necessary for the rule of law to protect intellectual property rights and more particularly pharmaceutical patents. Along with that, utilization of resources must take place afforded by increased foreign investment to ensure that people are not deprived of healthcare as a consequence to the country's economic endeavors. By maintaining such consciousness of balance, it may be feasible to reconcile India's global versus regional interests in its pharmaceutical industry. Following figures are indicators of the pharmaceutical company's economic analysis. Five major company's data is selected to show the recent trend with regard to the impact of patents.

Table: 9.3: Average Net Block (Million Rupees)[20]

Name of the Company	Pre TRIPS Position	Post TRIPS Position	Margin
Aurbindo	2755	8662	+5907
Cipla	3500	1674	-1826
Lupin	4599	93731	+89132
Ranbaxy	7115	15340	+8225
Dabur	24860	31892	+7032

Net block of all companies except Cipla has increased in the post TRIPS period. It is evident from the analysis that; net block of all companies except Cipla has increased in post TRIPS period. The increase is highest in Lupin followed by the Dabur.

[20] Teg Alam, and Rastogi Rupesh, (2016) *Pre TRIPS, Post TRIPS Patent Regime and the Indian Pharmaceutical Industry: An Empirical Study'* Indian Journal of Science and Technology, Vol. 9 (9)

Table: 9.4 Average Investment Amount (Million Rupees)[21]

Name of the Company	**Pre TRIPS Position**	**Post TRIPS Position**	**Margin**
Aurbindo	997	2785	+1788
Cipla	1684	164	-1520
Lupin	99	28769	+28670
Ranbaxy	4241	30496	+26255
Dabur	10689	32377	+21688

It is evident from the analysis that; investments of all companies except Cipla, has increased in post TRIPS period. The increase is highest in Dabur followed by the Ranbaxy.

Table: 9.5: Average Share Capital of Pharmaceutical Companies (Million Rupees)[22]

Name of the Company	**Pre TRIPS Position**	**Post TRIPS Position**	**Margin**
Aurbindo	223	273	+50
Cipla	600	134	-466
Lupin	449	6487	+6038
Ranbaxy	1682	2016	+334
Dabur	2857	9754	+6897

It is evident from the analysis that; Share Capital of all companies except Cipla has increased in post TRIPS period. The increase is highest in Dabur followed by the Lupin. The share capital of a company may be increased by issuing new shares (new issue) or by the company'sown funds being transferred from unrestricted equity to share capital (bonus issue). A new issue means that the company is supplied with new capital or reduces its debt.

---

[21] Supra Note 20.

[22] Ibid.

9.9. Conclusion

In spite of TRIPS compliance, section 3(d) is a very significant change made in the Indian Patent Act 1970. This section presumes that incremental innovations which are borne out of existing products are not eligible for patents unless they demonstrate an increase in efficacy. This section was enacted chiefly to curb an anti-competitive practice that is widely known as 'Ever-greening of Patents'. Because of Section 3(d), the Indian Patent Office's creative uses and the Judiciary's support to the legislation, the Indian legal regime is continuing to create conditions that favor Generic Drug Manufacturers, combat Ever-greening of patents and in the process, maximize value for the consumer by preventing prices from climbing the sky. On an international stage, India has come to assume the position as the leader alongside South American countries rallying for diluting patent-protection on improvement drugs, and at a broader level intellectual property protection. Based on the rapid growth of India's urbanization, it is expected that 590 million people will be migrated into the cities in the next 15 years, and therefore it is hard to imagine that the market for drugs will not match that pace. On a parallel, the rising GDP growth rate, creation of jobs and predictions of a decade-long bull run for the markets merge to make a powerful case for the growth of the industry, regardless of whether it is Big Pharma or Generic companies.[23]

Various markets of developing nations, as well as developed nations, are important for the progress of pharma companies. However, the basic argument against the framework of product patent by developing countries revolves around the facts that poor infrastructure, less developed economy and unemployment are holding back the development of the economy in developing countries. Therefore, pharmaceuticals are health inputs and are not to be treated at par with other consumables.

The World Health Organization (WHO), through its essential drug policy clearly, aims to ensure the accessibility of primary health care and medicine to all the human beings of the world, irrespective of colour, creed, care and economic status. It is continuously pressurizing governments of developed and developing countries alike to bring down prices of the drugs so that no one is deprived of medicines and suffers

[23] Supra Note 13

morbidity and mortality due to disease. The argument for product patent regime for pharmaceutical industries includes the high cost of patent filing and protection including maintenance of patents in WTO member countries. Another argument for the strong patent regime has been the availability of newer life- saving drugs and devices can only be ensured through the implementation of the TRIPS Agreement. Because of this product patent system, India will become dependent on the Multinational Companies for new drug inventions and also for obtaining permission to produce such patented drug and for that exorbitant charges or licence fees may have to be paid to them unless Indian companies are investing a substantial amount in the research and development of new drugs. The figures described above are clearly showing that today, Indian companies are also developing in the new patent regime.

It was assumed that the introduction of pharmaceutical product patents would have had a negative influence on the Indian pharmaceutical industry because it would have hampered its growth and the industry could no longer manufacture by reverse engineering or export drugs whose product patents are ineffective. However, against expectations, the Indian pharmaceutical industry has been growing since the post-TRIPS period, and its productivity is improving even in the post-TRIPS period which is visible from the abovementioned figures. It can be said that the introduction of pharmaceutical product patents has given rise to business opportunities for the Indian pharmaceutical industry and is promoting the growth of the industry. However, there are still concerns that the new patent act might reduce generic drug supplies and deteriorate access to medicines in India. Ensuring access to medicines at affordable prices is one of the most important tasks for the Indian government. Taking into consideration that India is a major supplier of affordable generic drugs, the issue of access to medicines is an essential one not only for India but for other poor developing countries, too. However, innovation is important for sustaining economic growth and development. Intellectual property is an important factor in promoting innovation. It should be noted that if the issue of access to medicines is abused in order to protect vested interests, it may retard innovation. Thus, the Indian government should seek an appropriate balance between the development of the Indian pharmaceutical industry and the improvement of public health.

Some suggestions are important with regard to the product patent system in India including:

- o A patent may be provided to the companies for a limited time and after some reasonable time, other companies may be given permission to prepare the drugs by usage of an alternative process.
- o Indian Pharmaceutical companies may also establish tie up agreements with some MNCs for providing the the facility for drug production and for research and development and because of that, the price may be controlled.
- o Some developed companies have applied the strategy to not grant product patent until their national companies acquire the technology and capacity to produce the required drugs. India can also think in such a direction in policy making.
- o The government may enact the legal provisions to put reasonable price fixing conditions on drugs for providing patent to the Multinational Pharmaceutical Companies. In developed countries, the medical expenses are paid for by health insurance so product patent system is not a big hurdle while in developing countries like India, 70% or more people pay for medical expenses from their own pocket and exorbitant prices of drugs can affect their right to health.
- o Moreover, the Indian Government has the right to grant a compulsory license on the basis of some conditions. Such a licence may be granted even before the expiry of the term of Patent and this provision of Compulsory license is also in compliance with TRIPs article 31.
- o For the safety of affordable medicines in India as well as for protection of Indian Pharmaceutical Industries, India needs a strong political system who can strongly bargain with MNCs and think in favour of the country. In order to do this, such MNCs may be brought under the preview of Indian Drug Price Control Acts so that before deciding price of the Patented Products, the government may check the reasonability of it.

Bibliography

Annual Report (2014-15) *The Office of Controller General of Patents, Trademarks, Designs and Geographical Indications*, Government of India Agreement on Trade-Related Aspects of Intellectual Property rights (TRIPS) (1994), Appendix 1A

Chaudhary Shubham, Pinelopi K. Godberg, and Panle J., (2006) *'Estimating the effects of Global Patent Protection in Pharmaceuticals: A Case Study of Quinolones in India'*, The American Economic Review 96, No. 5.

Dhar Biswajit & K. M Gopakumar., (2006) *'Post 2005 TRIPS scenario in patent protection in the pharmaceutical sector: The case of the generic pharmaceutical industry in India'*, UNCTAD/ICTSD Project on Intellectual Property Rights and Sustainable Development [online] Available at https://unctad.org/en/PublicationsLibrary/ictsd-idrc2006d2_en.pdf [Accessed 16 August 2016]

Feinberg Susan E and Majumdar Sumit K., (2001) *'Technology Spillovers from Foreign Direct Investment in the Indian Pharmaceutical Industry'*, Journal of International Business Studies (Palgrave Macmillan Journals) 32 No. 3.

Keayla B. K., (2005) *'India and the Patent Regime Amended Patents Act 1970: A Critique'*, Combat Law Vol. 4 Issue 4 June-July.

Kitch Edmund W., (1977) *'The Nature and Functions of the Patent system'*, Journal of Law and Economics, University of Chicago Press, Vol. 20, No. 2 (Oct., 1977) pp. 265-290 [online] Available at http://www.law.nyu.edu/sites/default/files/upload_documents/Kitch.pdf [Accessed 20 August 2016]

Lanoszka Anna, (2003) *'The Global Politics of Intellectual Property Rights and Pharmaceutical Drug Policies in Developing Countries'*, International Political Science Review, Sage Publications, 24 No. 2, April.

Nuno Pires de Carvalho, (2002) *'The TRIPS Regime of Patent Rights'*, Kluwer Law International, World Intellectual Property Organization. (WIPO) Annual Report 2000

Teg Alam, and Rastogi Rupesh, (2016) *Pre TRIPS, Post TRIPS Patent Regime and the Indian Pharmaceutical Industry: An Empirical Study'* Indian Journal of Science and Technology, Vol. 9 (9)

World Bank, (1999) *World Bank Development Report – Knowledge for Development*, New York: Oxford University Press.

Chapter 10

Governance of Nanomaterials in India: Learning from institutional analysis of the European REACH Regulation

Julian Schenten[1]

Abstract

Nanotechnologies such as the manufacturing and application of nanomaterials are deemed key enabling technologies and are therefore being pushed by funding measures, including in India. However, properties such as small size and increased surface reactivity link nanomaterials to specific but yet to a large extent uncertain or unknown risks. Hence, appropriate Indian governance strategies are required. Besides, there are discussions in India about modernizing their chemical legislation by shifting it to a regulatory system similar to the European REACH Regulation. Against this background, this chapter, after outlining the REACH system, analyses to what extent REACH contributes to adequate risk control of nanomaterials. To this end, the behavioural heuristics of the homo oeconomicus institutionalis are applied, which put individual actors working in companies that manufacture or import nanomaterials at the centre of an institutional analysis. At the same time, the chapter introduces an analytical framework which may support the Indian legislator identifying the "most harmonious fit" to solve the regulatory choice problem of ensuring safe and sustainable management of nanomaterials.

Keywords: Nanomaterials, Risk, Chemicals legislation, Institutional Analyses, Regulatory Impact Assessment

---

[1] Society for Institutional Analysis – sofia, Darmstadt University of Applied Sciences, Germany, Schenten@sofia-darmstadt.de

10. 1. Introduction

Since the early 2000s, the Indian government has made considerable efforts to promote nanotechnologies (Kumar, 2014) which are often referred to as key enabling technologies, providing the basis for innovation and new products (Giannopapa, 2010). The first phase of the current state funding program, the so-called "Nano Mission", had a volume of Rs. 1000 crore (DST, 2016). Indian funding for nanotechnologies addresses basic societal challenges, with nanotechnology-enabled innovations in the areas of, e.g. water purification and medical applications, but funding is also intended to boost economic growth (Beumer and Bhattacharya, 2013; Ali and Sinha, 2014).

At the same time, there are concerns over nanomaterials, i.e. chemical substances the manufacturing and application of which are essential parts of nanotechnologies. In the area of chemicals, the risk to human health and the environment is a function of a substance's inherent hazard potential and its exposure (van Leeuwen, 2007). As regards nanoscale substances, there is a high degree of uncertainty regarding both aspects (Savolainen et al., 2013). Against this background, concerns have been voiced that in India there is no adequate regulatory governance of nanomaterials (Srivastava and Chowdhury, 2008; TERI 2009). Adequate governance becomes all the more important as, after an initial government focus on establishing academia dominated nanotechnology excellence clusters, private companies increasingly are entering the nanotechnology arena (Sarma and Anand, 2012; Beumer and Bhattacharya, 2013). In 2010, the Indian Department of Science & Technology announced to create a Nanotechnology Regulatory Board (Business Standard, 2010). Draft "Guidelines for Safe Handling of Nanomaterials in Research Laboratories and Industries" have been released at the turn of the year 2015. However, legislative changes specific to nanomaterials have not yet been enacted (Sidal 2016).

Besides, as regards Indian regulation of chemical substances in general, in the XIIth Five Year Plan (2012-2017) for the national chemical industry the Department of Chemicals and Petrochemicals (DCPC) identifies a need to consolidate legislation to ensure the protection of human health and the environment against harm caused by chemicals. According to the DCPC, notwithstanding a wealth of chemicals-related legislation already in place, there are no specific requirements as to registration of substances, restrictions on hazardous substances, or detailed classification and labelling criteria (DCPC, 2011). Consequently, the XIIth Five Year Plan determines the "need to create REACH like legislation in India for the safe use of chemicals for the protection of human health & environment" (DCPC, 2011). The EU

Regulation concerning the Registration, Evaluation, Authorisation and Restriction of Chemicals (REACH) (OJ L 396, 30.12.2006) referred to is the basic legal framework for chemical substances manufactured or used in Europe or imported to Europe. REACH provides for a comprehensive risk management framework, addressing the entire life cycle of chemicals, and is based on the principle that actors in the chemical supply chains must ensure that neither humans nor the environment are harmed by their chemical products. At the same time REACH is, in general, deemed "the best possible framework for the risk management of nanomaterials"(European Commission, 2012a). A 2014 Indian Chemical Policy draft does not refresh the need for REACH like legislation but more generally calls for "an effective regulatory framework" (DCPC, 2014). Academia commentators, however, endorse the introduction of REACH-like legislation in India (Balaji et al., 2014; Sharma et al., 2014); besides, several other, mostly Asian countries, including China, have adopted or plan to adopt legislation comparable to REACH (Uyesato et al., 2013) thus putting pressure on India to gain on as regards state of the art chemicals governance in globalized markets. India's Ministry of Environment, Forests and Climate Change (MoEF&CC) is expected to propose a National Action Plan for Chemicals by 2018 (Chemical Watch, 2017) outlining a strategy for future Indian chemicals legislation, which might well be inspired by the European approach.

The following 2nd section elaborates on the specific but yet to a large extent unknown risks of nanomaterials and on how these are challenging regulation. Section 3 will briefly introduce the REACH system as a central piece of the European legislation to govern these risks. Section 4 analyses whether REACH ensures adequate risk control of nanomaterials. To this end, the assessment puts the individual actors manufacturing or importing nanomaterials at the center of an institutional analysis, which, based on the behavioural heuristics of the *homo eoconomicus institutionalis* as well as on a meta-analysis of a wealth of empirical data, asks for incentives and impediments with respect to adequate risk control. The final section draws conclusions as to a possible future governance of nanomaterials in India.

10. 2. Nanomaterial challenges

Legal definitions for the term nanomaterial vary according to jurisdictions and regulatory objects (Boverhof et al. 2015). One widespread approach however is also reflected by the International Organization for Standardization's (ISO) nomenclature, which defines "nanomaterial" as a "material with any external dimension in the nanoscale or having internal structure or surface structure in the nanoscale" (ISO, 2010), where nanoscale is defined as the size range from approximately 1 to 100 nm (ISO, 2008). Note that 1 nm corresponds to a millionth of a millimetre (10^{-9} m). Small size is thus one central feature of nanomaterials. Besides, in a nutshell, the number of atoms on a material's surface increases with decreasing material size, thus optimising or accelerating catalysis and other chemical reactions (Auffan et al. 2009). Consequently, nanomaterials can be useful to improve processes and products e.g. by reducing resource input or enabling new product features (Steinfeldt et al. 2010). Applications already on the market include medical science, energy storage and efficiency, environmental remediation and especially products intended for private consumers, including cosmetics, textiles and intelligent packaging in the food sector (WHO 2013, 1). In fact, quantities of nanomaterials available at least on the European market are considerable. For instance, in France alone, where companies are required to report quantitative statements, 300,822 t nanomaterials have been produced during the reporting period 2014; further 114,951 t were brought in by imports (Anses 2015). At the same time, individual volumes per manufacturer or importer are rather low (OECD, 2011; Gaia, 2012).

Usage in consumer products and high accumulative production volumes come along with a certain exposure of societies to nanomaterials, which raises thus the question about risks. In this respect, uncertainties play an important role due to the lack of data and methodical challenges. Any risk is, by definition, characterised by a two-fold uncertainty that exists with respect to the realisation of an event and its specific effect and consequences. Chemical substance-related risk assessment, in particular, is characterised by numerous uncertainties due to the complexity of the issue (NRC, 1983). In order to minimise uncertainty as much as possible, certain prudential aspects are considered intended to e.g. help to make appropriate assumptions where necessary (European Commission, 2000). Such rules, however, do not suffice to overcome the specific uncertainty in the risk assessment of nanomaterials.

With respect to single nanomaterials, existing data barely allows to define the dose or concentration below which no harm to human health or the environmental compartments is to be expected; fundamental prerequisites for a meaningful risk assessment and the identification of appropriate mitigating measures thus are often not met (Savolainen et al., 2013). Therefore, one can speak of a general uncertainty with regard to nanomaterial risks. This notion, however, merely outlines the known or at least perceived lack of knowledge, which can be measured e.g. by taking into account catalogues of relevant toxicity endpoints such as those established by the Globally Harmonised System of Classification and Labelling of Chemicals (GHS).

In addition, however, there is also ignorance, i.e. situations exist where both the realisation of an event as well as its effects and consequences are completely unknown ("unknown unknowns", c.f. Grieger et al., 2009). This phenomenon is of particular importance with respect to nanomaterials. Exposure patterns and adverse effects of nanomaterials are fundamentally determined by their physicochemical properties, including particle-number distribution, shape, surface properties (functionalisation, coating) and impurities (European Commission 2012b). However, these properties are subject to constant transformation processes in the substance's life cycle. Release into the environment creates a vast variability of potential exposure pathways and sites of action. Absorbed by organisms, dependent on the size, shape and solubility, nanomaterials can become systemically available and penetrate into individual cells and their components (Krug et al., 2013). Taken together, one can expect an unlimited number of possible interactions of nanomaterials with organic matter and biota (Nell et al., 2013). These complex causal relationships cannot be adequately controlled (Dupuy, 2004); the potential scale of adverse consequences cannot be estimated. Not least, the described uncertainty and ignorance are challenging legislators.

10. 3. Regulatory strategy in Europe: REACH

The EU Regulation concerning the Registration, Evaluation, Authorisation and Restriction of Chemicals (REACH) sets the framework for chemical substance-related risk regulation in the European Economic Area (EEA). REACH structures a systematic collection and evaluation of substance information by the manufacturers and downstream users before a substance enters the market. In addition, there are several instruments, which allow state actors to restrict certain substances or applications of concern (c.f. Bergkamp, 2013). In what follows, the regulatory approach and the instruments are presented. The potential strength of this approach becomes visible, in particular when compared to other approaches. Therefore, first, the legal situation before the entry into force of REACH is outlined.

10.3.1. Pre-REACH strategy

Prior to the entry into force of the REACH Regulation in June 2007, different requirements were imposed on "existing substances" already on the market in September 1981 and on "new substances". Directive 67/548/EEC (OJ L 196,16.8.67) required manufacturers and importers of new substances with a marketing volume of 10 kg or more to assess and evaluate the hazard potential of these substances for human health and the environment in a quantity-graduated stage test. According to the European Commission (2001), some 2,700 new substances were affected. By contrast, around 30,000 existing substances were marketed in relevant quantities at the beginning of the 21st century. Manufacturers and importers of these substances were permitted to place them on the market without prior safety assessment. Instead, Regulation (EEC) No 793/93 (OJ L 84, 5.4.1993) introduced a sovereign risk management program, which, during the course of its existence, involved a comprehensive risk assessment of some 140 priority existing substances (European Commission, 2001). This legal framework was therefore not sufficient to establish knowledge regarding the properties and applications of existing substances. Besides, it turned out to be an obstacle to innovation since only new substance developments triggered testing obligations for manufacturers and importers (Nordbeck and Faust, 2003).

10.3.2. Normative objectives of REACH

According to REACH Article 1(1) "[t]he purpose of this Regulation is to ensure a high level of protection of human health and the environment, including the promotion of alternative methods for assessment of hazards of substances, as well as the free circulation of substances on the internal market while enhancing competitiveness and innovation".

In order to achieve its protection objectives, pursuant to REACH Article 1(3) the regulation "is based on the principle that it is for manufacturers, importers and downstream users to ensure that they manufacture, place on the market or use such substances that do not adversely affect human health or the environment". Besides, according to REACH Article 1(3) sentence 2 the regulation's provisions "are underpinned by the precautionary principle".

10.3.3. Self-responsible risk management of the supply chain actors

Compared to the previous legal frameworks for chemicals, REACH marks a "paradigm shift" by obligating the actors in the supply chains to self-responsibly gather data on the substances they place on the market and to adequately control substance-related risks through suitable measures (Führ and Bizer 2007). Besides, after certain transitional arrangements, the last of which expired in Mai 2018, REACH legally equates existing substances and new substances.

Pursuant to the "no data, no market" rule set out in REACH Articles 5 et seq., substances manufactured or imported in annual volumes above 1 tonne need to be registered with the European Chemicals Agency (ECHA). The registration dossier, generally to be submitted by manufacturers and importers, shall include all physicochemical, toxicological and ecotoxicological information that is available to the registrant, however, as a minimum certain set of standard data, tiered according to substance tonnage bands, have to be submitted – even where this data is not available yet. REACH contributes therefore significantly to the generation of substance hazard and use data. As of 10th June 2018, the ECHA database of registered substances contains information on 20,677 unique substances (ECHA, 2018a). Furthermore, as regards substances in quantities of 10 tonnes or more per year, registration also includes a chemical safety report (CSR) in which "adequate control" of substance-related risks is documented. According to REACH Annex I, Section 6.4 evidence of adequate control is provided when throughout the life cycle of the substance for each exposure scenario the estimated exposure and concentration levels do not exceed the Derived No-Effect Level (DNEL) for effects toxic to humans and the Predicted No-Effect Concentration (PNEC) for ecotoxic effects. To this end, REACH Articles 10(b), 14 and Annex I require registrants to perform comprehensive risk assessments, to take adequate risk management measures and to communicate risk and hazard information to the downstream users, employing safety data sheets (SDS).

Downstream users, such as formulators or producers of products (articles in terms of REACH; c.f. REACH Article 3 No 3), are encouraged to support their suppliers in compiling all necessary risk information. Under certain conditions, however, if they are e.g. not willing to comply with risk management instructions communicated in the SDS, they might be obliged, in accordance with REACH Article 37, to prepare a CSR on their own behalf. In other words, REACH allocates primary responsibility to manufacturers and importers but downstream users are secondarily responsible, too.

In addition, the CLP Regulation (OJ L 353, 31.12.2008) applies according to which substances and mixtures, which entail a physical, health or environmental hazard have to be classified and labelled accordingly as well as packaged appropriately. The classification information is part of the REACH registration dossier. Conversely, the tests required for registration under REACH can help to improve the data basis for classification.

ECHA examines the quality of submitted dossiers on a random basis (REACH Article 40 et seq.).

10.3.4. Sovereign risk management

As regards certain problematic substances, the described approach relying on self-responsibility of the actors is deemed insufficient by the legislator. For such substances, REACH offers specific mechanisms of sovereign risk management. The authorisation scheme pursuant to REACH Article 55 et seq. establishes a ban of “substances of very high concern” (SVHC) with permit reservation; i.e. by applying for authorisation actors may (temporarily) overcome the barrier of the ban. For this they must, prior to the placing on the market or usage of the substance, prove that the risks are adequately controlled or that the socio-economic benefits outweigh the risks. In addition, substances posing an “unacceptable risk to human health or the environment” may become subject to general restrictions (REACH Article 67 et seq.), which may provide for e.g. article-specific or application-specific exceptions or limit values.

10.3.5. Transparency and participation

As seen in section 10.3.3., risk management is based *inter alia* on mechanisms for information, communication and cooperation within the supply chain (Führ and Bizer 2007). In addition, ECHA puts essential dossier contents into free-to-use online databases (ECHA 2018). Besides, REACH Article 33(2) provides consumers with an information claim against the suppliers of products (articles) with respect to SVHC contained in these articles.

In addition, prior to most final decisions of sovereign risk management (e.g. identification of SVHC, inclusion of SVHC in REACH Annex XIV, enactment of a new restriction) there is a public consultation giving interested actors such as companies, associations, NGOs as well as scientists or private persons the opportunity to submit incriminating or exculpatory evidence regarding the substance.

10.3.6. Interim results

Ten years after REACH came into force, setbacks such as high rates of non-compliance with the registration requirements (ECHA 2016b), a disputable granting practice with respect to applications for authorisation (Romano and Santos 2016) as well as flaws in design such as the exemption of imported articles with SVHC from the authorisation requirements (Schenten and Führ 2016) demonstrate that there is quite some potential to optimise the application of REACH and to some extent also its architecture (c.f. Hansen et al., 2007).

However, the underlying regulatory strategy could be a suitable approach to address risks and ignorance with respect to nanomaterials. As a reaction to of previous times' failed risk management, which was mainly driven by state actors, REACH highlights the self-responsibility of the actors in the supply chain who have to ensure that they manufacture, place on the market or use such substances that do not adversely affect human health or the environment. This principle is operationalized by substantive and procedural requirements which, in view of the complexity and variability of the regulatory object, nevertheless allow the actors some flexibility as to the development of appropriate strategies to meet their normative tasks. Besides, REACH structures cooperative processes along the entire supply chains while at the same time also integrating stakeholders such as representatives from science and civil society organisations, thus making the existing knowledge available for substance-related risk management. Further, transparency mechanisms allow targeted demand for substances and applications the safe handling of which is documented in the registration dossier and create thus incentives for compliant behaviour.

10.4. Nanomaterials in REACH

Nanomaterials are substances in terms of REACH Article 3 No 1 and are therefore subject to the legal requirements of this regulation. However, REACH does not yet contain specific rules for dealing with nanomaterials. Section 10.4.1. shows a lack of quantity and of quality as regards REACH registrations of nanomaterials. These findings contest the capability of REACH to ensure, as stipulated by Article 1(1), a high level of protection for human health and the environment. Against this background, an institutional analysis set out in sections 10.4.2. et seq. assesses whether REACH provides adequate incentives so that actors in companies manufacturing or importing nanomaterials ensure adequate risk control of these substances.

Basically, these sections summarize the key findings of a comprehensive institutional analysis which can be found in Schenten (2017). The analysis is based on the legal status quo. Besides, new nano-specific REACH provisions are expected to become applicable in 2020 (European Commission, 2018a). Section 10.4.4. comments on whether and to what extent these new legal requirements could have an effect on the institutional analysis provided in this chapter.

10.4.1. REACH registration data on nanomaterials

According to the European Commission, as of February 2012, in the ECHA database only 7 dossiers were found, the registrants of which ticked the voluntary information field "nanomaterial" (European Commission, 2012a). Later, ECHA reported that 4 further substances were registered as nanomaterials (Chemical Watch, 2013). However, it is to be assumed that further dossiers also cover nanomaterials without explicitly stating so. The European Commission assumes that nanomaterials, which are most common in terms of volume and turnover, are already registered (European Commission, 2012c). For a high number of other substances – the Commission assumes that a few hundred to a few thousand of nanomaterials are marketed in small quantities in the European Union – this is unlikely to be the case (Matrix 2014). Accordingly, a company survey shows very low rates of nanomaterial registrations (Schenten and Führ 2012).

A content analysis of dossiers identified to cover nanomaterials concludes that most of the data provided are not sufficiently specific and do therefore not allow adequate risk assessment of nanomaterials (Climent et al. 2012). Against this background, the European Commission, too, concludes that many of the registration dossiers on nanomaterials are not sufficiently clear as to what extent the specific risks of these substances have been addressed (European Commission 2012c).

Hence, it is open to question whether the REACH Regulation provides adequate incentives so that actors in companies manufacturing or importing nanomaterials ensure adequate risk control of these substances.

10.4.2. Institutional Analysis

The question has been raised whether REACH sets adequate incentives so that actors in relevant companies ensure adequate risk control of nanomaterials. In this respect, it has to be taken into account that these actors are not acting exclusively under the auspices of REACH. Rather, their behaviour is affected by a multitude of further factors. In order to approach the complexity of this research subject, it seems appropriate to make assumptions about these factors. To this end, the stage heuristics of the *homo oeconomicus institutionalis* (hoi) provide behavioural assumptions which can be employed (Führ and Bizer 2007). These heuristics use the *homo oeconomicus* as an analytical starting point but take into account that the assumptions made in this respect often explain behaviour only inadequately, and thus need supplementation. The heuristics thus assume different behaviours or specific perception patterns, such as professionally pre-determined perceptions, and therefore allow the systematic and comprehensible review of the behavioural effects of institutions. The term institution, in this context, does not refer to social entities (organisations) but to all formal and informal instructions that can have an effect on behaviour (North, 1991). Hence, the behavioural factors, including the requirements of REACH, form the individual actors' institutional framework, which guides their actions (c.f. Figure 1).

The stage heuristics of the hoi are embedded in the evaluation framework of Interdisciplinary Institutional Analysis. This framework combines normative test steps of regulatory impact assessment with an actor-related focus, taking into account the most relevant institutions (c.f. Bizer and Führ 2015).

Figure 10.1.: Homo oeconomicus institutionalis (Führ and Bizer 2007)

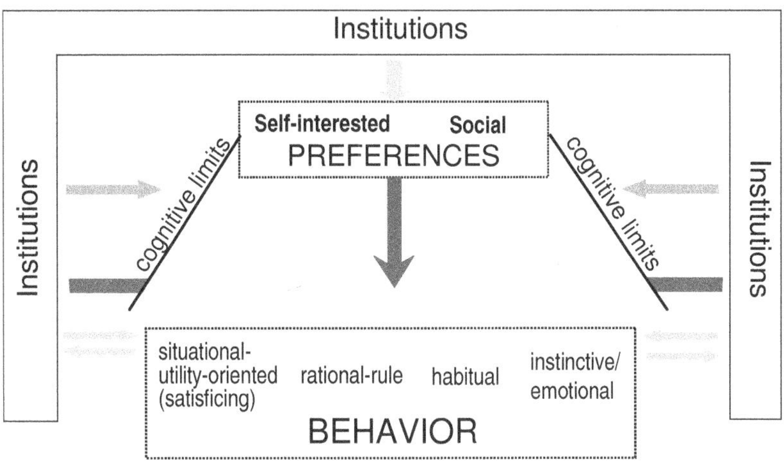

10.4.3. Preferences, incentives and impediments to ensure adequate risk control

Based on the behavioural heuristics of the hoi, this section assesses to what extent identified relevant institutions operate as incentives or as impediments regarding adequate risk control of nanomaterials. These factors can be structured using the categories of willingness, capacities and opportunities (Ashford, 2000). Besides, the analysis is focused on those actors working in companies that manufacture or import nanomaterials who are, compared to downstream users, particularly capable of originally preventing or at least sufficiently reducing nanomaterial risks.

Preferences of actors influence how they perceive risk and make cost-benefit assessments with regard to adequate control of nanomaterials. The actors' respective willingness is thus also driven by their preferences. Since single actors have different preferences due to divergent personal or professional imprints, different types of actors are to be assumed. On the basis of empirical data about, *inter alia*, risk management of nanomaterials (e.g. Schenten and Führ, 2012; Gaia 2012; Helland at al., 2008a; Helland et al., 2008b), which show the range of actors on the market, two types of actors can be modelled. One can be characterised as closed-defensive (type A), one as open-constructive (type B) (similar categories can be found in Pfister, 2009; Rossi, 2014). With regard to risk management, type A basically only makes the minimum effort necessary to generate a short-term benefit. In addition, he is not receptive to the views of other disciplines or groups of actors (e.g. representatives from NGOs). Type B basically makes every effort he can to achieve a longer-term benefit and is open to external influences; he acts proactively. The types of actors serve as an illustration of the range of possible actors for the analysis of incentives and impediments.

The capabilities of actors are related, among other things, to their professional qualifications, to organisational conditions in the company and to the available resources. Methodologically this aspect can be approached by analysing the capacities of companies, which can be considered linked with the capabilities of the actors employed. Companies in the field of nanomaterials are mostly small and medium-sized, often micro-enterprises as defined by the European Commission's recommendation for SMEs (c.f. Schenten, 2017). In general terms, SMEs are under particular pressure due to limited resources, less specialised staff and their dependence on local and regional markets. With the adoption of the REACH Regulation, the cost pressure increased even further. However, smaller companies are also considered more flexible due to their size. They are thus said to be able to respond more quickly and more specifically to customer requirements and market developments (Pelkmans et al., 2013; Nightingale et al., 2008).

Besides, the behaviour of actors is limited by their opportunities, i.e. the options and restrictions provided by the institutional framework. The REACH requirements constitute an essential component in this respect. Instruments in REACH are not sufficiently operationalised for nanomaterials. For instance, in general, no differentiations are made between conventional micro- or macro-scale "bulk" substances(e.g. silver) and nanoscale versions thereof (e.g. nanosilver). In fact, most nanomaterials are only representing versions of bulk substances (Pronk et al., 2009). Consequently, especially in cases where a company manufactures both a nanoscale and a non-nanoscale version of the same substance, nanomaterials might often simply slip through the framework's stitches as the instruments provided for in the legal text do yet not ensure that distinctions are drawn.

Furthermore, in REACH key legal tools, notably the registration obligation (including CSR) and sovereign risk management, often do not cover nanomaterials due to regulatory triggers tying in with conditions that nanomaterials often do not meet (quantities, conclusive knowledge of inherent hazard potential, conclusive knowledge of risk). In addition, even to the extent that certain nanomaterials are "caught" by the REACH instruments, lack of nano-specific obligations impedes

- substance identification (as opposed to bulk materials) as starting point of most legal obligations,
- fulfilment of standard physicochemical, toxicological and ecotoxicological data requirements, which are in addition not operationalised for nanomaterials, as basis for hazard assessment,
- risk assessment and risk management processes (Führ et al., 2007)

It follows that actors from businesses and law enforcement are facing legal uncertainties (Schenten and Führ 2012; Gaia 2012), constraining their abilities to act compliant and ensure adequate risk control.

Further opportunities to be considered include (c.f. Schenten 2017).

- complementary requirements from other legal frameworks (e.g. occupational health and safety, environmental law, product law) relevant for the actors,
- compliance costs in connection with the requirements of REACH and CLP,
- enforcement of REACH (including preferences, incentives and impediments of actors working in competent authorities);
- technical conditions relating to the production and risk management of nanomaterials (including availability of suitable methods, methodical constraints),
- preferences, incentives and impediments of stakeholders (consumers, downstream users, NGOs, economic associations, investors), market impulses due to the aforementioned factors.

In summary, the opportunities can be characterised as follows. There are indications of increasing public pressure linked with market impulses for "safe" application of nanomaterials. In turn, incentives for adequate risk control increase as well. At the same time, however, substance-related demand has so far been sufficiently diversified so that substances of lower quality, i.e. where e.g. hazard and risk data is missing or is not well documented, are selling, too. Besides, legal uncertainty in REACH and, not least, uncertainty about nanomaterial risks, also affect the marketability of these substances and thus restrict the willingness of actors to invest. Corresponding effects also result from technical restrictions (certain test methods for nanomaterials are not yet available), uncertain – but yet perceived as very high – compliance costs, as well as unclear loan conditions and insurance modalities. In this mixture of uncertainty factors, it seems difficult or impossible to predict the sales opportunities for individual substances and to make some reliable profit forecasts. Overall, there is a serious lack of planning security. In this situation of uncertainty, therefore, the willingness of the actors to invest in the risk management of nanomaterials can also be inhibited.

A relational analysis of the preferences, capabilities and opportunities of the two types of actors generates the following results: Closed-defensive actors' (type A) behaviour concentrates on the indispensable minimum requirements that meet clear legal obligations and satisfy clear demands of customers, and that help to avoid concrete threats of reputational losses. The latitude necessary for this strategy is provided by legal requirements that are not operationalised for nanomaterials, a lack of judicial sanctions in chemicals legislation and in product law as well and, in particular, the possibility of finding professional buyers of substances with poor quality. How rigorously type A applies this strategy depends *inter alia*on the degree of his company's popularity as this factor, in particular, influences the probability of extra-judicial sanctions. The vast majority of manufacturing companies, however, does not have to be concerned about reputational loss. This is because these companies are mostly acting outside the public perception and, besides, their contributions to e.g. final consumer articles, are too abstract for "scandalisation". Considering the strong preferences to generate short-term benefits while at the same time minimising costs, type A risk management of nanomaterials is most likely to a large extent based on data regarding the bulk versions and does not take into account initial concerns of substance risks in terms of the precautionary principle.

Behaviour of open-constructive actors (type B), on the opposite, is guided particularly by progressive demands for safety and quality products. Type B is therefore even open to over-commitment, if the legal framework fails appropriate operationalisation for nanomaterials and, consequently, products manufactured according to concrete legal requirements do not suit this demand. In order to overcome limited resources and to overcome uncertainties as to how nanomaterial risks can be adequately controlled, he cooperates with supply chain actors and other stakeholders. However, the high standard of quality is only affordable if the customers of the substances also contribute to these costs. Typically, type B makes every effort possible to achieve longer-term benefits. In this way, he strives for a behaviour, which is in line with the normative goal of REACH Article 1(1) to ensure "ensure a high level of protection" for humans and the environment. However, lack of capabilities (resources) and opportunities (methodical constraints) can create strong, sometimes absolute, barriers.

10.4.4. Interim results

In conclusion, institutional analysis shows that the REACH Regulation – in its institutional context – does not provide adequate incentives so that actors in companies manufacturing or importing nanomaterials ensure adequate risk control of these substance. Some actors (type A) are, in general, not willing to ensure adequate risk control of nanomaterials. Others (type B) are strongly motivated to do so but are constrained by deficient capabilities and opportunities.

At the same time, this identified "delta" can be used to determine alternative regulatory options within the REACH context to put both actor types in the position of adequately controlling risks. With respect to type B, institutional arrangements that even more intensify cooperation between supply chain actors or which increase the willingness of investors and professional users of nanomaterials to co-finance high safety and quality standards might be appropriate approaches. As for type A, to overcome his lack of willingness, alternative options must provide clear requirements for the risk management of nanomaterials, including effective judicial sanctions in cases of non-compliance, as well as effective intervention tools for the sovereign risk management. In particular, nanomaterials as such must become subject to the legal instruments – separated from their non-nanoscale micro and macro counterparts.

In fact, from 2020 on, new rules for nanomaterials will apply in REACH. Measured by the findings in this chapter, these regulatory changes, by providing clearer obligations regarding nanomaterials, will narrow down the latitude of type A actors. At the same time, legal uncertainties in the future legal text will offer room to act for type A, that he may use to maintain a, probably refined, strategy of concentrating on the indispensable minimum requirements that meet clear legal obligations. In particular, also the future legal text will not consider nanoforms of existing (non nano) substances as distinct substances. Consequently, legal uncertainties as to the extent to which existing substances and nanoforms thereof can be seen as identical substances in terms of the data requirements remain. Besides, the new provisions establish the standard rule that more than one dataset is not required, unless certain criteria – which are not fleshed out yet – are fulfilled: From 2020 on, a new obligation will apply pursuant to which "[m]ore than one dataset may be required for one or more information requirements whenever there are significant differences in the properties relevant for the hazard, exposure and risk assessment and management of nanoforms" (European Commission, 2018b). However, it is not specified which properties may trigger additional data requirements if they deviate significantly, it is not specified under what conditions a property deviates significantly and it is not specified which exact data requirements must be fulfilled whenever there are significant differences in the properties. There are thus obvious legal uncertainties, which might impede enforcement of the provision.

10.5. Conclusions

Nanotechnologies such as the manufacturing and application of nanomaterials are deemed key enabling technologies and are therefore being pushed by funding measures, including in India. However, properties such as small size and increased surface reactivity link nanomaterials to specific but yet to a large extent uncertain or unknown risks. Hence, appropriate governance strategies are required with respective calls also being formulated in India. Besides, there are additional discussions in India about modernizing chemical legislation by shifting it to a regulatory system similar to the European REACH Regulation. Against this background, this chapter analysed to what extent REACH contributes to adequate risk control of nanomaterials. By applying the behavioural heuristics of the *homo oeconomicus institutionalis* the assessment shows that some actors in the supply chain are not willing to ensure adequate risk control of nanomaterials while others are strongly motivated to do so but are constrained by deficient capabilities (e.g. resources) and opportunities (e.g. availability of appropriate test methods).

There are parallels in the incentive and impediment situations of European and Indian actors (e.g. limited access to venture capital, Sarma and Anand, 2012). In India, however, additional enforcement problems may arise due to the enormous share of un-registered MSME (KPMG and CII, 2015). Nevertheless, when modernizing its chemicals legislation and assessing ways to regulate nanomaterials India should take into account experiences made in other jurisdictions, such as Europe, in order to "leapfrog" certain initial flaws in the design and application of relevant frameworks. Besides, institutional analysis, informed by behavioural sciences, may support the Indian legislator identifying the "most harmonious fit" to solve the regulatory choice problem of ensuring safety and sustainable management of nanomaterials.

Bibliography

Ali A., and Sinha K., (2014) *Exploring the Opportunities and Challenges in Nanotechnology Innovation in India,* Journal of Social Science for Policy Implications, Vol. 2, pp. 227–251.

Anses, (2015) *Éléments Issus des Déclarations des Substances à l'État Nanoparticulaire – Exercice,* Rapport d'Étude, www.developpement-durable.gouv.fr/document162330 (accessed 28.10.2016).

Ashford N.A., (2000) *An Innovation-Based Strategy for a Sustainable Environment,* in: Hemmelskamp, J., Rennings, and K., Leone, F. (Eds.), *Innovation-Oriented Environmental Regulation: Theoretical Approach and Empirical Analysis,* Heidelberg and New York: Springer, pp. 67-107.

Auffan M., Rose J., and Bottero J.Y., *et al.*, (2009) *Towards a Definition of Inorganic Nanoparticles from an Environmental, Health and Safety Perspective,* Nature Nanotech, Vol. 4, pp. 634–641.

Balaji G., Potdar A., and Unnikrishnan S., (2014) *Environmental Legislation for Chemical Management in India: An Agenda for Reforms,* Journal of Environmental Research and Development, Vol. 9, pp. 494–596.

Bergkamp L., (2013) *The European Union REACH Regulation for Chemicals.* (Ed.), Law and Practice. Oxford: Oxford University Press,

Beumer K., and Bhattacharya S., (2013) *Emerging technologies in India: Developments, debates and silences about nanotechnology,* Science and Public Policy, Vol. 40, pp. 628–643.

Bizer K., and Führ M., (2015) *Compact Guidelines: Practical Procedure in Interdisciplinary Institutional Analysis, sofia-Diskussionsbeiträge zur Institutionenanalyse* Nr. 15-4, Darmstadt.

Boverhof D.R., Bramante C.M., and Butala J.H., *et al.*, (2015) *Comparative Assessment of Nanomaterial Definitions and Safety Evaluation Considerations,* Regulatory Toxicology and Pharmacology, Vol. 73, pp. 137–150.

Business Standard. (2010) *India to have Nanotechnology Regulatory Board soon,* http://nanotech.law.asu.edu/Documents/2010/06/india_459_8128.pdf (accessed 28.10.2016).

Chemical Watch. (2013) https://chemicalwatch.com/15076/2013-deadline-sees-only-four-nano-registrations (accessed 28.10.2016).

Chemical Watch. (2018) https://chemicalwatch.com/60306/india-to-have-a-national-action-plan-for-chemicals-by-2018 (accessed 9.6.2018).

Climent J.F., and Aschberger K., *et al.*, (2012) *Scientific Technical Support on Assessment of Nanomaterials in REACH Registration Dossiers and Adequacy of Available In-formation.* Final Report on Analysis and Assessment (Task I, step 3&4&5) and Options for Adapting REACH (Task II, step 1). NANO SUPPORT Project.

Department of Chemicals and Petrochemicals. (2011) *Indian Chemical Industry*, XIIth Five Year Plan 2012-2017, New Delhi.

Department of Chemicals and Petrochemicals. (2014) *Draft National Chemical Policy* (Final Draft NCP-2014), https://chemexcil.in/uploads/files/DRAFT_NATIONAL_CHEMICAL_POLICY_2014.pdf (accessed 28.10.2016).

Department of Science and Technology. (2016) http://nanomission.gov.in/ (accessed 28.10.2016).

Dupuy J.P., (2004) *Complexity and Uncertainty. A Prudential Approach to Nanotechnology, A Contribution to the Work in Progress of the "Foresighting the New Technology Wave,* High Level Expert Group, European Commission, Brussels.

ECHA. (2016) *Report on the Operation of REACH and CLP 2016*, Helsinki: ECHA-16-R-08-EN, ECHA, (2018) https://echa.europa.eu/de/information-on-chemicals/registered-substances (accessed 10.6.2018).

European Commission. (2000) *Communication on the precautionary principle.* Brussels: COM (2000)1.

European Commission. (2001) *White Paper on the Strategy for a Future Chemicals Policy*, Brussels: COM (2001)88.

European Commission, (2012a) *Second Regulatory Review on Nanomaterials*, Brussels: COM (2012) 572 fin,

European Commission. (2012b) *Types and Uses of Nanomaterials, Including Safety Aspects*, Brussels: Commission Staff Working Paper, SWD (2012) 288 final.

European Commission. (2012c) *Nanomaterials: Commission Proposes Case by Case Approach to Assessment.* MEMO/12/732.

European Commission. (2018a) *Draft COMMISSION REGULATION (EU) amending Regulation (EC) No 1907/2006 of the European Parliament and of the Council on the Registration, Evaluation, Authorisation and Restriction of Chemicals (REACH) as regards Annexes I, III, VI, VII, VIII, IX, X, XI, and XII to address nanoforms of substances*, D056122/02 (Draft implementing measure/act), http://ec.europa.eu/transparency/regcomitology/index.cfm?do=search.documentdetail&Dos_ID=15915&DS_ID=56122&Version=2 (accessed 10.6.2018).

European Commission. (2018b) *Annex to Draft COMMISSION REGULATION (EU) amending Regulation (EC) No 1907/2006 of the European Parliament and of the Council on the Registration, Evaluation, Authorisation and Restriction of Chemicals (REACH) as regards Annexes I, III, VI, VII, VIII, IX, X, XI, and XII to address nanoforms of substances,*

D056122/02 (Draft implementing measure/act), http://ec.europa.eu/transparency/regcomitology/index.cfm?do=search.documentdetail&Dos_ID=15915&DS_ID=56122&Version=2 (accessed 10.6.2018).

Führ M., and Bizer K., (2007) *REACh as a Paradigm Shift in Chemical Policy – Responsive Regulation and Behavioural Models,* Journal of Cleaner Production, Vol. 15, pp. 327–334.

Führ M., Hermann A., and Merenyi S., *et al.*, (2007) *Legal Appraisal of Nano Technologies. Existing Legal Framework, the Need for Regulation and Regulative Options at a European and a National Level,* ed. Umweltbundesamt (German Environment Agency). Dessau.

Gaia, (2012) *Study on REACH Contribution to the Development of Emerging Technologies.* Final Report.

Giannopapa. A., (2010) *Key Enabling Technologies and Open Innovation. New Impulses for the Space Sector.* ESPI Report 24, Vienna.

Grieger K.D., Hansen S.F., and Baun A., (2009) *The Known Unknowns of Nanomaterials: Describing and Characterizing Uncertainty within Environmental, Health and Safety Risks,* Nanotoxicology, Vol. 3, pp. 222–233.

Hansen S.F., Carlsen L., and Tickner J.A., (2007) *Chemicals Regulation and Precaution: Does REACH Really Incorporate the Precautionary Principle?* Environ Sci Policy, Vol. 10, pp. 395–404.

Helland A., Kastenholz H., and Siegrist M., (2008) *Precaution in Practice Perceptions, Procedures, and Performance in the Nanotech Industry,* J Ind Ecol, Vol. 12, pp. 449-458.

Helland A., Scheringer M., and Siegrist M., *et al.*, (2008) *Risk Assessment of Engineered Nanomaterials: A Survey of Industrial Approaches,* Environ Sci Technol, Vol. 42, pp. 640–646.

ISO. (2008) *International Organization for Standardization. Technical Specification: Nanotechnologies – Terminology and Definitions for Nano-objects – Nanoparticle, Nanofibre and Nanoplate.* ISO/TS 80004-2:2008.

ISO. (2010) *International Organization for Standardization. Nanotechnologies -vocabulary- part1: Core Terms.* ISO/TS 80004-1:2010.

Krug H., Wick P., Nowack B., *et al.*, (2013) *Human- und Ökotoxizität synthetischer Nanomaterialien. Erste Erkenntnisse für die Störfallvorsorge.* Umwelt-Wissen Nr. 1301: 43, Bundesamt für Umwelt, Bern.

Kumar A., (2014) *Nanotechnology Development in India, An Overview.* RIS Discussion Papers# 193, New Delhi.

Matrix Insight Ltd. (2014) *A Study to Support the Impact Assessment of Relevant Regulatory Options for Nanomaterials in the Framework of REACH,* Final Report, London.

Nell A. Xia, and T. Meng H., (2013) *Nanomaterial Toxicity Testing in the 21st Century: Use of a Predictive Toxicological Approach and High-Throughput Screening,* Accounts of Chemical Research, Vol. 46, pp. 607–621.

Nightingale P., Morgan M., and Rafols I., *et al.* (2008) *Nanomaterials Innovation Systems: Their Structure, Dynamics and Regulation.* A Report for the Royal Commission on Environmental Pollution, RCP (08)452.

Nordbeck R., and Faust M., (2003) *European Chemicals Regulation and its Effect on Innovation: An Assessment of the EU's White Paper on the Strategy for a Future Chemicals Policy,* Eur Env, Vol. 13, pp. 79–99.

North D.C., (1991) *Institutions.* The Journal of Economic Perspectives, Vol. 5, pp. 97–112.

OECD, (2011) *Information Gathering Schemes on Nanomaterials: Lessons Learned and Reported Information,* ENV/JM/MONO (2011)53, Safety of Manufactured Nanomaterials Series 31, Paris.

Pelkmans J., Schrefler L., and Gubbels I., (2013) *The Consequences of REACH for SMEs,* Note IP/A/ITRE/NT/2012-12.

Pfister J.A., (2009) *Managing Organizational Culture for Effective Internal Control. Contributions to Management Science.* Berlin and Heidelberg: Springer.

Pronk M.E.J., Wijnhoven S.W.P., and Bleeker E.A.J., *et al.* (2009). *Nanomaterials under REACH. Nanosilver as a case study,* Bilthoven: RIVM Report 601780003.

Romano D., and Santos T., (2015) *A Roadmap to Revitalise REACH. REACH Authorisation Progress - A Critical Assessment,* Brussels.

Sarma S.D., and Anand M., (2012) *Status of Nano Science and Technology in India.* Proceedings of the National Academy of Sciences, India Section B: Biological Sciences, DOI 10.1007/s40011-012-0077-2.

Savolainen K., Backman U., and Brouwer D., *et al.* (2013) *Nanosafety in Europe 2015-2025. Towards Safe and Sustainable Nanomaterials and Nanotechnology Innovations.* Helsinki.

Schenten J., (2017) *Rechtliche Gewährleistung eines hohen Schutzniveaus bei Nanomaterialien in REACH.* Defizitanalyse und Gestaltungsoptionen. Dissertation, Kassel University Press, Kassel.

Schenten J., and Führ M., (2012) *Law and Innovation in the Context of Nanomaterials: Barriers to Sustainable Development? Results of an Empirical Study,* elni Review 2, pp. 83–91.

Schenten J., and Führ M. (2016) *SVHC in Imported Articles: REACH Authorisation Requirement Justified Under WTORules,* Environmental Sciences Europe, 28:21.

Sharma B.G., Bharat G.K., and Tayal S., *et al.*, (2014) *The legal framework to manage chemical pollution in India and the lesson from the Persistent Organic Pollutants (POPs).* Sci Total Environ., Vol. 490, pp. 733–747.

Sibal P., (2016) *Why India Needs Nanotechnology Regulation Before it is Too Late,* www.thewire.in/45008/why-india-needs-nanotechnology-regulation (accessed 28.10.2016).

Srivastava N., and Chowdhury N., (2008) *Regulation of Health related Nano Applications in*

India: Exploring the limitations of the Current Regulatory Design (Draft Version). Paper presentedat International Conference on Mapping the Uncertainty of Nanotechnology. Challenges to Law, Ethics and Policy Making, held on May 22–24, 2008, at the University of Padua, Italy.

Steinfeldt M., v. Gleich A., and Petschow U., *et al.* (2010) *Environmental Relief Effects through Nanotechnological Processes and Products.* (ed)., Umweltbundesamt (German Environment Agency). Dessau-Roßlau.

The Energy and Resources Institute. (2009) *Regulatory Challenges posed by Nanotechnology Developments in India,* New Delhi.

Uyesato D., Weiss M., and Stepanyan J., *et al.*, (2013) *REACH's Impact in the Rest of the World,* in: Bergkamp, L. (Ed.), *The European Union REACH Regulation for Chemicals Law and Practice.* Oxford: Oxford University Press, pp.335–372.

v. Leeuwen C.J., (2007) *General Introduction, in: id., Vermeire,* T.G. (Eds.), Risk *Assessment of Chemicals. An Introduction.* Dordrecht: Springer, pp. 1–36.

WHO. (2013) *Nanotechnology and Human Health: Scientific Evidence and Risk Governance.* Report of the WHO Expert Meeting 10–11 December 2012, Bonn, Germany, WHO Regional Office for Europe, Copenhagen.

Chapter 11

Should a Constitution contain explicit anti-corruption mechanism?

Supruet Thavornyutikarn[1]

Abstract

There is a never-ending debate on whether a constitution should have clauses sketching a mechanism for the state to actively counter corruption. From the outset, it seems desirable. To many laypersons and academics – particularly anti-corruption advocates, it supposes to be the purpose of the constitution. This chapter argues that the more the state has the power/authority prescribed by the constitution, the chance of corruption increases and *vice versa*. In order to, philosophically, minimise corruption, the minimal state is needed. Thus, there is no explicit need for having any clause on anti-corruption in constitution. We should carefully inspect the real definition of constitution – which is a kind of social contract where people relinquish their rights and freedom to be controlled by the state. More state power implies more likelihood of corruption – as an abuse of power for private benefits. A dilemma arises when people expect more from the state. There are many things for the state to do, ranging from pure public goods to market intervention, and to a mere market transaction where the state acts simply as a buyer or seller. State and market are co-existed. If it is too expensive to allocate resources through the market, use of hierarchy cannot be denied. Since the transaction through hierarchy is not totally transparent (i.e. costless), corruption might be associated with its decision-makers. Particularly, governments of developing countries are demanded to be pro-active in order to stimulate the development; their constitutions might predetermine a lot of role to play, many institutions and hierarchies to be instituted, many non-market decision-makings, and, eventually, more

[1] Lecturer, Faculty of Economics, Thammasat University, Bangkok, 10200, THAILAND, Tel: +66899495109 Email: supruet@econ.tu.ac.th

opportunity for the abuse of authority. Thus, more demanding constitution automatically implies more corruptions and the mechanism to fight corruption would certainly create more corruption.

Keywords: Corruption, Constitution, Public Participation, Monitoring Cost, State, Market

11.1. Introduction

Corruption plagues countries' development all over the world. It harbours undesirable activities which spell out negative consequences to the society in various aspects – economic, political, and cultural. Therefore, it is universally accepted that corruption is detrimental and unwelcomed. There are relentless efforts to fight against corruption. Many jurisdictions, like Hong Kong, are particularly successful (Yeung, 2000; Kwok, 2005); many are not. One of the suggested solutions to fight against corruption is to have the anti-corruption mechanism or clauses embedded into the country's constitution forcing the state to have a duty to resist corruption. Post-2014-coup Thailand adopts this path. Corruption has always been a pretext for *coup d'état* in Thailand, as well as some other developing countries. Unfortunately, its world ranking in corruption does not improve after any coup at all (Thavornyutikarn, 2012; 2014). Thus, it is worth considering the attempt to include anti-corruption mechanism into the constitution if the corruption situation would be improving in Thailand. However, it is too early to evaluate that since the draft constitution is subject to a referendum in early August this year and the constitution would not be fully effective, awaiting its organic laws, in the short future. Taking a few steps back, the broader question of this paper is how appropriate an inclusion of anti-corruption mechanism into the constitution of any country would be, despite the fact that corruption is a universal evil to everyone.

This chapter argues that corruption is a price of having a state and it could not be fully eradicated. As long as the state is there, there is corruption. The only way to include an anti-corruption mechanism into the constitution is to properly define the optimal roles of the state and limit its authority to serve those roles only which is simply the principle of drafting the constitution. Therefore, explicit anti-corruption clauses in the constitution and forcing the state to have the duty to prevent corruption are irrelevant. Section 11.2 tries to clarify what corruption is from the perspective of law and economics. Section 11.3 illustrates constitution itself is an anti-corruption mechanism. The flaw of logic on corruption is identified in Section 11.4 and analysed in Section 11.5. Section 11.5 also establishes the pathway to understand corruption correctly and to optimise it. Concluding remarks are given in 11.6.

11.2. Genesis of Corruption

> *"All power tends to corrupt, and absolute power corrupts absolutely."*
>
> –Lord Acton

It is apparent from Lord Acton's quote that power is the ultimate source of corruption and the degree of corruption proportionately varies with the degree of power. The more power you have, the higher the chance of corruption. The preliminary question is how such power is formed.

Power is man-made; it is artificial. Alternatively, power is an institutional instrument for humans to solve a problem of public goods. In the absence of state, humans are living in pure nature and the Darwinian law of evolution applies. Human survivability is determined by its physical strength, brain power, and the ability to adapt. There would be no corruption since everyone is on its own to survive. Following the simple Prisoners' Dilemma game, it is less favourable to live our lives like that. When we live long enough to learn and human interaction is repeated indefinitely, the superior cooperative outcome prevails. That is how human construct the state and give it power through the agent – the government. The state becomes the invisible third person to assure the cooperative outcome among living human. Noting that such an outcome is collective; it benefits everyone in the society and, if anyone tries to enjoy that benefit alone, the society reverts to the inferior non-cooperative Darwinian outcome. The state exercises its power in order to punish those who deflect, keeping the cooperative equilibrium (Rajagopalan and Wagner, 2013). Systematic and repeated use of power emerges into law, particularly those that successfully could hold people to cooperate. And here is where corruption emerges.

The state exercises its power through an agent – a government which is a group of human beings. On one hand, the successive use of power could strengthen society through superior cooperative outcomes. On the other hand, agents who have their hands-on power could initially be altruistic, honest, and non-evil; but sooner or later, they start to impose their own version of what is good for the public through the legal enactment (Moreell, 1992). Moreell (1992) puts "That is a danger point! The more restrictions and compulsions he imposes on other persons, the greater the strain on his own morality." These agents, subsequently, start to have an enthusiasm for using power to control people and see the opportunity to bend the rule for achieving what is 'good' for them and, in the end, their private benefits (Moreell, 1992). This is corruption and injustice.

11.3. Constitution as an anti-corruption mechanism

"When injustice becomes law, resistance becomes duty."

–Thomas Jefferson

The battle between state and its people is evident. The state, by the implicit consent of its citizen, controls the citizen to achieve superior cooperative outcomes. However, state agents can be perverted, extracting the surplus from such outcome for their own benefits. Consequently, its people fight back by determining what the state can and cannot do. For instance, a later Charter of *Magna Carta* becomes the model for modern constitution because it effectively constrained the rulers with citizen's readiness to protect their rights if the rules did not comply (Leeson and Suarez, 2016). Constitution demarcates what is *ultra vires* and *intra vires* of the state and provides the mechanism to incentivise the state not to do any *ultra vires* for the protection of its citizen's rights. Essentially, constitution itself is an anti-corruption mechanism (Teachout, 2009; 2014).

"A Constitution is not the act of a Government, but of a people constituting a government, and a government without a constitution is a power without right."

–Thomas Paine

The definition of constitution in the simplest form is "a set of rules which constrain the activities of persons and agents in the pursuits of their own ends and objectives" (Buchanan, 1977). Evolution of constitution is simply the mirror image of the state discussed earlier. It could be seen here in connection with the previous section that constitution is another set of law emerging to control the state, particularly enforcers of state authority using their discretion for their private benefits (Gordon, 1999).

Thus, the positive constitutional economic explanations show that constitution itself controls the state, which, in turn, limit corruption; meanwhile, other laws (particularly administrative and public laws) determine how the state controls its people, which allow discretion and corruption. It could be said there are complimentary to each other or there is reciprocity between the state and its citizen as per social contract explanation. The sole purpose of constitution is to limit the state authority (which implies protect the citizen's rights) (Voigt, 1999).

11.4. Curbing Corruption: not only concern Constitution

The bottom line role of state from an economic point of view is the minimal state that provides only public goods since it is impossible to allocate resources by using other means apart from fiat or hierarchy. Subsequently, the constitution must allow the state to deal solely with the production and distribution of public goods. Even with only public goods, the state needs an authority to produce and deliver them and that opens a chance for corruption. The easiest example would be how much the state will tax its people to produce such public goods. If the tax revenue exceeds the cost of public goods production, how the state deals with the residue. However, the opportunity of corruption would be minimised given the existence of state. As the state engages in more and more roles, the probability of corruption increases, *ceteris paribus,* because the state may embark on an inefficient duty that could be achieved alternatively (i.e. through the market) and use taxpayers' money paying someone to do it.

Again, it is worth reiterating that there would be no corruption if there is no state or government but society has to pay for it. The guaranteed absence of corruption has its price – the society has to sacrifice its cooperative surplus. Nevertheless, having the state does not always imply corruption; the likelihood of corruption just simply increases.

Providing what we have discussed in two previous sections, it becomes apparent that corruption cannot be totally eliminated. As long as we have the state, corruption is there. It is not about how to eliminate or reduce the level of corruption, but it is about the optimal and socially acceptable level of corruption. To determine that, it requires at least a two-pronged approach: on one prong, carefully crafting constitution concerns because it is about how to limit the role of the state; on another prong, all other non-constitutional laws must be simultaneously reviewed in order to evaluate how much authority the state has under existing legislations. Despite the fact that in most jurisdictions, constitution has supremacy and prevails over any other law; those statutory laws may commit to its people with a certain duty which then could let corruption takes place by state agents.

Therefore, to curb corruption, the constitution must delineate the exact role of the state and the government in relation to all law it upholds. And the interpretation of constitution must not allow the state to engage in *ultra vires* exercise of authority. However, this is only one side of the story. Before we could draft the constitution, we must know what the people expect or want the state to do. The more they demand from the state, the more authority the state has, implying a higher chance of corruption. Citizens of many developing countries require their states to do a lot of things, much more than mere provisions of public goods; while demand their states not to corrupt. This is incongruous.

To reduce corruption is to reduce the role of the state. Not the other way around. Thus, calling the state to be actively fighting with corruption is equivalent with asking the state to kill itself. By adding more authorities to combat corruption in the constitution, it is giving the state more authorities to corrupt. There is a contradiction here. Limiting the role and duty of the state is the key to curb corruption. Who will do that? Definitely, the citizen has to demand less from the state and the government first. The puzzle is solved now. A real origin of corruption is the demand of people for the state to do something for them.

11.5. People as a source of and solution to Corruption

11.5.1 Demand for state intervention creates Corruption

Essentially, from the discussion, people are at the centre of corruption. If not because of the failure to cooperate among the people themselves and call for the third party intervention, there would be no state; if there is no state, there is no power and authority; without power, there would be no discretion and no exploitation of authority for private benefits; without discretion and exploitation, there would be no corruption. Rajagopalan and Wagner (2013) described "...law is an abstract noun, and abstract nouns can't rule. Only people can rule." Citizens are usually insisting that the state does something for them, which automatically implies they are calling for more use of authority and the backside of it is corruption.

Economically speaking, corruption is the price of state intervention. It is acceptable as long as the service provided by the state is valued more than the private benefits extracted by state agents. If we can deter the private exploitation of state authority, values of public services would be increased. This is the reason why we should fight against corruption. But it is not the end of the story because it is costly to deter corruption and it is a taxpayers' money.

Suppose the value of public service offered by the state is V (and it is presumably fully funded by tax from taxpayers). State agents extract or corrupt c out of that value. As long as $V - c > 0$, it seems to be fair to allow those agents to continue their corruption. However, it is worth investing in an anti-corruption activity, say k (which is also paid for fully by taxpayers), to save this c to make V highest. How much should we invest? It is quite straightforward that k should be less than c ($k < c$) in order to justify an efficient anti-corruption investment. What k is essentially? It is a monitoring and enforcing cost for people to control state agents. If $k = c$, the society is 'indifferent' between having someone corrupt and no corruption at all. As V grows larger (such as healthcare or education), c tends to increase and so does k. When $V - c$ is getting smaller, i.e. more corruption, k could be increased and return on k would be very high. This implies, other things being equal, it is worth targeting big public projects to find corruption. It also implies that petty corruption would usually get away with it. Corruptors do not want to be detected; thus, they would be extremely careful to make sure $V - c$ remains positive and substantial enough not to cause any consternation.

11.5.2 Downsizing the state

Considering, now, the type of public services provided. If it is a pure public good, V will be very high since it is non-rival and non-excludable. Subsequently, corruption would be more likely too (higher c) and we should invest more in the anti-corruption activity to save the value of this service (higher k) as long as it is efficient to do so ($k < c$). If it is not a public good, V would be lower for the sake of rivalry or excludability and the same arguments still hold. However, moving to another extreme, if a particular service can be offered through other channels, or even through market exchange in the case of a pure private good (where there is a rivalry and excludability), V would be compared to its alternative values, for instance, price, P, if it has been exchanged through the market. If $V - P > 0$, this means it is economically efficient for the state not to provide this service and purchase it from the supplier in the market. What follows is there would be no corruption (no c) since state agents cannot seize any c out of P as P is the minimum possible market value of this service. State agents may negotiate with a private provider to mark up the price from P to $P + c$, but this would be a self-signalling for corruption. People wonder why they can buy the same thing at P, but the state buys it at $P + c$. As long as the market is sufficiently efficient, the state shall not try to offer what market does and shall consider such attempt as *ultra vires*.

Now it is clear that the market can help by offering a benchmark to evaluate whether there is a clue for corruption, particularly when the price is higher than the market price. The implication is the state shall abstain from involving in any transaction or exchange which can be done through the market unless there is a market failure. This further implies, to reduce corruption, eliminating some products and services used to be provided by the state and substituting them to be delivery by other intermediaries (i.e. market or other non-state institutions) which means the people have to demand less from the state. This implication coincides with Boettke and Suarez (2013) saying that the state should be smaller and the philanthropic role of the state should be structured to ensure efficiency. It is also coincided with Rajagopalan and Wagner (2013) mentioning people have to choose rules and enforce on the agreed rules in order to reflect their real needs, not let the state to subjectively interpret those rules. Therefore, if there is other cheaper alternative to allocate resources than the state on a particular transaction, the state shall not intervene in that transaction. Constitution must be drafted to restrict the state authority on such transaction correspondingly. Although it sounds like the indirect confirmation for the state not to allow corruption, in fact, it is the most fundamental way to prevent corruption by not authorising the state to do something. It is a flaw to explicitly tell the state that it has the duty to fight corruption because doing so actually results in more corruption.

11.5.3 Constitutional amendment and revision of other Organic Laws

Downsizing the state by drafting a restrictive constitution is necessary but not sufficient to reduce corruption. There are plenty of existing legislations allowing state agents (namely government officials and civil servants) to use their authorities to achieve genuine purposes but prone to discretion and corruption. These laws are organs of the state. Without revision of these legislations, constitutional amendment would simply cut its head off but its tentacles are still functioning, or we could say state departments are having their own lives – uncontrolled. This is even worse and more corruption is predicted. Revision of all organic laws must be done after the amendment in order to put some state functions to an end or to orderly adjust them to synchronise with the constitution. Otherwise, as described in Rajagopalan and Wagner (2013), the rule of law could be delusional since instating rules and enforcing rules are not the same. Thus, carefully amending constitution to manifest the underlying essential role of the state is crucial as well as cautiously revising organic laws not to allow the unintended use of authority by state agents for the sake of the rule of law is equally vital.

This stage is the most difficult thing to do since it is sentimental and affecting many stakeholders, particularly government officials themselves. There would definitely be resistance from state agents as well as from its people because people think their benefits would be banished or their cost of living would be increased. This transition is tough. Often, because of this treacherous transition, the society has the impression to assign the state a duty to fight corruption. This is why most anti-corruption attempts logically fail and fighting against corruption as a constitutional duty becomes an urban myth. This myth, then, becomes self-propagating due to frequent discourse reproduction, particularly anti-corruption advocates. In fact, drafting the constitution to have anti-corruption duty is simply suicide. It leads to even more corruption. An anti-corruption mechanism would be discretionally disguised to hide actual corruption and to blame authorities' enemies or opponents as their scapegoats. To be more precise, anyone who advocates constitutional duty of state to fight against corruption is either negligent due to the myth or a potential corruptor.

11.5.4. Empowering people

Since there is no commitment from state agents to resist corruption, people's movement to fight against corruption is necessary and an only available – and viable – option. A big dilemma arises because people are diverse and transaction cost for coordination among them is prohibitively astronomical. This sounds like a cyclical reasoning in which the state should do anti-corruption activities. Corruption is simply a dark side of the state. When it is too costly to monitor state's behaviour, and everyone is free-riding, state agents can corrupt for their private benefits.

Boettke and Suarez (2013) say "[a] current system of government does not have the appropriate institutional structure to provide effective countervailing constraints to government power. Neither the political structure nor the voting booth provides enough disciplinary feedback to keep government policy in check." They argue further that, as the state is getting smaller, the society should grow bigger. The scope of state and government should be redefined by a decentralised society. Many social functions could be done locally through re-energised community and making the state less irrelevant.

With an advancement in information and communication technology (ICT), transaction cost for monitoring state agents and coordination among people become significantly lower. The value of k is much lower and, in many cases, lower than individual's private cost of corruption (despite the fact that the cost of corruption *per capita* is negligible as population rises). Many countries, including India, Bolivia, and other African nations, adopt mobile application as a tool to monitor and complain about corruption (Grönlund *et al.*, 2010; Chêne, 2012). Features of mobile devices are fully exploited to provide the channel to report as well as to create instant evidences of corruption. These help ordinary people to discipline state agents much easier and more effective without requiring a legal mechanism. Of course, its corrective purpose may not be effective without such mechanism because officials may help each other to cover up, not to press charge, or just discard complaints. But all evidences could be shared on the internet at a low cost causing state agents to fear themselves of being exposed and making corruption less attractive due to higher cover-up cost. Simply, state agents or government officials are now afraid of ordinary people. When corruption is less lucrative, state's resistance reduces considerably. Officials do not worry much about losing their authorities. And the whole society can work backward to what we have discussed, up to the point of constitutional amendment. Similarly, empowered people gain self-confident and realise their abilities to do many things on their own. They are less dependent on the paternalistic role of state. It is worth-noting the power of ICT. Despite enabling people to coordinate and re-energise community, it also enables the state to offer many public services more efficiently and eliminate unnecessary public duties by using ICT to facilitate alternative modes of delivery. This would facilitate the process of state downsizing and, simultaneously, the process of socialisation by people.

11.6. Conclusion

It is flawed and catastrophic to specify in the constitution that the state has a duty to fight against corruption. Doing so would eventually induce more corruption and less transparency. Constitution itself is already an anti-corruption mechanism depending on how much people want from the state. More duties of the state come at a price – higher probability of corruption – and *vice versa*. Developing countries face with the dilemma of how big the state should be because the state is believed to be an agent for growth and development. Usually, constitutions in these countries demand their states to do many things and, of course, grant their states with authorities profusely to achieve those tasks. In hindsight, people should have known they practically allow more corruption. Thus, the basic tradeoff of the state is how much the state could create surpluses from cooperative outcomes and how much society loses from corruption (including cost of combating corruption). To reduce corruption, the role of the state should be reduced and limited by constitution; not to explicitly specify in constitution that the duty of the state is to resist corruption.

People are at the centre of corruption. They create corruption through creating the state and they combat corruption through constitution. Therefore, the first step to curb corruption is to determine the optimal role of state – as long as state is the least cost provider of certain tasks, it should be constitutionally authorised to carry out those tasks. If alternative intermediaries can deliver some tasks cheaper than the state, those tasks shall be constitutionally restricted.

Essentially, the myth of the constitutional role for the state to combat corruption creeps out from the distinction between "choosing rules" and "choices within rules", put forwarded by Rajagopalan and Wagner (2013). A real task of people is to choose proper rules to control themselves but if they neglect that fact they are allowing the state to create rules to confine their choices from within. While losing the control of state, people inadvertently consent the state to rule and state agents are finding corruption more attractive.

At the same time, people must be empowered to privately fight against corruption. Modern ICT allows them to do just that. Corruptive activities could be cheaply caught on mobile phone's camera and posted on social media in no time and virtually no cost, bypassing any anti-corruption agency (which may be corrupted too since it has a legal authority). Corruption would eventually be discouraged. Also, people will gain more confident and learn what they could do by themselves without the state. These two forces fortify each other to reform the government and the state. Lastly, all organic laws allowing state to exert its power and authorities must be revised, corresponding to people's will and constitution. Unfortunately, most people still live in myth, believing that it is the duty of the state to combat corruption.

Bibliography

Buchanan J. M., (1977) *Freedom in Constitutional Contract - Perspectives of a Political Economist.* College Station, TX Texas: A&M University Press.

Chêne M., (2012) *Use of Mobile Phones to Detect and Deter Corruption.* U4 Expert Answer, No. 321, http://www.u4.no/publications/technological-innovations-to-identify-and-reduce-corruption/downloadasset/3122 (accessed 11.07.2016).

Gordon S., (1999) *Controlling the State: Constitutionalism from Ancient Athens to Today.* Cambridge, MA: Harvard University Press,

Grönlund Å., *et al.*, (2010) *Increasing Transparency and Fighting Corruption through ICT Empowering People and Communities.* Stockholm: SPIDER.

Kwok T. M., (2005) *Formulating an Effective Anti-corruption Strategy – the Experience of Hong Kong ICAC.* UNAFEI Resource Material No. 69, United Nations Asia and Far East Institute for the Prevention of Crime and the Treatment of Offenders, pp. 196-201.

Leeson P.T., and Suarez P.A., (2016) *An Economic Analysis of Magna Carta,* International Review of Law and Economics, http://dx.doi.org/10.1016/j.irle.2016.05.001 (accessed 11.07.2016).

Moreell Ben, (1992) *Power Corrupts.* Religion and Liberty, Vol. 2, No. 6. http://www.acton.org/pub/religion-liberty/volume-2-number-6/power-corrupts (accessed 11.07.2016).

Rajagopalan S., and Wagner R.E., (2013) *Constitutional Craftmanship and the Rule of Law,* Constitutional Political Economy, Vol. 24, pp. 295-309.

Teachout Z., (2009) *The Anti-Corruption Principle,* Cornell Law Review, Vol. 94, No. 341, pp. 342-413.

Teachout Z., (2014) *Constitutional Purpose and the Anti-Corruption Principle,* Northwestern Law Review, Vol. 108, pp. 200-217.

Thavornyutikarn S., (2012) *The Implications of Thailand's Military Expenditure on Intervention in Politics and Governance Quality,* National Anti-Corruption Commission Journal, Vol. 5, No. 2, pp. 138-160.

Thavornyutikarn S., (2014) *Did the Military spearhead the Fight against Corruption in Thailand?* 18th Annual Conference of the International Society for New Institutional Economics (ISNIE) in Duke Law School, Durham, NC, USA. http://extranet.isnie.org/uploads/isnie2014/thavornyutikarn.pdf(accessed 11.07.2016).

Voigt S., (1999) *Constitutional Law,* in: Bouckaert B., De Geest G., (eds.), *Encyclopaedia of Law and Economics, Volume I.* The History and Methodology of Law and Economics. Cheltenham: Edward Elgar. http://encyclo.findlaw.com/9100book.pdf (accessed 11.07.2016).

Yeung J.A., (2000) *Fighting Corruption – the Hong Kong Experience.* Seminar on International Experiences on Good Governance and Fighting Corruption, Bangkok, Thailand,http://unpan1.un.org/intradoc/groups/public/documents/APCITY/UNPAN002750.pdf (accessed 11.07.2016).

Chapter 12

The Way Ahead: Towards A Social Economics?

Upendra Baxi[1]

Abstract

The Chapter explores, within the context of law and economics, some key ideas in the movement of towards 'social economics'. May we instead of law and economics consider law as economics and economics as law? Are there ways to integrate considerations of efficiency' with 'justice'? How is one to view 'efficiency' both as 'static' and 'dynamic' social process? How does the judicial process and the law shape the free market and stand shaped by it? Does the 'nudge' theory implicitly extend to Indian social action litigation in India?

Keywords: Efficiency, Justice, Neoclassical Economics, Markets, Nudge Theory, Social Economics

12.1. Introduction

The IIT Kanpur, the NLUG, and IIM, Ahmedabad have made notable Indian contributions to the understanding of the difficult relationship between law and economics. My disappointment at not being with you today is not compensated fully, if at all, by sharing these inaugural notes.

The conference themes are indeed wide ranging: they cover almost all the important themes in constitution, law, and jurisprudence in their current development. I wish you well, although I think you will run out of time in every one of these. I wish you a lot of moral luck in your deliberations.

---

[1] Dr Upendra Baxi, Emeritus Professor of Law, University of Warwick and Delhi Distinguished Professor of Law, NLUD, Delhi.

Even as I express my gratitude at your kindly inviting me on this occasion, I salute your determination to explore the dynamic relation between law and economics. I have read with a lot of learning experience the fine book *Economic Analysis of Law: An Indian Perspective.*[2]

I hope you will want to agree with me that the work is a fine blend of student and faculty effort and brings to bear the importance of a distinctively economic analysis and understanding of law in action (the daily diet - and practice- of both Indian legislation and adjudication). Of importance is the principal text to each chapter which gives an overview of law and economic themes, issues, and literature in Euro-American theory and a micro-study of Indian cases or legislations. At times, there is innovation through specific Indian examples, as in Chapter 18 deploying Kaushik Basu's theories about sexual harassment, Chapter 12 on the proposed GST, or Chapter 16 offering an 'economic analysis of crime and punishment.

The question one must ask, with the book, is whether economic theory is universal in its scope and method or is culturally specific. I think that the book beautifully evades this intransigent question by talking about Indian 'perspectives', which seems to suggest that while theory is 'universal', perspectives have to be' cultural' and local. Or, perhaps, the juxtaposed 'perspectives' interrogate the idea of a meta-theory. I hope that this Conference will give a thought to what is generally understood to be a law (in the sense of invariability, and vulnerability to the local) and 'reconceptualization of lawhood' entailed by *ceteris paribus law.*[3] The latter (by now an inarticulate premise of economic theory) in any event leans more towards "explanatory generalizations" than towards the prescriptive ones (the state-law combinatory specializes in these).

---

[2] Edited by Drs. Bimal Patel, Ranita Nagar, and Hitehshkumar Thakkar (Delhi, LexisNexis,2014); hereafter referred to as *EAOL*.

[3] See, for example. James Woodward., 'Explanation and Invariance in the Special Sciences", British *Journal for the Philosophy of Science*, 51: 197–254.(2000); 'There is no Such Thing as a Ceteris Paribus Law", in *Ceteris Paribus laws,, Erkenntnis*, 52 (Special Issue): 303–328(2002); ,., *Making Things Happen:* Id: *A Theory of Causal Explanation* (Oxford University Press, 2003); Id., 'Causation in Biology: Stability, Specificity, and the Choice of Levels of Explanation", *Biology and Philosophy*, 25: 287–318 (2010); and the extremely valuable discussion in James Woodward, and Christopher Hitchcock, 'Explanatory Generalizations, Part I: A Counterfactual Account", *Noûs*, 37:1: 1–24 (2003). But for a historical approach, see Toni Vogel Carey, 'Always or Never: Two Approaches to "Ceteris Paribus" *'Erkenntnis* 77: 3, 317-333 (2012).

It is all for the good that Dr. Ranita Nagar and you all pursue the famous prophecy of Justice Oliver Wendell Holmes, Jr., in 1897 that:' For the rational study of the law the blackletter man may be the man of the present, but the man of the future is the man of statistics and the Master of Economics'.[4]

Holmes did not say what he meant by the term 'economics' but we all know that he thought. For example, in his famous dissent in *Lochner* he ruled that: '...a constitution is not intended to embody an economic theory, whether of paternalism and the organic relation of the citizen to the State or of laissez faire. ...It is made for people of fundamentally differing views, and the accident of our finding certain opinions natural and familiar or novel and even shocking ought not to conclude our judgment upon the question whether statutes embodying them conflict with the Constitution of the United States'.[5] In other words, judicial self-restraint in matters of micro and macroeconomic and development matters was to be a rule, not an exception—this is also the view that the Supreme Court of India has generally followed, despite an impressive edifice of administrative jurisprudence and demosprudential judicial leadership.[6]

This faith in legisprudence (the prudence and the wisdom of the legislatures) is quite touching until we recall the famous dictum of Lord Keynes: 'The ideas of economists and political philosophers, both when they are right and when they are wrong are more powerful than is commonly understood. Indeed, the world is ruled by little else. Practical men, who believe themselves to be quite exempt from any intellectual influences, are usually slaves of some defunct economist.'[7] Incidentally, the last phrase has a flavour of arrogance that only economic theory as a social science discourse can bring to us; when we see the neoliberal world consensus before us it would seem that economic theorists are more like 'defunct' beings led by a globalizing universal middle class in quest of security and welfare within a political- industrial-military complex!

---

[4] 'The Path of Law' *Harvard Law Review* 10:457 (1897).

[5] *Lochner v. New York*, 198 US 45 (1905). See also Jack M. Balkin, 'Wrong the Day It Was Decide'": *Lochner* And Constitutional Historicism', *Boston University Law Review*,.85:677 -725 (2005).

[6] Upendra Baxi, 'Demosprudence and Socially Responsible/Response-Able Criticism: The NJAC Decision and Beyond' WBNUJS Law Rev. 9: 153-172.

[7] As cited by Robert Skidelsky, *Keynes: The Return of the Master* 88 (London, Allen Lane, 2009).

Despite this observation, what is named as 'social economics' has developed as a master narrative frame, and it is more conducive to legal theory and movement than some other law and economic frames (such as the 'neoclassical'. 'rational choice', 'welfare', 'development'. 'comparative' and 'institutional' approaches).[8] Of what 'social economics' may consist in is an issue much debated—at least ever since in 1993 when Steven Medema published his classic article' "Is There Life beyond Efficiency?...[9] wherein he articulated the ways in which social economics may make a vanguard contribution to the economic analysis of law. Yet, the situation has not noticeably improved. We ought to ask 'Why?'

Social economics appears as a strange idea that stresses that both law and economics are human artefacts and inescapably linked to each other. This is an insight that Max Weber (1864–1920) fully developed, but Weber is of course of no interest to economics theorist or economistic policy discourse.[10] In this zodiac, one must fall back on more recent thinkers who reiterate Weber's central insights. Thus, Medema recalls Samuels who speaks of the 'the numerous attributes of the legal-economic nexus' as 'the social process in which are (re)worked out power structure, law, distribution, and societal values and definitions' and 'in which government operates to (re)define and (re)create the economy, and in which nominally private interests, perhaps especially economic interests,

---

[8] See Upendra Baxi, 'Global Development and Impoverishment' in Mark Tushnet and Peter Cane (ed.) *The Oxford Handbook of Legal Studies*, DOI: 10.1093/oxfordhb/9780199248179.013.0022; Id., 'International development, global impoverishment and human rights' in Scott Sheeran and Sir Nigel Rodley (ed.) *Routledge Handbook of International Human Rights Law* 597-614(2013); Id.,

[9] Steven G. Medema, 'Is There Life Beyond Efficiency? Elements of a Social Law and Economics, *Review of Social Economy*, 51:2, 1 a, 38-153 (208). See also, Nicholas Mercuro and Steven Medema, 'The Jurisprudential Niche of Law and Economics' (being Chapter 1 of *Economics and the Law: from Posner to Postmodernism and Beyond*) http://ssrn.com/abstract=889641; and further, Mark D. White (ed.), *Law and Social Economics: Essays in Ethical Values, Theory, Practice, and Policy* (New York, Palgrave Macmillan, 2015).

[10] Max Weber, *Max Weber on Law in Economy and Society* (Harvard University Press; Edited and translated by Max Rheinstein, 1954). See the interesting analysis in Max L. Stackhouse 'Weber, Theology, and Economics', *The Oxford Handbook of Christianity and Economics* (Oxford University Press, Paul Islington, ed, 2014; DOI: 10.1093/oxfordhb/9780199729715.013.017); David M. Trubeck, 'Max Weber's Tragic Modernism and the Study of Law in Society', *Law and Society Review* 40:4, 573- 603 (1996); Id., 'Complexity and Contradiction in Legal Order: Balbus and the Challenge of Critical Social Thought About Law '*Law and Society Review* 11:529-568(1977).

operate to (re)define and (re)channel government, given the dominant belief system, which is itself reformulated and rechannelled through the uses selectively imposed upon or made of it'.[11] This, as you may agree, is a rather complex description but the focus on 'socio-economic nexus' is quite central to social economics; equally crucial is the invitation to 'create', 'redefine' and 'recreate' the economy. These processes remain bidirectional: even as the economy gets transformed, the governance processes are also themselves changed. Law and economics shape, as well are shaped, by governance processes and social change. Perhaps, then we may (even ought?) speak not of law *and* economics but law *as* economics and economics *as* law. Max Weber, we should remind ourselves, accomplished this a long time ago.[12]

As against the neo-classical economists, 'social economics' views persons as complex entities; they are not just simple ('barebones') utility - maximizing individuals but are 'unique, socially-oriented persons, and... [they] make-up ... socially-oriented persons ..., encompassing numerous cultural, moral, and ideological forces, of which Catholic solidarist man, Kantian man with his corpus of binding duties, Marxian man, and humanistic man are particular manifestations'.[13] Not merely does this confront the notion of *homo economicus* as proselytized by high economic theory but it also confronts possessive individualism as the sole basis of describing human species itself. The consuming self of course matters but does not exhaust human beings as constitutionally sincere citizens, moral agents, and spiritual beings.

The other theme relates to efficiency as justice and justice as efficiency plus. The notions of economic efficiency vary widely.[14] Efficiency plus is

---

[11] Supra note 8 at 143. See also, Mark Lutz and Kenneth Lux, *Humanistic Economics: The New Challenge* (New York, Rowman & Littlefield Publishers / Apex, 1988).

[12] A useful beginning in this interface has been recently made by Catherine L. Fisk and Robert W. Gordon: see their 'Foreword: "Law As . . .": Theory and Method in Legal History' *UC Irvine Law Review* 1:3, 519-541(2011).

[13] Id.at 144.

[14] Se the brief but pointed discussion mapping the difference between the Paretian optimality and Kaldor- Hicks formula, *EAOL* Chapter 8 (in the context of FDI policies in India). See also, Upendra Baxi, 'Introduction' to Massey's *Administrative Law* LI-LVI (Lucknow, Eastern Law Book Co., 2013); Id., 'Notes on Constitutional and Legal Aspects of Rehabilitation and Replacement' on W. Fernandes & E. G. Thukral, (ed.). Development, Displacement and Rehabilitation, 164-170. (New Delhi: Indian Social Institute (1989); Id., 'Development, Displacement, and Resettlement: A Human Rights Perspective'

an ethical conception that may not be derived from the 'morals free' zones of market institutions and processes. While high economic theory defines and measures market efficiency, discourse on justice is non-quantitative.

Social economics follows and develops the distinction between 'static' and 'dynamic' efficiency. The latter is considered essential to social justice tasks. In contrast, the standard economic way of thinking about efficiency is provided by the rational actor model thus: "rational agents are self-interested maximisers of utility; . . . utility can be best understood . . . as a single item varying only in quantity; . . . utility is best analysed in terms of preferences; . . . preferences are . . . not significantly shaped by law and institutions; and . . . ends adopted by an agent cannot be the subject of rational deliberation, although agents may deliberate about instrumental means to ends'.[15] Put another way, efficiency consists in the means-ends relationship; once you decide the ends or purposes, the question is how to achieve these best by rational means and those means are rational which involve the least transaction costs. However, as John Rawls has notably demonstrated what an actor considers as rational may not always be reasonable.[16]

Efficiency is also important for justice. If efficiency plus is to amount to justice, how does one define and measure it? Are we to think of justice according to its forms or types (of justice as social, political, distributive, commutative, restorative, and corrective justice? Or, as a first virtue of social institutions and outcomes? Or, in terms of good order that respects humane governance and actualities and aspirations of human rights, providing at once both morality of duty as well as an ethic of aspiration?

---

http://csdindia.org/publications/social-development (visited 15 August 2016).

[15] Martha Nussbaum, 'Flawed Foundations: The Philosophical Critique of (A Particular Kind of) Economics', *University of Chicago Law Review*, 66: 197-214 (1997).

[16] John Rawls, (*Political Liberalism* New York, Columbia University Press, 1993) has consistently guided us to think this difference. Reason signifies relating means to an end. But not every decision or choice that is rational remains reasonable. Rational actors chose to maximize their power, influence, or authority but doing so may not always be reasonable. Colonialism was rational this ay but surely not reasonable. The Bhopal settlement orders were rational in this sense, but they were not reasonable. The decision in *Shiv Kant Shukla* denying habeas corpus even on grounds of mistaken identity was "rational" in terms of the furthering the ends of Emergency Rule but was not reasonable. It would be interesting to study the jurisprudence of the duty to give reason from this perspective. See further the interesting discussion, concerning 'legality' and 'legitimacy', the contributions in David Dyszenhaus (ed.), *The Unity of Public Law* (2004, Oxford, Hart Publishing).

Are there spheres of justice resting on different principles (as Michael Walzer notably argues)[17] for market and nonmarket institutions or are we to regard these differences as immaterial to law as economics and economics as law?

But of course, conceptions of justice, or even morality, may not apply at all if, as David Gauthier maintains, perfectly competitive markets (PCM) are 'morally free zones'. By definition a PCM is conceived as a state of pure freedom:' ...no one is subject to any form of compulsion, or to any type of limitation not already affecting her actions as a solitary individual'[18]: a PCM rules out decisions based on force and fraud. Postulating, of course, the enormous advantages of methodological individualism, and assuming that all forms of PCM are thus, what may we say then when we come to the real world where they are flawed? Are actual market forms free of 'force' and 'fraud'? And, to raise another related large question. what theory about the' 'politics 'of regulation/deregulation may be adopted?[19]

Widely conceived, the social economics is 'primarily concerned with prescribing what should and should not be done; with passing value judgments upon economic ends, institutions, behaviour, etc. . . . If used in this sense economics patently cannot be divorced from ethics'.[20] The question, of course, is how far one is to convert core (neoclassical) economic theory into social ethics. Adjudicatory discourse must necessarily do this as it has to make behaviour consistent with moral and ethical values in the constitution and the law. However, very often justices and courts counsel that they stay away from the task of macroeconomic management. Listen to what the Supreme Court of India most recently

---

[17] *Spheres of Justice: A Defense of Pluralism and Equality* (New York, Basic Books, 1984).

[18] David Gauthier, *Morals by Agreement*, (Oxford, Oxford University Press, 1986 at 96. See also, 123: *Ethics*: A Symposium: David Gauthier's *Morals by Agreement* (2013). And see also, Gauthier, *Limits of Liberty* (Chicago: University of Chicago Press, 1975).

[19] See, for example, Mercruro and Madema, *supra* note 8; Peter Shuck, *The Limits of Law: Essays on Democratic Governance*167-138 (Boulder, Colorado, 2000); Michel Aglietta, 'Capitalism at the Turn of the Century: Regulation Theory and the Challenge of Social Change', *New Left Review*, 232 (1998); Andrei Shleifer, 'Understanding Regulation', *Financial Management* 11:4, 439-451(2005); Hertog, J.A. den, 'General Theories of Regulation', *Encyclopaedia of Law and Economics*, 223 – 270 (1999).

[20] William R. Waters. Evolution of Social Economics in America in Mark Lutz, (ed.), *Social Economics: Retrospect and Prospect*' 91-117 (Boston: Kluwer Academic Publishers, 1990).

said in 2G decisions: 'as far as "trusteeship" is concerned, there is no cavil that the State holds all natural resources as a trustee of the public and must deal with them in a manner that is consistent with the nature of such a trust but it simultaneously holds that the ' public trust doctrine is a specific doctrine with a particular domain and has to be applied carefully'.[21] What may the caveat signify- is good law always poor economics or good economic theory is always good law?

To make a major but brief detour, the theme of environmental justice as developed in the recent decades by the High Courts and the Supreme Court of India, and now notably by the National Green Tribunal, lends itself a great deal to social economics. This arena is underdeveloped in India, particularly in terms of environmental economics and green political theory. I suppose that the environmental economics that may fully develop will stress sustainable development, with 'developmental' aspect more fully accentuated. However, social economics will reinforce 'sustainability'. What urgently matters are not even states of 'sustainability' but just sustainabilites at local, regional, national, supranational, and global levels. In the Anthropocene era what matters decisively are the levels of reversal of present-day environmental and economic harms and a near-future extinction of humans (and many other species and ecology on planet earth); we urgently need theories of global climate change justice.[22]

What we call environmental jurisprudence and justice also aggravates inequality and injustice in India. A careful study by Geetanjoy Sahu demonstrates that the Court's invigorating 'pro-environment approach has largely 'upheld the concerns of middle-class environmentalism' and it has failed to recognize' the strong linkages between livelihood and environmental protection in India. And in matters of infrastructure projects, it has yielded to 'public purpose' as defined by the executive and privileged development over rights and justice.[23] Would economics of environment also adopt the same approach, or is there evidence elsewhere that social economics has, or could, make a difference.

---

[21] RE: SPECIAL REFERENCE NO.1 OF 2012 [Under Article 143(1) of the Constitution of India], per D.K. Jain, J. [For S.H. Kapadia, CJI, Dipak Misran and Ranjan Gogoi, JJ., with an additional concurring opinion by Jagdish Singh Khehar J.]

[22] Upendra Baxi, 'Towards a Climate Change Justice Theory?' *Journal of Human Rights and the Environment*, 7: 1. 7–31 (2016).

[23] See Geetanjoy Sahu, *Environmental Jurisprudence in India*, Orient Blackswan, Delhi, 2014, at 67—68. I hope that the authors of *EAOL* would incorporate environmental dimensions of development in the second edition.

For social economics theory, the deeper question is: How do we distinguish between the rhetoric and reality of dispossession? Rhetorically, natural resources are said to 'belong to the people' but the Court immediately adds that 'the State legally owns them on behalf of its people'.[24] How are justices and legislators to prescribe norms or structures of normative discursivity? Are they in devising norms to follow free market institutions or are they to avoid 'unconstitutional economics'?[25] Whether or not that latter term articulates a viable concept, it remains apt for social economics theory if only because it redirects attention to the need for a constitutional theory of state and the place of adjudicatory law and policy making within that realm. Should Justices only (in a rich phrase of Judge Richard Posner) 'mimic the market' or shape/reshape market institutions in the name, and power, of 'justice'? [26] There is a great contention (and even strife) among ethical philosophers and interpreters (as well as makers) of the constitution, concerning whether justice is an individual, social, or political virtue and in what the 'justice' may consist of [27] but one thing is clear: while economic theory and thought are necessary for doing the tasks of law and justice, these are not sufficient. Social economics may not perform these tasks without a theory of, and about, justice. That truism remains poignantly articulated by social economics perhaps best serving the objectives of law and economics?

May I extend to you all felicitations and offer a secular prayer for the very best in this endeavour?

10.2. Postscript, 2018

Since this paper was presented in 2016 at the conference, I have become interested in the so-called 'nudge' function enunciated notably in behavioural economic theory. That theory is not directly interested in law,

---

[24] See also, Paras 75-76 of the 2G Reference.

[25] Kishen Mahajan embryonically formulated this fecund notion in his essay 'Law and Developments' in Upendra Baxi (ed.) *Law and Poverty: Critical Essays* 438-439 (Bombay. Tripathi, 1988).

[26] Richard Schamelbeck, 'The Justice of Economics: An Analysis of Wealth Maximization as a Normative Goal' https://scholarship.law.duke.edu/cgi/viewcontent.cgi?article=2449&context=faculty_scholarship (visited 15 August 2016).

[27] See, for example, John Mukum Mbaku, 'Preparing Africa for the Twenty-first Century: Lessons from Constitutional Economics' *Constitutional Political Economy*, 6:139-160 (1995).

being more addressed to rational choice being influenced by the ways of market and governance. A nudge is a stimulus guiding someone to make a choice, without any quotients of coercion.

A nudge has been explained, by Pelle Guldborg Hansen as a 'function of any attempt at influencing people's judgment, choice or behaviour in a predictable way'; because of 'cognitive boundaries, biases, routines, and habits in individual and social decision-making posing barriers for people to perform rationally in their own self-declared interests', and which 'works by making use of those boundaries, biases, routines, and habits as integral parts of such attempt'. A nudge 'works independently of forbidding or adding any rationally relevant choice options' and is also different from 'changing incentives', incentives that would also modify rational behaviour'. [28]

It is maintained that nudges, constitute a 'genuinely distinct mode of governance, with a corresponding distinct normativity'.[29] Accordingly, one may regard, nudge agenda, or nudging behaviour, as legal or extralegal, depending on one's conception of law.[30] Good examples of nudge agenda are to be found in respectively in the Preamble of the Constitution, Part IV and Part IVA of the Indian Constitution, which respectively stipulate the objectives, directive principles of the State Policy, and prescribe the Fundamental Duties of Citizens. On a legal positivist conception of that equates law with enforceability, these constitutional provisions may be regarded as parts of the *constitution* but not of the constitutional *law*. However, a broader view complex recognition of a variety of nudge agendas remain as paramount as a constitutional culture of obedience and resistance.

Writing earlier, I had painstakingly described the processes of 'creeping jurisdiction' over other state institutions, and 'hope and trust orders' and directions that were passed in the charismatic (founding) phase of

---

[28] Pelle Guldborg Hansen, The Definition of Nudge and Libertarian Paternalism: Does the Hand Fit the Glove?', *European Journal of Risk and Regulation*, 7: 1-20. (2016). The idea that one may go beyond mere enforceability as a measure of effectiveness has often been reinforced by the idea of rewards as positive sanctions. However, nudging is to be considered as positive sanctions (incentives) but as an affair of choice.

[29] Ibid.

[30] Péter Cserne 'Is nudging really Extra-legal?' The Tocqueville Review/La revue Tocqueville, 37: 1, 159-180, at 151 (20160.

epistolary jurisdiction and the emphasis in SAL on the non-adversarial nature.[31]

In a broader normative framework, the law, along with other regulatory techniques is integral to the project of good governance. Such a project is not distinct from law but encompasses various forms of legality accompanying the judicial endeavour.[32] Many flayed the early phase of SAL as issuing non-enforced directions, but the court was aware that the SAL offered a dialogical mode of redress, not an either-all adversarial result.[33] Not enough attention is paid to the fact that in institutionalizing a new jurisdiction, Justices considered contempt motions not the best way to proceed. In any event, understood in terms of behavioural economic theory, SAL certainly has since promoted a 'nudge' function theory based on principled respect for the framework of the individual choice making.

Nudging is often regarded as an aspect of state paternalism, and there are many aspects why moral paternalism displayed by the law and the state is regarded as problematic.[34] in direct opposition, the sparse but substantial literature claims that nudging fosters various public goods such as autonomy, rationality, and choice. This notion of nudge agenda and nudge functions (roughly put here) holds interest in terms of the idea of law without sanctions, which legal anthropologists have variously pursued; that is the intelligibility of the very concept of law minus sanctions. The concepts of law floated by Jeremy Bentham[35] and H. L. A.

---

[31] Upendra Baxi, 'Taking Suffering Seriously: Social Action Litigation Before the Supreme Court of India', *Third World Legal Stud.* ,107-132(1985).

[32] See also, Richard H. Thaler, Cass R. Sunstein, *Nudge: Improving Decisions about Health, Wealth, and Happiness*, (New Haven, Yale University Press, 2008); Cass R. Sunstein, *Why Nudge? The Politics of Libertarian Paternalism*, (New Haven, Yale University Press, 2014); Alberto Alemanno, Anne-Lise Sibony (eds.), *Nudge and the Law: A European Perspective*, (Oxford, Hart 2015; Alberto Alemanno, Alessando Spina, 'Nudging Legally: On the Checks and Balances of Behavioural Regulation', *International Journal of Constitutional Law*, 12 (2014) 429; Hansen, Note 27 supra.

[33] Upendra Baxi 'Uprooting Injustice, Organizing Negation: The Enduring Contribution of Justice P.N. Bhagwati', (forthcoming, A Festschrift for Justice P.N. Bhagwati, M. C. Sharma ed.)

[34] Chatrapati Singh, 'The Ideological Roots of Legal Paternalism in India', *Journal of the Indian Law Institute*, 24:844-101 (1982).

[35] Jeremy Benham, *The Theory of Legislation* (Bombay, NM Tripathi/Delhi, Lexis Nexis, with an Introduction, 1986; Upendra Baxi, ed.)

Hart[36] fascinated me for this reason, as did the work of Max Weber[37] and Emile Durkheim the latter with his strong thesis on what he called 'non-contractual elements in contract'.[38]

Clearly, as I have said elsewhere,[39] the SAL as developed by the Supreme Court of India takes the nudge function seriously as a way of taking human suffering, and its alleviation by constitutional law, quite seriously. The impact of the nudge function needs to be studied as a species of symbolic judicial action, as modifying the constitutional aptitudes and attitudes of several impact constituencies. To ignore the symbolic dimension of SAL is to miss out on its long-term mission of making power increasingly accountable, governance more just, and state incrementally ethical.[40]

Bibliography

Adolphus H.H.L., (1961) The Concept of Law. Oxford: Oxford University Press.

Aglietta M., (1998) *Capitalism at the Turn of the Century: Regulation Theory and the Challenge of Social Change,* New Left Review, 232.

Alemanno A., and Sibony A.L., (2015) *Nudge and the Law: A European Perspective.* (Ed) Oxford: Hart Publishing.

Alemanno A., and Spina A., (2014) *Nudging Legally: On the Checks and Balances of Behavioural Regulation,* International Journal of Constitutional Law, 12, 429

Balkin J. M, (2005) *Wrong the Day It Was Decided: Lochner and Constitutional Historicism,* Faculty Scholarship Series, 236. Online. Available at https://digitalcommons.law.yale.edu/fss_papers/236, (Accessed 18 October, 2018).

Baxi U., (2016) *Towards a Climate Change Justice Theory?,* Journal of Human Rights and the Environment, 7: 1. 7–31.

Baxi U., (2016) *Demosprudence and Socially Responsible/Response-Able Criticism: The NJAC Decision and Beyond, WBNUJS Law Rev.* 9: 153-172.

Baxi U., (2015) *Symbolic and Instrumental Dimensions of Impact Analysis: Some Marginal Notes,* Delhi Law Review 34: 1-8.

---

36 H.L. A. Hart, *The Concept of Law* (Oxford, Clarendon Press, 1961).

37 See Note 9, *supra.*

38 Stewart Macaulay, 'Non-Contractual Relations in Business: A Preliminary Study, 28 *Am. Soc. Rev.* 55 (1963). But see, Robert W. Gordon,' Macaulay, Macneil, and the Discovery of Solidarity and Power in Contract Law', Wis. L. Rev. 85: 565 (1985).

39 *Supra* Note 32.

40 See, Upendra Baxi, 'Symbolic and Instrumental Dimensions of Impact Analysis': Some Marginal Notes', 34 *Delhi Law Review,* 1-8 (2015).

Baxi U., (2013) *Introduction to Massey's Administrative Law.* Lucknow: Eastern Book Company.

Baxi U., (2013) *International development, global impoverishment and human rights,* in Scott Sheeran, and Sir Nigel R., (ed.) Routledge Handbook of International Human Rights Law 597-614.

Baxi U., (2005) *Global Development and Impoverishment,* in Mark Tushnet and Peter Cane, (ed.) The Oxford Handbook of Legal Studies, 1-18.

Baxi U., (1985) *Taking Suffering Seriously: Social Action Litigation Before the Supreme Court of India,* Third World Legal Stud. ,107-132.

Baxi U., *Uprooting Injustice, Organizing Negation: The Enduring Contribution of Justice P.N. Bhagwati* in A Festschrift for Justice P.N. Bhagwati, M. C. Sharma (eds.) (forthcoming).

Bentham J., (1894) *The Theory of Legislation.* London: Trubner & Co., Online.available at https://archive.org/details/legislation00bentuoft/page/n3, (Accessed 18 October, 2018).

Carey T. V., (2012), *Always or Never: Two Approaches to "Ceteris Paribus",* Erkenntnis, 77: 3, 317-333.

Cserne P., (2016) *Is nudging really Extra-legal?* The Tocqueville Review/La revue Tocqueville, 37: 1, 159-180. Online. Available at https://muse.jhu.edu/article/626856 (Accessed 18 October 2018).

Den Hertog J.A., (1999) *General Theories of Regulation,* Encyclopedia of Law and Economics, 223 – 270.

Dyzenhaus D., (2004) *The Unity of Public Law.* (Ed) Oxford: Hart Publishing.

Fisk C. L., and Gordon R. W., (2011) *Foreword: "Law As…": Theory and Method in Legal History.* UC Irvene Law 1:3, 519-541. Online. Available at https://scholarship.law.uci.edu/cgi/viewcontent.cgi?article=1010&context=ucilr (Accessed 19 October, 2018).

Gauthier D., (1986) *Morals by Agreement.* Oxford: Oxford University Press.

Gordon R. W, (1985) *Macaulay, Macneil, and the Discovery of Solidarity and Power in Contract Law,* Wis. L. Rev. 85: 565.

Hansen P. G., (2016) *The Definition of Nudge and Libertarian Paternalism: Does the Hand Fit the Glove?,* European Journal of Risk and Regulation, 7 (1), 155-174. Online. Available at https://rucforsk.ruc.dk/ws/portalfiles/portal/57294350/ejrr_2016_01_020.pdf (Accessed 18 October 2018).

Holmes O. W., (1897) *The Path of the Law* Harvard Law Review 10:457.

Lutz M., and Lux K., (1988) *Humanistic Economics: The New Challenge.* New York: Rowman & Littlefield Publishers / Apex.

Macaulay S. (1963) *Non-Contractual Relations in Business: A Preliminary Study,* Am. Soc. Rev. 28, 55-67.

Mahajan K., (1988) *Law and Developments* in Upendra Baxi (ed.) Law and Poverty: Critical Essays Bombay: Tripathi.

Mbaku J. M., (1995) *Preparing Africa for the Twenty-first Century: Lessons from Constitutional Economics,* Constitutional Political Economy, 6 (2),139-160. https://doi.org/10.1007/BF01303254

Medema S. G, (1993) *Is There Life Beyond Efficiency? Elements of a Social Law and Economics,* (ed.), Review of Social Economy, 51:2, 1 a, 38-153.

Nussbaum M., (1997) *Flawed Foundations: The Philosophical Critique of (A Particular Kind of) Economics,* University of Chicago Law Review, 64 (4), 1197-1214. DOI: 10.2307/1600214. Online. Available at https://www.jstor.org/stable/pdf/1600214.pdf (Accessed 18 October 2018).

Patel B. N., Nagar R., Thakkar H. (eds.), *Economic Analysis of Law: An Indian Perspective,* Delhi: Lexis Nexis.

Rawls J., (1993) *Political Liberalism.* New York: Columbia University Press.

Sahu G., (2014) *Environmental Jurisprudence in India,* Orient Blackswan, Delhi.

Schmalbeck R. L, (1983) *The Justice of Economics: An Analysis of Wealth Maximization as a Normative Goal,* Book Review: The Economics of Justice Posner R. A. Mass.: Harvard University Press, 1981. Online. Available at https://scholarship.law.duke.edu/cgi/viewcontent.cgi?article=2449&context=faculty_scholarship. (Accessed 18 October 2018).

Shleifer A., (1999) *Understanding Regulation,* European Financial Management,11 (4), 439-451.

Shuck P. H, (2000) *The Limits of Law: Essays on Democratic Governance.* Colorado: Boulder.

Singh C., (1982) *The Ideological Roots of Legal Paternalism in India,* Journal of the Indian Law Institute, 24: 844-101.

Skidelsky R., (2009) *Keynes: The Return of the Master 88.* London: Allen Lane.

Stackhouse M. L., (2014), Weber, Theology and Economics in *The Oxford Handbook of Christianity and Economics.* Paul Oslington: Oxford University Press. Pp. 107-336.

Sunstein C. R., (2014) *Why Nudge? The Politics of Libertarian Paternalism.* New Haven: Yale University Press.

Thaler R. H., and Sunstein C. R., (2008) *Nudge: Improving Decisions about Health, Wealth, and Happiness.* New Haven: Yale University Press.

Trubek D. M., (1986) *Max Weber's Tragic Modernism and the Study of Law in Society,* Law and Society Review 20 (4), 573- 603. DOI: 10.2307/3053467

Trubek D. M., (1978) *Complexity and Contradiction in Legal Order: Balbus and the Challenge of Critical Social Thought About Law.* Law and Society Review 11 (3), 529-568. DOI: 10.2307/3053131

Walter F., and Ganguly T.E., (1989) *Development, Displacement and Rehabilitation.* New Delhi: Indian Social Institute.

Walzer M., (1984) *Spheres of Justice: A Defense of Pluralism and Equality.* New York: Basic Books.

Waters W.R, (1990) *Evolution of Social Economics* in America. In Lutz M. A., (ed.), Social Economics: Retrospect and Prospect. Boston: Kluwer Academic Publishers.

Weber M., (1954) *Max Weber on Law in Economy and Society.* Harvard: Harvard University Press.

White M. D., (2015) *Law and Social Economics: Essays in Ethical Values, Theory, Practice, and Policy.* New York: Palgrave Macmillan.

Woodward J., (2010) *Causation in Biology: Stability, Specificity and Choice of Levels of Explanation,* Biology and Philosophy, 25: 287-318.

Woodward J., (2003) *Making Things Happen: A Theory of Causal Explanation,* Oxford University Press.

Woodward J., and Hitchcock C., (2003c) *Explanatory Generalizations, Part I: A Counterfactual Account,* Noûs, 37:1, 1-24.

Woodward J., (2003f) *There is no Such Thing as a Ceteris Paribus Laws,* Erkenntnis, 57: 303-328.

Woodward J., (2000) *Explanation and Invariance in the Special Sciences,* British Journal for the Philosophy of Science, 51: 197–254.

Index

J

K

L

M

N

O

P

R

S

T

U

V

W

www.ingramcontent.com/pod-product-compliance
Lightning Source LLC
LaVergne TN
LVHW010721210926
848485LV00007B/1407/J
* 9 7 8 1 6 2 2 7 3 4 5 2 8 *